Chemical Dependency

OPPOSING VIEWPOINTS®

D0167541

Other Books of Related Interest in the Opposing Viewpoints Series:

American Values
America's Children
America's Prisons
Censorship
Civil Liberties
Criminal Justice
The Death Penalty
Drug Abuse
The Health Crisis
The Homeless
Poverty
Social Justice
Violence in America
War on Drugs

Chemical Dependency

OPPOSING VIEWPOINTS®

David L. Bender & Bruno Leone, *Series Editors*

Charles P. Cozic & Karin Swisher, *Book Editors*
Stacey L. Tipp, *Assistant Editor*

OPPOSING VIEWPOINTS SERIES ®

Greenhaven Press, Inc.   PO Box 289009   San Diego, CA 92198-0009

Library of Congress Cataloging-in-Publication Data

Chemical dependency : opposing viewpoints / Charles P. Cozic & Karin Swisher, book editors ; Stacey L. Tipp, assistant editor.
      p.   cm. — (Opposing viewpoints series)
   Includes bibliographical references and index.
   Summary: Presents opposing viewpoints about the causes and treatment of alcohol, tobacco, and other drug addiction. Includes critical thinking skill activities and a list of organizations to contact.
   ISBN 0-89908-179-7 (lib.) — ISBN 0-89908-154-1 (pap.)
   1. Drug abuse—United States.   2. Narcotics, Control of—United States.   3. Alcoholism—United States.   [1. Alcoholism. 2. Drug abuse. 3. Smoking.]   I. Cozic, Charles P., 1957-   . II. Swisher, Karin, 1966-   . III. Tipp, Stacey L., 1963-   . IV. Series: Opposing viewpoints series (Unnumbered)
HV5825.C44   1991
362.29—dc20   91-12228

"Congress shall make no law . . . abridging the freedom of speech, or of the press."

First Amendment to the U.S. Constitution

The basic foundation of our democracy is the first amendment guarantee of freedom of expression. The Opposing Viewpoints Series is dedicated to the concept of this basic freedom and the idea that it is more important to practice it than to enshrine it.

Contents

Chapter 6: How Can Chemical Dependency Be Reduced?

Why Consider Opposing Viewpoints?

"It is better to debate a question without settling it than to settle a question without debating it."

Joseph Joubert (1754-1824)

The Importance of Examining Opposing Viewpoints

The purpose of the Opposing Viewpoints Series, and this book in particular, is to present balanced, and often difficult to find, opposing points of view on complex and sensitive issues.

Probably the best way to become informed is to analyze the positions of those who are regarded as experts and well studied on issues. It is important to consider every variety of opinion in an attempt to determine the truth. Opinions from the mainstream of society should be examined. But also important are opinions that are considered radical, reactionary, or minority as well as those stigmatized by some other uncomplimentary label. An important lesson of history is the eventual acceptance of many unpopular and even despised opinions. The ideas of Socrates, Jesus, and Galileo are good examples of this.

Readers will approach this book with their own opinions on the issues debated within it. However, to have a good grasp of one's own viewpoint, it is necessary to understand the arguments of those with whom one disagrees. It can be said that those who do not completely understand their adversary's point of view do not fully understand their own.

A persuasive case for considering opposing viewpoints has been presented by John Stuart Mill in his work *On Liberty*. When examining controversial issues it may be helpful to reflect on this suggestion:

The only way in which a human being can make some approach to knowing the whole of a subject, is by hearing what can be said about it by persons of every variety of opinion, and studying all modes in which it can be looked at by every character of mind. No wise man ever acquired his wisdom in any mode but this.

Analyzing Sources of Information

The Opposing Viewpoints Series includes diverse materials taken from magazines, journals, books, and newspapers, as well as statements and position papers from a wide range of individuals, organizations, and governments. This broad spectrum of sources helps to develop patterns of thinking which are open to the consideration of a variety of opinions.

Pitfalls to Avoid

A pitfall to avoid in considering opposing points of view is that of regarding one's own opinion as being common sense and the most rational stance, and the point of view of others as being only opinion and naturally wrong. It may be that another's opinion is correct and one's own is in error.

Another pitfall to avoid is that of closing one's mind to the opinions of those with whom one disagrees. The best way to approach a dialogue is to make one's primary purpose that of understanding the mind and arguments of the other person and not that of enlightening him or her with one's own solutions. More can be learned by listening than speaking.

It is my hope that after reading this book the reader will have a deeper understanding of the issues debated and will appreciate the complexity of even seemingly simple issues on which good and honest people disagree. This awareness is particularly important in a democratic society such as ours where people enter into public debate to determine the common good. Those with whom one disagrees should not necessarily be regarded as enemies, but perhaps simply as people who suggest different paths to a common goal.

Developing Basic Reading and Thinking Skills

In this book, carefully edited opposing viewpoints are purposely placed back to back to create a running debate; each viewpoint is preceded by a short quotation that best expresses the author's main argument. This format instantly plunges the reader into the midst of a controversial issue and greatly aids that reader in mastering the basic skill of recognizing an author's point of view.

A number of basic skills for critical thinking are practiced in the activities that appear throughout the books in the series. Some of the skills are:

Evaluating Sources of Information. The ability to choose from among alternative sources the most reliable and accurate source in relation to a given subject.

Separating Fact from Opinion. The ability to make the basic distinction between factual statements (those that can be demonstrated or verified empirically) and statements of opinion (those that are beliefs or attitudes that cannot be proved).

Identifying Stereotypes. The ability to identify oversimplified, exaggerated descriptions (favorable or unfavorable) about people and insulting statements about racial, religious, or national groups, based upon misinformation or lack of information.

Recognizing Ethnocentrism. The ability to recognize attitudes or opinions that express the view that one's own race, culture, or group is inherently superior, or those attitudes that judge another culture or group in terms of one's own.

It is important to consider opposing viewpoints and equally important to be able to critically analyze those viewpoints. The activities in this book are designed to help the reader master these thinking skills. Statements are taken from the book's viewpoints and the reader is asked to analyze them. This technique aids the reader in developing skills that not only can be applied to the viewpoints in this book, but also to situations where opinionated spokespersons comment on controversial issues. Although the activities are helpful to the solitary reader, they are most useful when the reader can benefit from the interaction of group discussion.

Using this book and others in the series should help readers develop basic reading and thinking skills. These skills should improve the reader's ability to understand what is read. Readers should be better able to separate fact from opinion, substance from rhetoric, and become better consumers of information in our media-centered culture.

This volume of the Opposing Viewpoints Series does not advocate a particular point of view. Quite the contrary! The very nature of the book leaves it to the reader to formulate the opinions he or she finds most suitable. My purpose as publisher is to see that this is made possible by offering a wide range of viewpoints that are fairly presented.

David L. Bender
Publisher

Introduction

"Regardless of political affiliation and ideology, socioeconomic status and ethnicity, or geographical and occupational location, most Americans continually rank 'drugs' among the major problems facing the nation."

—James A. Inciardi

Millions of Americans are dependent upon mood-altering drugs. These substances range from illicit drugs such as crack cocaine and heroin to legal drugs such as tobacco, alcohol, and prescription drugs. Use of these drugs often leads to chemical addiction, which in turn leads to high rates of debilitating illness, crime, and even death. Despite the "war on drugs" waged by both the Reagan and Bush administrations, chemical addiction remains a very serious problem. The government, law enforcement officials, sociologists, and public health experts continue to seek remedies for the drug problem that some say is eroding the very foundation of the nation.

The United States government has long sought ways to reduce the overwhelming human, social, and financial costs of drug addiction. The most popular strategy for reducing drug addiction has always been prohibiting the addictive substance. Many drugs, such as heroin, cocaine, and marijuana are prohibited. Others, such as amphetamines and morphine, are strictly regulated and can be used only under medical supervision. Still others, such as tobacco and alcohol, are limited to use by adults. State and federal governments advocate stricter enforcement of drug laws by dedicating more police officers to arresting drug users and by imposing harsher prison sentences on those who break them. According to Carlton Turner, who was Ronald Reagan's principal adviser on narcotics issues, "Drug arrests are going to continue to rise, because the number of arrests is really a measure of our law enforcement effectiveness, and if there's any one group in our society that has been effective in fighting drugs, it has been the law enforcement community." To carry out this strategy, the police arrested approximately 750,000 people for drug-law offenses each year in the late 1980s. Judges have assigned strict penalties for even first-time offenders. In addition, some criminal justice experts and private citizens have even advocated the death penalty for established drug dealers.

Continued widespread drug use and abuse, however, have caused many experts to reject prohibition. Critics such as Nobel Prize-winning economist Milton Friedman and former secretary of state George P. Shultz maintain that enforcing America's drug laws has not only failed to reduce chemical dependency but has caused a dramatic increase in violent crime in the 1980s and 1990s. The number of assaults and murders in the deadly wars of drug-dealing gangs over unpaid debts and territory continues to escalate. Those who argue that drug laws are ineffective propose either decriminalization—reducing the penalties for drug crimes—or legalization—abolishing laws against using drugs altogether. Decriminalization or legalization, these experts contend, would reduce drug-related crime and release millions of dollars currently allocated to drug-law enforcement to more important programs. These programs could use education and treatment to reduce the incidence of addiction to illegal drugs.

Many experts agree that prevention and treatment are the real keys to ending America's drug problem. Secretary of health and human services Louis W. Sullivan states, "Treatment is one of the most important tools we have in alleviating the pain and misery that drug addiction has wrought upon our nation." Many programs are already in place. Most schools attempt to educate students on the dangers of alcohol, tobacco, and illegal drugs. Public health programs use television and print advertising to educate both adults and children about the dangers of drug use. Other programs are designed to treat those already addicted to these drugs and to provide long-term residential care for hardcore addicts. Treatment advocates argue that the federal government should allocate a larger portion of its drug budget to treatment programs. More programs would alleviate the shortage of available spaces in existing programs and provide special programs for jailed addicts and pregnant women. They maintain that most prevention and treatment programs succeed in reducing chemical dependency and that more programs would reduce the problem even further.

Not everyone agrees that treatment can significantly reduce chemical dependency. Even the most effective programs, critics maintain, have a high rate of failure. According to the Comprehensive Assessment and Treatment Outcome Research program at the Ramsey Clinic in St. Paul, Minnesota, only 50 percent of cocaine users treated are abstinent one year after treatment. In New York City, only 10 percent of heroin addicts managed to stay off the drug.

So, what is the solution to the complex problem of chemical

dependency? Prohibition, enforcement, education, and treatment all have advocates. But they also have critics. *Chemical Dependency: Opposing Viewpoints* presents a wide variety of opinions on several important issues that reflect these varied concerns. The questions debated are: What Are the Causes of Chemical Dependency? Is Smoking Harmful? How Harmful Is Alcohol? Should Drug Laws Be Reformed? Should Pregnant Women Be Prosecuted for Drug Abuse? How Can Chemical Dependency Be Reduced? When addressing many of these questions, the need to reduce the alarming levels of chemical dependency seems paramount. How society can best work toward this reduction is one of the most important objectives of the chemical dependency debate.

What Are the Causes of Chemical Dependency?

**Chemical
Dependency**

Chapter Preface

Most people agree that a serious drug problem exists in the United States. Indeed, in 1985, the number of cocaine users alone reached six million. According to Robert DuPont, former director of the National Institute on Drug Abuse, "Never before in world history has so large a segment of a national population used such a large number of dependence-producing drugs."

Many different theories have been advanced to explain the causes of widespread drug abuse. One disagreement hinges on whether the causes are societal or related to the addictive properties of the drugs themselves. Gabriel Nahas, author of *Cocaine: The Great White Plague*, points out that some drugs produce a pleasurable feeling, a "reward" that commands repeated drug use. Nahas writes, "Drugs abridge the freedom of the individual by enslaving him in a habit which he may no longer control." Nahas further notes that abstinence from these drugs results in unpleasant and painful reactions due to withdrawal, which increases the need for the drug.

However, other theorists do not agree that the blame for chemical addiction lies primarily with the drug. Some sociologists and others claim, for example, that a breakdown in traditional values and family unity leads to drug abuse. J.A. Parker, editor of the conservative black journal *Lincoln Review*, asserts that a collapse of strong families, schools, and religious institutions denies youths the moral strength to resist drugs. Parker says the lack of supervision in many one-parent families also provides opportunities for drug abuse.

The authors in this chapter debate the various social, cultural, and psychological causes of chemical dependency.

"The natural pursuit of intoxicants . . . functions like a drive, just like our drives of hunger, thirst and sex."

Chemical Dependency Is Instinctual

Ronald K. Siegel

Some addiction experts maintain that the desire to use drugs is the fourth instinctual drive, after those of hunger, thirst, and sex. In the following viewpoint, Ronald K. Siegel presents as proof the fact that almost every animal species has sought intoxication, and that people worldwide have historically used drugs such as alcohol and other mind-altering substances. Siegel is a psychopharmacologist at the University of California at Los Angeles School of Medicine and author of *Intoxication: Life in Pursuit of Artificial Paradise.*

As you read, consider the following questions:

1. In Siegel's opinion, how is the war on drugs a war against ourselves?
2. Does the author favor the development of safe drugs? Why or why not?
3. Does Siegel believe drugs have a legitimate place in society?

Ronald K. Siegel, "It's a Drive as Natural as Food or Sex," *Los Angeles Times*, March 15, 1990. Reprinted with permission.

There is a silent spring of intoxicants that flows through our lives and bodies. Whether we wake up with a cup of coffee or a line of cocaine; whether we take a break with a cigarette or a beer; whether we relax after work with a cocktail or a joint of marijuana; whether we go to sleep with something we bought at the pharmacy or on the street—we use drugs to change the way we feel. Nobody wants this to be unhealthy or dangerous. Nobody wants people living out their lives inside crack houses, dying from cancer caused by tobacco or lying dead on the highways as a result of drunk drivers. . . .

Sure, we can discourage the use of a drug such as cocaine. Already, the image of cocaine has been transformed from a glamorous drugs for the rich and famous to one found in dirty crack pipes on inner-city streets. This new image has turned off many users but the lower price of "crack" has attracted many more.

Futile Drug War

So we blockade their streets and bulldoze their crack houses. When we uncover huge warehouses full of cocaine, we find out who sent it. Then we go after them, encouraging extradition, kidnaping if we must, even invading a country to capture just one of the kingpins. The federal budget escalates as we provide military support for coca eradication in the jungles of South America and coerce foreign governments reluctant to help. At home, we use urine tests to uproot users from their jobs and write tough laws to treat dealers like so many coca shrubs.

If the domestic cultivation of coca now beginning in several states—Florida, Hawaii, Arizona, California—is curtailed, and the development of synthetic-coke labs can be avoided, these efforts might reduce cocaine use. Let's say they do.

What if cocaine simply disappeared from the face of the Earth? The war on drugs would still be lost. Why? Because the drive to use drugs is unstoppable and the supplies are unlimited.

As Natural as Hunger

History shows that we have always used drugs. In every age, in every part of this planet, people have pursued intoxication by consuming drugs derived from plants, alcohol and other mind-altering substances. Surprisingly, we're not the only ones to do this. Almost every species of animal has engaged in the natural pursuit of intoxicants. This behavior has so much force and persistence that it functions like a drive, just like our drives of hunger, thirst and sex. This "fourth drive" is a natural part of our biology, creating the irrepressible demand for drugs. In a sense, the war on drugs is a war against ourselves, a denial of our very nature.

Of course, this "fourth drive" sometimes runs amok and overshadows the other drives, as is the case when animals and people pursue an intoxicant to the exclusion of everything else in their lives. This tells us that we are doing the right thing when we try to curtail cocaine use. But there is simply no end to the supply of dangerous drugs. Already, there is a methamphetamine ("ice") epidemic looming on the horizon, ready to recruit ex-cocaine users to its ranks. Designer chemistry, exotic plants, even over-the-counter medicines provide endless sources of new highs. And so the war on drugs will continue, as it has throughout history.

Legalizing Drugs Is No Solution

Some people want to stop the war, putting an end to its enormous societal costs, by legalizing drugs such as cocaine or heroin. The voices calling for legalization are not only well-intentioned, they are also louder and more respectable than ever. But calling a drug legal doesn't change its basic pharmacology or safety any more than saying "no" changes our basic drive to pursue intoxication.

Inherent Need

I have come to the view that humans have a need—perhaps even a drive—to alter their state of consciousness from time to time.

Lester Grinspoon, *Time*, August 21, 1989.

Making some dangerous drugs illegal while keeping others legal is not the solution. Outlawing drugs to solve drug problems is much like outlawing sex to win the war against AIDS. We recognize that people will continue to have sex for non-reproductive reasons, whatever the laws or mores. Thus, we try to make sexual practices as safe as possible in order to minimize the spread of the AIDS viruses. Similarly, we continually try to make our drinking water, foods and pharmaceutical medicines safer.

To solve the drug problem, we must recognize that intoxicants are medicines, treatments for the human condition. Then we must make them as safe and risk-free and—yes—as healthy as possible.

Make Safe Drugs Available

Dream with me for a moment. What would be wrong if we had perfectly safe drugs? I mean drugs that delivered the same effects as our most popular ones but never caused dependency, disease, dysfunction or death. Imagine an alcohol-type drug that never caused addiction, liver disease, hangovers, reckless driv-

19

ing or workplace problems. Would you care for a cigarette that is as enjoyable as marijuana but as harmless as clean air?

This is not science fiction. There are such intoxicants available now. If former drug czar William J. Bennett can switch from smoking tobacco to chewing nicotine gum, why can't crack users chew a cocaine gum that has already been tested on animals and found to be relatively safe?

Even safer drugs may be just around the corner. They could be made available early in the next century. What would it cost to develop them? Probably less than this year's budget for the war on drugs. But it will first take a national commitment equal to putting a man on the moon.

We must begin by recognizing that there is a legitimate place in our society for intoxication. Then we can join in building new, perfectly safe intoxicants for a world that will be ready to discard the old ones as the corroding pieces of junk they really are.

"A variety of psychological factors are commonly part of a person's addiction."

Chemical Dependency Is Psychological

Dennis C. Daley

In the following viewpoint, Dennis C. Daley argues that a person's attitudes and beliefs can cause some drug and alcohol users to become chemically dependent. Many addicts use chemicals to mask insecurity or guilt, Daley asserts. Daley is the clinical administrator for the Comprehensive Drug and Alcohol Abuse Program at the University of Pittsburgh School of Medicine in Pennsylvania.

As you read, consider the following questions:

1. According to Daley, why do most chemically dependent people never seek help?
2. In the author's opinion, how do "reinforcing factors" sustain alcoholism or drug addiction?
3. What does Daley state are the traits of people with unhealthy personalities?

Excerpted and reprinted, with permission, from *Surviving Addiction* by Dennis C. Daley. New York: Gardner Press, 1988.

21

There are various reasons why people use substances. For many, drinking alcohol in moderation is a normal part of their lives. It is served with meals, as part of special celebrations such as weddings, and at social and recreational events. Some drink alcohol to "fit in" with their peers, relax, change their mood, or reduce the pressures of day-to-day living. The majority of people who drink alcohol do not develop alcoholism or experience problems with its use.

Other types of drugs are used for similar reasons. In addition, some people use drugs to treat medical and psychiatric problems, whereas others experiment with drugs introduced to them by their peers, particularly during the teenage and young adult years. Like the majority of people who use alcohol, most who use drugs do not develop an addiction or experience use-related problems. . . .

A variety of psychological factors are commonly part of a person's addiction. These include his or her motivations, attitudes, and beliefs; psychological defense mechanisms such as denial; coping abilities related to handling problems or feelings; learned behaviors that are reinforced or "rewarded" by other people in the social environment; and personality patterns.

Human behavior is influenced by both our conscious and unconscious needs, feelings, and motivations. Conscious factors are those things we are aware of that influence what we say or how we act. Unconscious factors refer to influences on us of which we are not aware. An addicted person may consciously choose to get high to "relax and feel good" or to "blot out the hassles of the world." Another person may be unable to identify a particular reason for using drugs and may be unconsciously attempting to "self-destruct." Or, that person may even be expressing deeply hidden angry feelings that he or she has been harboring toward another person, perhaps a family member.

Denial: A Deadly Enemy

A major psychological defense mechanism that contributes to addiction and helps to maintain it is denial. Denial occurs unconsciously and allows an addicted person to continue using alcohol or other drugs despite any problems that are created by such use, however severe they may be. It is probably the major reason why the overwhelming majority of people with chemical addictions never seek or receive help.

According to Dr. Daniel Anderson, a pioneer in the field of addiction, denial is the "fatal aspect" of this disease, ultimately contributing to the addict's death if it is not confronted. In such cases, denial can take various forms:

1. The user does not believe that a problem exists even though there is sufficient evidence to the contrary. Everyone

22

else may see the addiction and yet the addict does not. Addiction is sometimes referred to as the only disease whose major symptom is not knowing that you have it.

2. The user recognizes that a problem exists, but feels that "it's not that bad." This feeling is particularly common among people who do not use substances every day, who do not always end up getting high or drunk, or who are not experiencing major life problems from such use. If one sees others who are worse off in terms of their alcohol or drug use, the denial is reinforced and one becomes even more convinced that one is not that bad off.

3. The user feels there are legitimate reasons to use alcohol or drugs—calm shaky nerves, help cope with job pressures, and so forth.

4. The user admits to having a problem with alcohol or other drugs, but does not do anything about it. Many alcoholics and drug addicts recognize their addiction but continue to use substances. Most are actually afraid of what it would be like to live without drugs or alcohol, and may also question whether they could actually cope with life without substances as a crutch.

5. The user believes that by cutting down or limiting the amount used, "things will be under control." Most addicted people would like to be able to control their use of substances, and some actually do so for awhile.

6. The user believes he or she cannot be addicted because alcohol or drugs are not used "every day." This is a very common fallacy. Many addicted people are not daily users, but are weekend alcoholics or drug addicts in the sense that they wait until the weekends before using substances excessively.

7. The user rejects the idea of addiction because he does not "use too much alcohol or drugs." As discussed before, the symptoms of addiction can be present regardless of the amount of alcohol or other drugs actually used.

8. The user believes addiction is not possible because he or she holds a job, takes care of a family, and does not have a lot of problems resulting from the use of substances.

Other psychological defenses that contribute to addiction include rationalization, projection, and intellectualization. In a sense, they are just other forms of denial. *Rationalization* refers to the tendency to explain the reasons for using alcohol or drugs in order to justify it ("Everyone else uses," "I don't drink any more booze than other people I know," "My job has a lot of pressure"). *Projection* refers to placing the blame on others for using substances ("My wife nags me and drives me to drink"). *Intellectualization* refers to approaching alcohol or drug use objectively or philosophically ("Marijuana ought to be legalized since so many in our society smoke it," "It can't be as bad as 'hard' drugs"). Whatever the form denial takes, the result is the same—addiction continues, increasing the chances of suffering for the affected person and the person's family.

23

One's thinking affects one's expectations and beliefs. Expectations and beliefs, in turn, guide one's behavior. For example, people who expect alcohol or drugs to make them feel better or to help them cope with life's difficulties are likely to continue using them. And those who believe that alcohol and drugs are needed to have fun or fit in with a peer group, are likely to use in order to "have fun" or "fit in" with the peer group.

Some people even believe that if they possess certain attitudes or qualities, they cannot develop alcoholism or drug addiction. For example, Jake is a respected member of his community and highly regarded by his family. He is a much decorated combat veteran of World War II who survived a devastating experience as a prisoner of war. He is a strong-willed man who prides himself on his work and who held two jobs for many years in order to provide sufficiently for his wife and children.

Emotional Relief

Drug use is not commonly viewed as a pleasure-seeking activity but rather as a means of reducing emotional pain. Specific drugs are chosen by different individuals for their specific pharmacological properties and capacity to reduce psychological distress.

Howard J. Shaffer and Stephanie B. Jones, *Quitting Cocaine*, 1989.

When Jake developed alcoholism in his late 50s, he was stunned and refused to admit that he "could no longer handle booze." This stubbornness was a major factor in his insistence that he could stop on his own without anybody's help. It was not until his alcoholism worsened to the point that he was threatened with losing a job that he had held for over 30 years that he sought treatment. Although he is doing quite well now, he struggled for quite awhile with the idea that he was an alcoholic and would be unable to drink liquor. He could not accept the fact that here he was, a successful husband and father, a hard-working and strong-willed man, and a war hero, and yet he was unable to control his use of alcohol.

Coping Mechanisms

People may use alcohol or other drugs to reduce anxiety, forget problems, mitigate unpleasant emotional states such as anger, guilt, loneliness, or boredom, or deal with difficulties in living. But in the process of using alcohol or drugs to cope, they can gradually become dependent and the substances become a "crutch."

In some instances, unpleasant feelings or physical discomfort created by withdrawal lead to a continued need for alcohol or other drugs. For example, someone who uses stimulants such as cocaine or speed may utilize alcohol or tranquilizers to relax while coming off of cocaine. The user copes with the problems related to one type of drug with another drug. Or a person may become furious with his or her spouse, for example, over disagreements on how to budget the family's finances, but rather than work this out, will choose to deal with it by drinking—thus adding new problems.

Human behavior is often repeated as a result of learning that there is a reward, or "reinforcing factor" following the behavior. For example, we work hard in anticipation of a reward in the form of a raise or praise for a job well done. A child works hard at earning good grades in school because of the teacher's praise or his or her parents buy the child something special. An alcoholic or drug addict repeats the behavior of consuming alcohol or drugs to reap the reward of feeling "good," "euphoric," or "buzzed up." Or it may be to "not feel bad or sick" in those instances in which the person uses substances to prevent withdrawal sickness.

Personality Traits

Many addicted persons also receive reinforcement or support for their substance use from the members of their social groups, particularly those who also have alcohol or drug addictions. This support may be evidenced in being provided with free drugs, in being made to feel part of the group, or in verbal rewards for behaviors related to using substances or getting them.

Personality traits are patterns of relating to the world. With a healthy personality, a person is able to display a broad range of traits in a flexible manner. For example, he or she may feel equally comfortable as a leader or a follower, depending on the situation, or to demonstrate the quality of being greatly organized and in control, or to be disorganized and not feel anxious about not being in control of every situation.

A person with an unhealthy personality tends to be rigid and inflexible—traits that can cause personal distress or problems in life. Among common personality traits are dependence, independence, aggression, passivity, impulsiveness, openness, suspiciousness, warmth, coldness, empathy, and self-centeredness. A person with strong dependency needs is prone to developing a dependency on chemicals. Some drug-dependent people have difficulty controlling their impulses and develop other addictions as well—gambling, sex, work, overeating, compulsive shopping and the like. Many believe that they have an "addictive personality." Not every alcoholic or drug-addicted person can be considered to have an addictive personality, however, but some can.

"Without . . . values, all things become possible—one of which is the plague of drugs. "

Moral Failure Causes Chemical Dependency

Allan Brownfeld

The American drug crisis is often attributed to a breakdown in traditional values. In the following viewpoint, Allan Brownfeld argues that children lack a strong moral foundation to resist drug use. Since the family, church, and community no longer play a major role in teaching traditional values, children lack the moral framework and self-esteem to live without drugs. Brownfeld is a syndicated columnist whose editorials appear in conservative publications such as the *Washington Inquirer* and the *Conservative Chronicle*.

As you read, consider the following questions:

1. In Brownfeld's opinion, how are some families responsible for their children's lack of morality?
2. What does the author mean when he states that society is blamed for antisocial individual behavior?
3. How does Brownfeld describe the "alternative life-styles" of some people?

Reprinted, with permission, from "Drug War Unwinnable Without Social Values," by Allan Brownfeld, *The Washington Inquirer*, October 13, 1989.

Four out of ten Americans now view drugs as the nation's most severe problem. A *Washington Post*-ABC News poll found that 44 percent of those interviewed ranked drugs as the country's most serious problem, easily eclipsing all other domestic or foreign concerns. Among those most troubled are black Americans. Nearly seven out of ten blacks interviewed said drugs are the country's biggest problem.

Yet even as the Bush administration has launched a "war on drugs," U.S. officials concede that an all-out effort to get large numbers of addicted people off drugs, whether they are in the inner cities or not, is not being planned. That aim, they say, is too complicated and the problems in reaching it too intractable to be achieved in the near future. The true goals of the "war on drugs," one drug-policy aide told *The New York Times*, is to move the nation "a little bit" beyond where current trends would put it anyway.

White House Chief of Staff John H. Sununu says that the anti-drug effort would not "undo all the social problems of the inner cities." But he said he would consider it progress if the plan helped reduce the casual use of illegal drugs and made some headway in reducing habitual use that would "bring some tranquility in terms of the criminal problems that people face in the cities."

Anti-Drug Strategy

Another senior White House official says that there is little hope for weaning drugs from large numbers of young people who are at the heart of much of the current crisis. Of more concern, he said, "is doing better by the next generation of kids.". . .

In the inner cities, drug use seems to be out of control. In Washington, D.C., for example, the infant mortality rate, already among the highest in the U.S., increased by nearly 50 percent in the first half of 1989 because of a surge of babies born to cocaine-addicted women. An estimated 169 babies died before their first birthdays during the first six months of 1989, an infant mortality rate of 32.3 deaths per 1,000 live births, according to preliminary city data. By contrast, the infant mortality rate for all of 1988 was 23.2 deaths per 1,000. "It is like a bomb has gone off," said one city official. "No one in this are knows what to do. I don't know what to do about social pathology and decay in half the city."

Drugs, sadly, are part of a larger social pathology in our inner cities and throughout the larger American society as well. More and more children find themselves in one-parent families and do not receive the care and nurturing which previous generations took for granted. We live, more and more, in a value-free society—in which it is considered inappropriate to be "judgmental." We blame "society" for the anti-social behavior of individuals, and refer to what was once viewed as aberrant behavior as "alternative lifestyles." In such an atmosphere, how are young people to determine what is right and what is wrong?

Loose Society to Blame

We don't have a drug problem. We have a culture problem.

Sure, drugs are addictive, but the precise nature of addiction is poorly understood by scientists and varies from individual to individual. And yes, drugs do give rise to crime—but mostly indirectly, by creating a market for an illegal substance. This is not to say that widespread drug use is not a problem. It is. But the problem inheres in the kind of society which has so loosened its traditional supports—family, church, community—that its individual members are flying off in all directions like rivets from an exploding steel drum. It is the disintegration of traditional values, not the drugs themselves, that causes people to smoke and snort their lives away.

Mona Charen, *The Washington Times*, August 29, 1989.

Our families, schools and, all too often, our religious institutions as well, have turned their backs upon the Biblical injunction: "Train up a child in the way he should go, and when he is old, he will not depart from it" (Proverbs 22.6).

What young people are not learning is the moral compass by which action and lives are to be judged. Joe Clark, the tough black high school principal from Paterson, New Jersey, who turned a drug- and crime-ridden school around, declares: ". . . in many cases these youths do not learn morality. That is, a sense of fairness to serve as a guide for their actions. The schools should teach them this, if the schools were run with the right intentions, the right spirit. I am not suggesting the removal of the separation of church and state. What I am saying is that education, properly understood and practiced, requires an energetic commitment from teachers and administrators, not only to provide career skills, but also to elevate the mind and the heart to the whole story of life; its wonders and dangers, its joys and sorrows, its struggles and possibilities. The dynamic of right and wrong runs throughout the whole story—from Lexington to Los Alamos, from Hippocrates to Macbeth, from the earliest myths to the headlines of this morning's newspaper—and the truly dedicated teacher cannot help but project the rightness of his or her task, which is the genuine preparation of the next generation for the challenge of life."

One reason for widespread drug addiction is the fertile field we have created. Dr. Robert DuPont, former head of the National Institute of Drug Abuse, states, "Never before in world history has so large a segment of a national population used such a large number of dependence-producing drugs." The reason, DuPont argues, is a shift in values in the U.S. He notes, "The shift has to do with moving away from centering one's life around values having to do with religion, tradition, family or community, and thinking instead of one's self only. The goal becomes doing what feels right to you. If the purpose of your life is to feel good you are tremendously vulnerable to drugs because drugs produce good feelings. On the other hand, you might say: 'Wait a minute. I'm here in the world for some purpose larger than my feelings.' . . ."

The war on drugs will fail until we recognize that there are causes for the widespread proliferation of drug use beyond what occurs in Colombia, Peru or Washington, D.C. One cause which has been largely overlooked is the national abandonment of its traditional moral values. Without such values, all things become possible—one of which is the plague of drugs.

"On some level, this [addictive] personality will always be searching for an object or some type of event to form an addictive relationship."

An Addictive Personality May Cause Chemical Dependency

Craig Nakken

Why one person can use a drug occasionally while another grows dependent on it is a key question in addiction research. In the following viewpoint, Craig Nakken argues that some people with addictive personalities satisfy their emotional needs with chemical substances rather than personal relationships. Nakken maintains that an addict's emotional instability results in an increasing loss of self-esteem and self-control. Nakken is a certified chemical dependency practitioner and lectures at the Rutgers School of Alcohol Studies in Piscataway, New Jersey.

As you read, consider the following questions:

1. How does Nakken define "dry drunk"?
2. In the author's opinion, how is there potential for an addictive personality within everyone?
3. What type of denial is necessary for an addiction to progress, according to Nakken?

Addiction is a set of experiences that indicates a specific movement in a specific direction, bringing a series of changes that takes place within a person. It is through the commonalities of these experiences and changes that we are able to describe addiction.

As addiction develops, it becomes a way of life. Rather than being rigid, addiction is continually changing. As it changes, it inflicts changes on the person suffering from the addiction. . . .

The true start of any addictive relationship is when the person repeatedly seeks the illusion of relief to avoid unpleasant feelings or situations. This is nurturing through avoidance—an unnatural way of taking care of one's emotional needs. At this point, addicts start to give up natural relationships and the relief they offer. They replace these relationships with the addictive relationship.

Consequently, addicts seek serenity through an object or event. This is the beginning of the addictive cycle. If one were to diagram addiction there would be a downward spiraling motion with many valleys and plateaus.

This cycle causes an emotional craving that results in mental preoccupation. For an addict, the feeling of discomfort becomes a signal to act out, not a signal to connect with others or with oneself. The amount of mental obsession is often an indication of the stress in the addict's life. Some addictions produce physical dependency that creates physical symptoms upon withdrawal (as with alcohol and other drugs). Many other types of recovering addicts—sex addicts, addictive gamblers, and addictive spenders—also report physical symptoms when they stop acting out. Whether this is part of the grief process in ending an addictive relationship or actual withdrawal symptoms is unclear—it's probably a combination of both. Addicts who have stopped acting out report feeling edgy and nervous, and these symptoms can last up to a few months. . . .

The Addictive Personality

The reason the idea of the addictive personality is so important to understand is that eventually a person forms a dependent relationship with his or her own addictive personality.

Once an addictive personality is established within a person, the specific object or event takes on less importance. When an addictive personality is firmly in control, addicts can (and often do) switch objects of addiction as preferences change or when they get into trouble with one object. Addicts who switch objects of addiction know it's a good way to get people off their backs.

The addictive personality is very important for recovering addicts to understand because the addictive personality will stay with them for life. On some level, this personality will always be searching for an object or some type of event to form an addictive relationship. On some level, this personality will always give the person the illusion that there is an object or event that can nurture them.

Activating the Addictive Personality

There seem to be two different motivating factors behind the classic addictive personality. On the one hand, his personality structure may be so weak that he needs a constant supply of his drug just in order to keep from falling apart. This qualifies such an individual as a pathologically dependent personality, with drug use being the object of his dependence.

These people tend to look for their fulfillment in areas outside their own selves. Such a dependency object may or may not initially be drugs or alcohol; it could just be a job or a spouse. But once these dependency objects are lost, the addictive personality feels driven to use some other type of dependency object to substitute for them. Drugs and alcohol remain two of the most popular ways of performing this substitution.

Michael A. Corey, *Kicking the Drug Habit*, 1989.

The term "dry drunk" describes a person whose life is being controlled by an addictive personality without any drug being present. Dry drunks still trust in the addictive process and cut themselves off from the natural relationships they need in order to be nurtured.

People in a recovery program for alcohol addiction need to clearly understand that they are prone to form a possible addictive relationship with another object or event—food, for example. For these people, sobriety acquires a new dimension: instead of only monitoring their relationship with alcohol, they also need to learn how to monitor the addictive part of themselves.

I am using the example of alcohol and food here because it's common for a recovering alcoholic to become a food addict. I've met persons who, within three or four years of leaving an alcoholism treatment center, have gained 40 or 50 pounds and are as unhappy and emotionally isolated as they were the day they entered treatment. To quote one such person, "I now find myself eating for all the same reasons I drank: I'm lonely, I'm afraid." Many of these people attend A.A. [Alcoholics Anonymous] regularly, are working good recovery programs, and their lives are much better, but something stands in their way of serenity—another addiction.

It's in understanding the addictive personality, even in recovery, that the words, "cunning, baffling, powerful!" show their true meaning. It's the addictive relationship inside oneself that the recovering addict will need to break, not just the relationship with an object. This is when total recovery takes place.

The foundation of the addictive personality is found in all persons. It's found in a normal desire to make it through life with the least amount of pain and the greatest amount of pleasure possible. It's found in our negativism and our mistrust of others and the world, whether our pessimism is big or small, valid or not valid. There is nothing wrong with this part of us; it's natural for all of us to have these beliefs to some degree. It's when these beliefs control one's way of life, as it does in addiction, that people get into trouble. There are persons who are more susceptible to addiction. These are persons who don't know how to have healthy relationships and have been taught not to trust in people. This is mainly because of how they were treated by others while growing up, and they never learned how to connect.

If you were raised in a family where closeness was just a word, not a reality, you are much more prone to form an addictive relationship. This is for two reasons. First, you were taught to distance yourself from people instead of being taught to connect with them. Second, growing up in this type of family left you with a deep, lonely emptiness that you've wanted to have filled. Addiction offers the illusion of fulfillment. If you were raised in a family where people were treated as objects rather than as people, you have already been taught addictive logic. The sad part for many of these people is that many of them struggle hard in recovery; for them, recovery is not a return to a healthier self, but needing to develop a new personality.

Choosing the Addictive High

Addiction is an active belief in and a commitment of oneself to a negative lifestyle. Addiction begins and grows when a person abandons the natural ways of getting emotional needs met, through connecting with other people, one's community, one's self and spiritual powers greater than oneself. The repeated abandonment of oneself in favor of the addictive high causes the addictive personality to develop and gradually gain power.

The development of an addictive personality is similar to a person who gets up each morning and throughout the day says to himself, "Why bother? Life is hard." The more people tell themselves this, the more they will develop the lifestyle and personality of someone who has given up on life. Every time addicts choose to act out in an addictive way, they are saying to themselves one or more of the following:

- "I don't really need people."
- "I don't have to face anything I don't want to."

- "I'm afraid to face life's and my problems."
- "Objects and events are more important than people."
- "I can do anything I want, whenever I want, no matter who it hurts."

This type of thinking forms a pattern in which a person continually supports and reinforces an addictive belief system found inside oneself. A subtle personality change starts to take place. The fact that in most cases these changes are subtle and gradual over long periods of time adds to the seductiveness of addiction.

As time goes on and a person continues to act out and is preoccupied and emotionally distant from others, the addictive personality starts to assert more control over the person's internal life. At this stage, the person suffering from addiction will start to feel a "pull" inside. This may come in the form of emotional restlessness or pangs of conscience.

Personality Mosaic

Personality factors have been shown to be common to both substance and activity addictions. A landmark report released from the National Academy of Sciences in 1983 identified many of the common characteristics. Addicts are more likely to have low self-esteem (where the addiction is a search for self-fulfillment and enhancement of self-image); to be depressed and trying to find escape; to feel alienated; to behave impulsively and unconventionally; to have difficulty in forming long-term goals; and to cope less effectively with stress (and, I would add, to experience a higher level of anxiety from which they seek relief).

Archibald D. Hart, *Christianity Today*, December 9, 1988.

Addiction now starts to produce a by-product—shame. This happens both consciously and unconsciously to addicts, but mostly on an unconscious level. The more addicts seek relief through addiction, the more shame they'll start to experience and the more they will feel a need to justify the addictive relationship to themselves.

Shame creates a loss of *self*-respect, *self*-esteem, *self*-confidence, *self*-discipline, *self*-determination, *self*-control, *self*-importance, and *self*-love. In the beginning, this shame may be a general uneasiness. It's the first cost an addict pays for the addictive relationship. The person starts to feel shame about the signs of loss of control that are beginning to appear within. There may be an occasional incident of behavioral loss of control, but the major forms of loss of control happen on the emotional, thinking level. The person is more apt to feel bad about the internal withdrawal from others. For as the person slowly starts to become more committed to an object or event, there is a gradual emotional withdrawal from intimate relationships with people or a Higher Power.

Addiction starts to create the very thing the person is trying to avoid—pain. In creating pain, the process also creates a need for the continuation of the addictive relationship. *The addict seeks refuge from the pain of addiction by moving further into the addictive process.* The addict seeks happiness and serenity in the high, but because the addict has started to withdraw from self and others, the addict can't see that the pain he or she feels is created by acting out.

Long before episodes of being out of control behaviorally appear, the person has fought and lost many battles with his or her Addict on the emotional level, where the addictive personality gains control. An addictive personality starts its development here, at the emotional level. This is the first part of one's personality that becomes controlled by the addictive process.

Addicts act like kids—if it feels good, they do it. They explore; they follow their emotional impulses. Emotions are at the very core of most people's being. This is easily understood when we remember emotions existed long before we had words to describe them or words to help us understand them.

At this stage, the person emotionally feels uneasy, restless, and guilty. These are some of the internal warning signals that one may feel, but part of the addictive process is learning how to deny these warning signals. Addiction is also a process of denial—denial of reality, but mainly denial of the Self. This denial must be accomplished for the addiction to progress.

"Talk therapy" hasn't proven very effective in treating addicts, for the core of the illness exists on an emotional level, not on a thinking level.

How the Addictive Personality Gains Control

Much of an addict's mental obsession results from denial or refusing to recognize the loss of control that is happening on the emotional level. Avoiding the reality of the situation allows the creation of more pain, which will eventually create the need to explain to oneself what is happening. This will evolve into obsessive thoughts or preoccupation and rationalizations. The obsessive thoughts occur more often and consist of constant questioning: *Why?* Preoccupation has to do with acting out and creating a mood change. We've all heard the saying, "Just change your thoughts and you'll feel better." No one knows this better than addicts. If practicing addicts don't like the way they're feeling, they'll think about acting out and a subtle mood change occurs. Each time this happens, the person loses a small piece of control that is transferred to the addiction.

We are starting to see how the gradual loss of the Self occurs in addiction, and how the addictive personality slowly gains more and more control. *The decrease in the Self causes an increase in the addictive personality.*

The Addictive Cycle

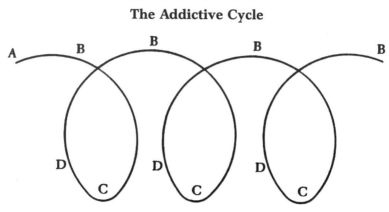

A = pain; B = feel the need to act out; C = act out, start to feel better; D = pain resulting from acting out; B = feel the need to act out; C = act out, start to feel better.

Craig Nakken, *The Addictive Personality*, 1988.

In addiction, there is an almost constant internal conflict between the Self and the Addict. In this struggle, the Addict wins. This is what is meant by "loss of control." The longer the struggle, the more control the addictive personality gains and establishes. Each time the Self struggles against the addiction, the Addict becomes stronger. To fight and struggle against something that has more power than you drains your energy. For each defeat there is some loss of self-esteem. This is why in recovery people are taught to surrender. It is through accepting that one can't conquer his disease that the person finds strength to start connecting with others. . . .

The addictive relationship is an internal relationship based on the interaction between the Self and the Addict; it is a one-to-one relationship; it is based on emotional logic; it creates an inward focus and isolation; it is sustained by the mood change produced by acting out in the addictive process. The longer the interaction between the Self and the Addict, the stronger the addictive personality becomes; the longer the interaction, the more developed the addictive relationship within becomes. In addiction, the Addict becomes the dominant personality.

People and family members often desperately ask themselves and others, "Why does he act like this? Doesn't he care about us anymore?" The truth is that the Addict within doesn't care about them. What it cares about is acting out, getting the mood change. The Addict doesn't care about the Self either. A statement such as, "At least if you won't stop for me, stop for yourself!" falls on deaf ears. The person who suffers from an addiction often asks the same question long before anyone else: "Why do I act this way? Don't I care?"

I've seen many families gather together in tears, realizing it's the Addict, the illness, the addiction they all hate and fear, not the person. It's often a great relief for people suffering from an addiction to realize that they are not "bad people," as they believed, that their addictive personality is not all of them, but only a part of them, having grown as a result of the illness.

"Addiction engages age-old questions about will power, self-control, personal responsibility, and values. "

Personal Choice Causes Cocaine Addiction

Stanton Peele

Health researcher Stanton Peele believes drug addiction is a matter of personal choice and responsibility. In the following viewpoint, Peele maintains that substance abusers deliberately choose a life-style that includes drug use and that cocaine's chemical composition does not cause addiction. Peele is a senior health researcher at Mathematica Policy Research in Princeton, New Jersey, and the author of *Diseasing of America: Addiction Treatment Out of Control.*

As you read, consider the following questions:

1. In Peele's opinion, why is a cocaine habit easier to quit than a cigarette habit?
2. Why does the author believe most middle-class cocaine users avoid addiction?
3. To what does Peele attribute an increase in addictive behaviors?

Stanton Peele, "Control Yourself." Reprinted, with permission, from the February 1990 issue of *Reason* magazine. Copyright © 1990 by the Reason Foundation, 2716 Ocean Park Blvd., Suite 1062, Santa Monica, CA 90405.

America is clearly moving into the 21st century in addictionology—the identification and explication of new addictions, defined as diseases. In addition to the standard drug and alcohol habits, these addictions include shopping and debt, sex and love, gambling, smoking, overeating, and just about anything people can do to excess. There are now A.A.-type support groups organized around several hundred types of activities. The crucial first step of the 12-step program that Alcoholics Anonymous and its derivatives have made famous is the obligation for the alcoholic or addict to admit he or she is "powerless over alcohol," or whatever the person's habit happens to be. This symptom is central to the disease, and A.A. focuses on loss of control as the definition, the etiology, and the excuse for addiction and addictive misbehavior.

It is not science that is fueling the movement to label so many activities as addictions. The tendency to see all addictions as cut from the same cloth returns us to 19th-century (and earlier) usage, in which to be addicted meant to be given over to a vice or activity in some unwholesome and morally reprehensible or weak-willed way. The observation that alcoholism (called inebriation and drunkenness in the last century) and drug addiction are items in a much larger class of human behavior is a fundamental realization that has been accepted throughout most of human history, but which American addictionologists have recently been rediscovering.

What is new in the 20th century is the claim that these compulsive activities somehow represent codifiable diseases. In the case of alcoholism, the inability to control one's drinking is today described as an inherited trait. This is wrong. In fact, even biologically oriented research has shown that loss of control is not an inheritable trait, as A.A. originally claimed.

A Preference to Drink

Rather, to the extent that genetic transmission of drinking patterns is indicated (and the scientific underpinnings for even this minimal proposition are far weaker than most lay readers suspect), researchers see alcoholism as the cumulative result of a long history of drinking. Some genetic theorists claim people continue drinking heavily for long periods of time to resolve neuro-psychological deficiencies or because they lack the inherited mechanism to determine when they have drunk enough.

These theories nonetheless leave room for any number of environmental and personal factors to influence the development of alcoholism.

Research has shown decisively that alcoholics, even while drinking, are crucially influenced by value choices and environmental considerations. Alcoholics who seem to be out of control on the street are actually pursuing deliberate drinking strategies designed to achieve specific levels of drunkenness. Street alcoholics allowed to earn credit for booze in a laboratory will work until they accumulate enough chits to attain the exact level of intoxication they seek. Or, allowed to drink freely in an isolation booth, they will voluntarily cut down their drinking to spend more time in a comfortable, abstinent environment with other alcoholics watching television. Such alcoholics do get drunk a lot, and they prefer drinking to most other options available to them in their natural environments. Nonetheless, alcoholic drinking is a largely purposive behavior, even if alcoholics' purposes are quite alien to most people and even though alcoholics frequently regret their choices after they become sober (at least, until they become drunk again).

The Cocaine and Crack Myth

Much of the work on alcoholics' intentions while drinking has been conducted at the Baltimore City Hospital, part of the federally supported Addiction Research Center. But many of these same investigators are now giving their work with cocaine addicts a very different slant from the one they gave their alcohol research. This research group is often shown on television working with addicts attached to electrodes or giving responses recorded on a computer as they take or come down from their cocaine doses. A researcher then explains to the interviewer how cocaine provides a tremendous uplift, followed by an enervating down.

Actually, this process is a standard one observed in human beings engaged in activities ranging from eating carbohydrates to sexual intercourse (hence the readiness with which these activities are equated with drug addictions). Often, the researchers observe how the anticipation of the cocaine high or the need to reintroduce cocaine to alleviate the low will drive the addict to do anything. Sometimes reference is made to laboratory studies in which animals continue to inject cocaine through an implanted catheter until they kill themselves.

Just how addictive are cocaine and crack? Cocaine in any form is less addictive than cigarettes by the two key behavioral measures of addiction. Five times as many regular cigarette as crack smokers become addicted, according to Jack Henningfield, a researcher at the National Institute on Drug Abuse, and addicts indicate it is easier to give up crack than cigarettes. In fact, if we go by the NIDA survey to which George Bush alluded in his nationally televised speech in September 1990, very few cocaine users become addicted. The survey found that 21 million Americans had used cocaine, 8 million had used it in the last year, and 3 million were current users, but only 300,000 used cocaine daily or nearly so. Government statistics thus show that 10 percent of current users and 1.5 percent of all users take the drug close to every day.

What are we to make, then, of the addict who explains that he needed to steal or kill to get more of his drug, or the woman who sells sex—one notorious addict prostituted her teenage daughter—to get money for crack? Aren't these behaviors drug effects? No, they are not, and it is a mark of naiveté—not science —to mistake the behavior of some drug users with the pharmacological effects of the drug, as though addictive loss of control and criminal behavior were somehow chemical properties of a substance.

Responsibility and Values

Notwithstanding all the pseudoscience associated with it, addiction engages age-old questions about will power, self-control, personal responsibility, and values. How are some people able to turn down a fattening dessert or an after-dinner cigar which they might enjoy consuming, but which they have decided is bad for them? Do those who instead indulge themselves have a disease? Or do they have less self-control or think it is less important to be healthy?

In fact, science, like law, cannot accurately proceed without taking into account individual responsibility and values. For example, given that cigarettes are harder to quit than crack, what should we learn from the fact that William Bennett gave up smoking to take his post as drug czar? The only possible answer is that he was wise enough to recognize that he couldn't hold an antidrug post and be a cigarette addict, and that he wanted the drug post more than he wanted to continue smoking.

Few Users Become Addicted

In spite of widespread availability and declining prices, most people never use cocaine; of those who do, most use it only once or a few times; of those who become casual or regular users, most do not become dependent or addicted; of those who become dependent or addicted, most return to moderate use or voluntarily abstain without treatment.

Bruce Alexander, *Reason*, December 1990.

Of course, self-control and sound values are not immutable, Platonic ideals either. After all, Bennett inappropriately maintained his cigarette addiction throughout his tenure as secretary of education. Smokers and fat people demonstrate similarly weak self-control for years, until they successfully stop smoking or lose weight, after which we all envy them for their superior will power. People do refocus their values as their lives progress and they have different opportunities and options and become better prepared or more willing to change long-term habits. This is the nature of the beast, and nothing we learn about the chemistry of one drug versus another can change it. *Try* to say something sensible about nicotine's addictive properties as a way of explaining Bennett's newfound ability to abstain from smoking.

Avoiding Addiction

Why do we think crack/cocaine is so much more addictive than cigarettes, or heroin, or alcohol (all of which addicts with multiple addictions say are harder to quit than cocaine, whether smoked, injected, or snorted)? The drug's current reputation seems strange when we consider that cocaine was an ingredient in Coca-Cola and other soft drinks into the 20th century, and that research on cocaine's effects was conducted for 50 years before cocaine was announced to be addictive in the mid-1980s, coinciding with the explosion of recreational cocaine use in this country. Cocaine came to be addictive among some inner-city users and among a very small percentage of middle-class users who tried the drug.

Why didn't most of these people become cocaine addicts? The answer is so simple that we are left wondering why scientists can't figure it out: Most people have better things to do than to become addicted to cocaine. This is an example of a scientific concept—addiction—developing a symbolic meaning which is contradicted by the data. Nothing about drug use or any other addiction rules out choices and individual values. Without taking these facts of life into account, we cannot understand who becomes addicted and who does not, and why.

A study of middle-class users of cocaine by the Addiction Research Foundation of Toronto found not only that most regular users do not become addicted, but also that most of those who develop a steady craving for cocaine eventually cut back or quit the drug on their own. In other words, cocaine use resembles just about every other compelling experience in its potential to upset people's equilibrium, but this is not a permanent or inexorable condition for most people.

Teach Respect and Ethics

Counterpoised with these data are reports by the few who despair of kicking their cocaine habits on their own and enter private treatment centers, or by the addict-criminals who testify on television that you would kill and prostitute your children—as they did—if only you took crack. These claims are preposterous, the scientists and clinicians who encourage them are misrepresenting the facts, and we have reached a strange impasse in our civilization when we rely for information and moral guidance about habits on the most debilitated segments of our population—groups who attribute to addiction and drugs what are actually their personal problems. What, really, are we to learn from people who stand up and testify that they couldn't control their shopping sprees, that they spent all their money and went bankrupt to get material possessions we were smart enough to resist, and that they now want us to forgive them and their debts?

The message in all this is that one of the best antidotes to addiction is to teach children responsibility and respect for others and to insist on ethical standards for everyone—children, adults, addicts. Crosscultural data indicate, for instance, that when an experience is defined as uncontrollable, many people experience such loss of control and use it to justify their transgressions against society. For example, studies find that the "uncontrollable" consequences of alcohol consumption vary from one society to another, depending upon cultural expectations. In arctic Finland, drinking sessions regularly lead to knife fights and killings; in Mediterranean countries such as Greece, on the other hand, such violence is virtually unheard of, and people do not perceive a link between alcohol and aggression.

Preventing Addiction

The modern "scientific" view of alcoholism and addiction has actually caused addictive behaviors of all kinds to grow. It excuses uncontrolled behavior and predisposes people to interpret their lack of control as the expression of a disease which they can do nothing about. Treatment advocates attack those who don't accept the disease model of addiction as being "unscientific" and "moralistic," or as practicing "denial." On the contrary, the refusal to accept the loss-of-control myth seems to inoculate people against addiction.

One of the worst consequences of the idea that addiction and alcoholism are diseases is the notion that substance abuse can be treated away, a view continuously propagated by a large and growing addiction-treatment establishment and bought by well-meaning public officials and private citizens. In fact, these treatments are exorbitantly expensive ($7,500 to $35,000 a month in a private treatment center) while being demonstrably ineffective.

One of the most remarkable works of addictionology of the 1980s was a tome by psychiatrist George Vaillant entitled *The Natural History of Alcoholism*. Vaillant defended throughout his book the medical model of alcoholism, but then revealed that the alcoholics he treated at Cambridge Hospital in Massachusetts with detoxification, compulsory A.A. attendance, and counseling fared no better than comparably severe alcoholics who went completely without treatment. Several times in this strange book, Vaillant warns professional readers not to interfere with "the natural healing process"—this, in a work by a psychiatrist who insists that we need to get more alcoholics into treatment.

43

What works in fact for alcoholism and addiction is giving people the options and values that rule out addictive drug use. Investing more in futile but expensive treatment programs simply subtracts from the resources that are available to influence people's actual environments in ways that can reduce their vulnerability to addiction. Even Dr. Herbert Kleber, Bennett's deputy in charge of "demand reduction," has indicated that addicts can only be treated by being "given a place in the family and social structures" that they may never have had before. In other words, as Kleber puts it, they require "habilitation more than rehabilitation."

Social Structures and Abstinence

The head of the NIDA, Charles Schuster, indicates that in treating drug addicts, "the best predictor of success is whether the addict has a job." Of course, the best way to avoid addiction in the first place is to have in place social structures, jobs, and values that militate against habitual intoxication. But these are hardly treatment issues, and to approach them as such is to attack the problem in a belated, piecemeal, and ultimately self-defeating way. . . .

Clearly, although we convinced those with the most personal resources and responsibility to stop experimenting with drugs, those who are unable or unwilling to control their drug use grew more numerous and found themselves in a deeper hole. At the same time, as we have seen, the NIDA survey to which Bush alluded found that minuscule numbers of those who experiment with cocaine become addicts. Here we see how the administration's own statistics disprove the link between recreational drug use and addiction that Bennett seeks to claim.

In the area of addiction, what is purveyed as fact is usually wrong and simply repackages popular myths as if they were the latest scientific deductions. To be ignorant of the received opinion about addiction is to have the best chance to say something sensible and to have an impact on the problem.

"Cocaine causes both psychological and physiological dependence. "

The Drug Itself Causes Cocaine Addiction

Cardwell C. Nuckols

Cardwell C. Nuckols, a recovered drug addict and a cocaine-addiction specialist, is a consultant for chemical dependency treatment programs. In the following viewpoint, Nuckols argues that chemicals in cocaine cause addicts to be physically and psychologically dependent on the drug. He believes cocaine's pleasurable effect on the brain and the physical pain of withdrawal results in repeated drug abuse.

As you read, consider the following questions:

1. Why does Nuckols believe it is difficult for some addicts to use cocaine sparingly?
2. Why are cocaine freebasers compelled to use again, according to the author?
3. Besides cocaine, what other substances does Nuckols believe cause mental and physical dependence?

Andrew Weil, in *Chocolate to Morphine*, says there is nothing wrong with drugs. They are neither inherently good nor bad. People use them for reasons that often lead to serious problems, creating bad relationships between the consumer and the drug. Tragically, that appears to be the norm when the drug is cocaine.

I was in Connecticut lecturing on cocaine, intimacy, and sexual relationships. I noticed a lady crying in the audience. During the break I took her aside and said, "What happened? It seems there's something occurring in your life related to what we're talking about." She said, "Yes, my husband is a doctor and he just picked cocaine over me. We're getting a divorce."

I hear this a lot. "Cocaine can't hug me or kiss me; it can't give me affection. Yet I will pick this damned white substance over people who can do all the nice things in the world for me. I pick it over my job. Pick it over anything. Half of the time, I pick it over sex—but I would prefer to have sex with it."

The Allure of Cocaine

This is cocaine addiction and it simply means we're saying, "This person can't stop." I've often asked patients who were cocaine addicts, "What do you think about this stuff? Do you think it causes physical dependency?" The reply has generally been, "I used to think cocaine wasn't physically addictive but when, for the thousandth time, I tried but couldn't stop using it, I figured I had a problem. Maybe I was dependent."

When you ask people who use cocaine regularly if they have a dependency problem, what you hear is, "Yes, I do, because I can't stop. Even when I want to stop, I can't stop. Nine out of ten times I can't refuse cocaine. Nine out of ten times, even when I don't want to use cocaine, just being physically close to it causes me to use again. If I take one line, I'll take every bit I can get my hands on. I may even start calling people at 4 A.M. to get more."

Alcohol and cocaine dependents share the same patterns of initial reactions to the drug experience. Cocaine dependents often say, "I remember a time when I thought I could never do more than a half or one gram of cocaine a night." Then there are those who are immediately captivated, who "get down" in their first episode. With cocaine, however, the progression of the drug dependency is different from alcohol.

Drugs and the Brain

An alcoholic may spend from five to thirty years developing the addiction we call alcoholism, all the psychological, behavioral, social, spiritual problems of chemical dependency. With adolescents freebasing cocaine, we see a progression to a situation requiring intensive treatment in from two to six months.

With adults, we're seeing anywhere from six months to three or four years of heavy use, to develop the same levels and types of difficulties it takes twenty years for chronic alcoholics to develop.

Instant and Protracted Addictions

It may take several minutes to feel the effects of snorting coke, and the "high" lasts for about 20 minutes to half an hour. Crack, on the other hand, is felt within a few seconds, and the short but very intense high lasts only for five or 10 minutes, followed by a very intense crash. Cocaine is psychologically and physically addictive to many people, but it usually takes from two to five years for the addiction to develop. Crack, because it operates so quickly, is also very quickly addictive. Almost without exception, users become addicted within the first few uses, sometimes from the very first use.

Elizabeth A. Ryan, *Straight Talk About Drugs and Alcohol*, 1989.

Dr. Doug Talbot, a well known addictionologist, believes there is a drug dependency progression that occurs within the brain itself. When a person starts using drugs, conscious choice governs. The cerebral cortex, the computer part of the brain, enables this person to turn off the drug use early, get to bed, and do the things he needs to do. But as drug use continues, something happens so that the person becomes dependent upon the drug, physiologically and psychologically.

Dr. Talbot believes what happens is that at some point the drug takes on a property which the brain interprets as an instinct, something necessary for survival. After watching my father die of alcoholism and others die of addiction, this is the only explanation that makes sense to me. The drug having taken on an instinctive quality equated with survival is the only way I can explain the behaviors I see among cocaine addicts.

No Control

Related to the inability to stop is the inability to conserve the drug, to put some away for tomorrow. This is also true of people who have become dependent upon marijuana, heroin, alcohol, tranquilizers, sedatives, and the "Heinz 57" variety of drugs that alter consciousness. Why is it when people become chemically dependent they can't leave a little bit for tomorrow? It's rare to find a cocaine addict who is going to save any at all. They say things like this to themselves: "I have two grams left and I want to put some of it away." They can't bring themselves to do it though. The anguish of coming off this drug and the strong components of addiction involved in using cocaine make it practically impossible for dependents to conserve.

The *Diagnostic and Statistical Manual* of the American Psychiatric Association (the *DSM-III*) declares cocaine abstinence a disorder that induces people to use cocaine because the dysphoria or anguish of coming off this drug is profound. When you are getting off a drug like alcohol, you are coming down for several hours. Distributing the experience of coming down over several hours doesn't seem to result in the intense anguish of cocaine abstinence. Cocaine "takes you up" quickly, but drops you quickly too. If it hits your brain within six to eight seconds, in the time it takes to get the freebase pipe from your mouth to the table, you experience a "coming down" that is also precipitous.

Coming off cocaine is one of the most anguished, depressing experiences. I've watched people talk about coming off freebase and one of the things I noticed was the nonverbal maneuvers they use to describe it. It looks like they're describing a heart attack. They have fists clenched to the chest. You can see that it hurts. They can recreate that hurt for you because it's a devastating event. They'll do almost anything to keep from crashing on cocaine. And on top of that they'll do just about anything to keep their supply coming. Postcocaine anguish is a strong inducement to use again—to keep the pain away.

Cocaine, Mind, and the Body

There are moral and legal issues pertaining to using cocaine. It is an illegal drug. This raises serious questions about the notion of the "recreational use" of cocaine. From a clinical perspective it is difficult to answer the question, "What is recreational cocaine use?" Are there people who can use cocaine without experiencing trouble with it? There may be a subpopulation of people who can "do a little bit" of cocaine, put it away, "do a little bit more later," and not have problems. But therapists and counselors don't have people coming to them saying, "I snorted two lines of cocaine last night. Can you help me? I enjoyed the hell out of it." The people may be out there somewhere but they aren't part of the clinical scene. The cocaine users whom therapists and counselors see are those who have lost families, health, jobs and hope. They are victims of a progressive addiction.

Unfortunately, some of the basic reference materials used by psychologists, psychiatrists and other clinicians in the past, for example the *DSM-III* mentioned earlier, described cocaine as a substance of abuse—but not a substance of dependence. A later edition of this manual, *DSM III-R*, describes cocaine as a drug of dependence-producing potential. The notion is that you can distinguish between the mind and the body, and that the crucial issue is what happens to the body. Dependence is a physical phenomenon. But I don't think you can differentiate the mind from the body. In terms of consequences for the drug user, his family and the community, what difference does it make if his destruction has arisen from a psychological dependence or from a physical dependence? The truth is, he can't stop using cocaine and is in desperate trouble.

Shattered Lives

I have worked with people who have used cocaine for less than a year and whose lives were already shattered. One gentleman in particular comes to mind. In nine months he had blown $150,000, had lost his whole family, owed another $50,000, and was in an auto wreck. He had blown everything . . . from job to family. The progressive nature of the illness is astonishing.

I am convinced, from my work with drug users, that cocaine causes both psychological and physiological dependence, just as alcohol, Valium and many other drugs do. We see consistent patterns of electroencephalogram changes and biochemical changes, and we repeatedly observe the same set of symptoms in early recovery. These facts tell me that cocaine is a chemical which causes physical dependency.

a critical thinking activity

Understanding Words in Context

Readers occasionally come across words they do not recognize. And frequently, because they do not know a word or words, they will not fully understand the passage being read. Obviously, the reader can look up an unfamiliar word in a dictionary. By carefully examining the word in the context in which it is used, however, the word's meaning can often be determined. A careful reader may find clues to the meaning of the word in surrounding words, ideas, and attitudes.

Below are excerpts from the viewpoints in this chapter. In each excerpt, one of the words is printed in italics. Try to determine the meaning of each word by reading the excerpt. Under each excerpt you will find four definitions for the italicized word. Choose the one that is closest to your understanding of the word.

Finally, use a dictionary to see how well you have understood the words in context. It will be helpful to discuss with others the clues that helped you decide on each word's meaning.

1. Andrew Weil, in *Chocolate to Morphine*, says there is nothing wrong with drugs. They are neither *INHERENTLY* good nor bad.

   INHERENTLY means:

   a) nearly   c) described as
   b) essentially   d) very

2. People may use alcohol or other drugs to *MITIGATE* unpleasant emotional states such as anger, guilt, loneliness, or boredom.

   MITIGATE means:

   a) increase   c) lessen
   b) express   d) achieve

3. An alcoholic or drug addict uses alcohol or drugs in order to feel good, *EUPHORIC*, or "buzzed up."

   EUPHORIC means:

   a) elated　　　　　c) lazy
   b) firm　　　　　　d) smart

4. Cocaine use may upset some people's equilibrium, but this is not a permanent or *INEXORABLE* condition for most people.

   INEXORABLE means:

   a) painful　　　　c) pleasing
   b) quiet　　　　　d) unavoidable

5. The idea that addiction or alcoholism are diseases that can be treated is a view *PROPAGATED* by the addiction-treatment establishment.

   PROPAGATED means:

   a) attacked　　　　c) denied
   b) believed　　　　d) spread

6. We generally blame "society" for the antisocial behaviors of some people and we refer to these *ABERRANT* behaviors as "alternative life-styles."

   ABERRANT means:

   a) calm　　　　　c) abnormal
   b) wise　　　　　d) violent

7. The government believes that anti-drug education programs can help Americans *CURTAIL* their drug use.

   CURTAIL means:

   a) curl　　　　　c) support
   b) outlaw　　　　d) reduce

8. An all-out effort to get large numbers of people off drugs is too *INTRACTABLE* to be achieved in the near future.

   INTRACTABLE means:

   a) unfair　　　　c) simple
   b) difficult　　　d) peaceful

9. To capture drug dealers who have escaped to foreign countries, the U.S. encourages these countries to *EXTRADITE* drug dealers to the U.S.

   EXTRADITE means:

   a) surrender　　　c) demonstrate
   b) elect　　　　　d) execute

Periodical Bibliography

The following articles have been selected to supplement the diverse views presented in this chapter.

Jonathan Beaty — "Do Humans Need to Get High?" *Time*, August 21, 1989.

William Ira Bennett — "Patterns of Addiction," *The New York Times Magazine*, April 10, 1988.

Maureen Dowd — "Addiction Chic," *Mademoiselle*, October 1989.

David Gelman — "Roots of Addiction," *Newsweek*, February 20, 1989.

Stuart Greenbaum — "Youth and Drug Abuse," *USA Today*, November 1989.

Pete Hamill — "Crack and the Box," *Esquire*, May 1990.

Archibald D. Hart — "Addicted to Pleasure," *Christianity Today*, December 9, 1988.

John Leo — "The It's-Not-My-Fault Syndrome," *U.S. News & World Report*, June 18, 1990.

Art Levine — "America's Addiction to Addictions," *U.S. News & World Report*, February 5, 1990.

Linda Marsa — "Addiction and IQ," *Omni*, October 1989.

Michael Massing — "Desperate over Drugs," *The New York Review of Books*, March 30, 1989.

Elayne Rapping — "Hooked on a Feeling," *The Nation*, March 5, 1990.

Anastasia Toufexis — "The Struggle of Kitty Dukakis," *Time*, February 20, 1989.

Linda Troiano — "Addicted States of America," *American Health*, September 1990.

Maxine Waters — "Drugs, Democrats and Priorities," *The Nation*, July 24, 1990.

William L. Wilbanks — "The New Obscenity," *Vital Speeches of the Day*, August 15, 1988.

Is Smoking Harmful?

**Chemical
Dependency**

Chapter Preface

Because public smoking is an issue of both personal rights and health, it generates many arguments. Both smokers and non-smokers argue that their rights are breached when one group's desires are allowed to prevail over the other's.

In the battle over smoking, nonsmokers argue that second-hand cigarette smoke, also called passive or secondary smoke, is a health hazard to nonsmokers. They cite research showing that long-term exposure to passive smoke increases the risk of heart disease and lung cancer. Health researchers say passive smoke, containing more than forty carcinogens, is responsible for as many as fifty thousand deaths in America every year. In efforts to protect people from secondhand smoke, nonsmokers' groups have campaigned for legislation restricting public smoking. In 1990, for example, California members of Americans for Nonsmokers' Rights helped pass a Sacramento city ordinance that completely banned smoking in workplaces and in public.

Conversely, pro-smoking groups, such as The Tobacco Institute, which lobbies for the tobacco industry, object to classifying passive smoke as a cause of cancer. As Institute spokesperson Brennan Dawson says about passive smoking causing cancer, "The science is so lacking, it's impossible to believe the conclusions will hold up." In addition, many smokers object to public-smoking restrictions, believing these laws discriminate against them. These advocates argue that smoking is a personal choice that the government has no business restricting, particularly in the workplace. Dave Brenton, president of Smokers' Rights Alliance, says, "It's unethical to try to dictate private behavior. Smoking is just one of many private behaviors which . . . cannot legally be forbidden."

The debate between smokers and nonsmokers will continue regardless of which side legislation may favor. The authors in the following chapter debate the issues of personal rights and health regarding smoking.

"No drug ever ingested by humans can rival the long-term debilitating effects of tobacco."

Cigarette Smoking Is Harmful

K. H. Ginzel

K. H. Ginzel, a professor of pharmacology and toxicology at the University of Arkansas in Fayetteville, has studied nicotine and its effects on the body. In the following viewpoint, Ginzel argues that cigarette smoking is one of the most powerful addictions known. He states that the chemicals and toxic gases in cigarettes can cause cancer, heart disease, and emphysema.

As you read, consider the following questions:

1. What does Ginzel say is the irony concerning chemicals in cigarettes and identical chemicals found elsewhere?
2. How does the author view the imagery surrounding cigarettes?
3. According to the author, how many people die worldwide from the effects of tobacco usage?

K.H. Ginzel, "What's in a Cigarette?" *Priorities*, Fall 1990. Reprinted with permission from the publisher, the American Council on Science and Health.

For those who still don't know—let me emphatically state that cigarette smoking is a true addiction, more powerful than a dependence on alcohol, heroin or cocaine. To grasp this well-documented fact, one really doesn't have to study all the supporting scientific evidence. One simply needs to consider that no other drug is self-administered with the persistence, regularity and frequency of a cigarette. At an average rate of ten puffs per cigarette, a one to three pack-a-day smoker inhales 70,000 to 200,000 individual doses of mainstream smoke during a single year. Ever since its large-scale industrial production early in this century, the popularity of the modern cigarette has been spreading like wildfire. Here is the first, and perhaps the most significant answer to the question [What's in a cigarette?]: Addiction is in a cigarette.

Probing into what makes a cigarette so irresistible, we find that much of the recent research corroborates earlier claims: It is for the nicotine in tobacco that the smoker smokes, the chewer chews, and the dipper dips. Hence, nicotine is in a cigarette.

In contrast to other drugs, nicotine delivery from tobacco carries an ominous burden of chemical poisons and cancer-producing substances that boggle the mind. Many toxic agents are in a cigarette. However, additional toxicants are manufactured during the smoking process by the chemical reactions occurring in the glowing tip of the cigarette. The number is staggering: more than 4,000 hazardous compounds are present in the smoke that smokers draw into their lungs and which escapes into the environment between puffs.

Pollution and Disease

The burning of tobacco generates more than 150 billion tar particles per cubic inch, constituting the visible portion of cigarette smoke. According to chemists at R.J. Reynolds Tobacco Company, cigarette smoke is 10,000 times more concentrated than the automobile pollution at rush hour on a freeway. The lungs of smokers, puffing a daily ration of 20 to 60 low to high tar cigarettes, collect an annual deposit of one-quarter to one and one-half pounds of the gooey black material, amounting to a total of 15 to 90 million pounds of carcinogen-packed tar for the aggregate of current American smokers. Hence, tar is in a cigarette.

But visible smoke contributes only 5-8% to the total output of a cigarette. The remaining bulk that cannot be seen makes up the so-called vapor or gas phase of cigarette "smoke." It contains, besides nitrogen and oxygen, a bewildering assortment of toxic gases, such as carbon monoxide, formaldehyde, acrolein, hydrogen cyanide, and nitrogen oxides, to name just a few. Smokers efficiently extract almost 90% of the particulate as well as gaseous constituents (about 50% in the case of carbon monoxide) from the mainstream smoke of the 600 billion cigarettes consumed annually in the U.S. In addition, 2.25 million metric tons of sidestream smoke chemicals pollute the enclosed air spaces of homes, offices, conference rooms, bars, restaurants, and automobiles in this country. Hence, pollution is in a cigarette.

Bill Schorr, © 1987 Los Angeles Times Syndicate. Reprinted with permission.

The witch's brew of poisons invades the organs and tissues of smokers and nonsmokers, adults and children, born as well as unborn, and causes cancer, emphysema, heart disease, fetal growth retardation and other problems during pregnancy. The harm inflicted by all other addictions combined pales in comparison. Smoking-related illness, for example, claims in a few days as many victims as cocaine does in a whole year. Hence, disease is in a cigarette.

Chemicals in Cigarette Smoke

The irony is that many of the poisons found in cigarette smoke are subject to strict regulation by federal laws which, on the other hand, specifically exempt tobacco products. "Acceptable Daily Intake," ADI, is the amount of a chemical an individual can be exposed to for an extended period without apparent

detriment to health. A comparison of the actual intake of selected chemicals in mainstream smoke with their ADIs reveals
the enormity of toxic exposure incurred by the smoker (this includes the presence of methyl isocyanide, the toxicant of the
Bhopal disaster).

In addition, there is the chemical burden from sidestream
smoke, afflicting smokers and nonsmokers alike. Based on the
reported concentrations in enclosed, cigarette smoke-polluted
areas, the estimated intakes of nicotine, acrolein, carbon monoxide, nitrogen dioxide, and formaldehyde peak at 200, 130, 75, 7,
and 3 times the ADI, respectively. The high exposure to acrolein
is especially unsettling. This compound is not only a potent respiratory irritant, but qualifies, according to current studies, as a
carcinogen.

Regulatory policy aims at restricting exposure to carcinogens
to a level where the lifetime risk of cancer would not exceed 1
in 100,000 to 1,000,000. Due to a limited database, approximate
upper lifetime risk values could be calculated for only 7 representative cigarette smoke carcinogens. The risk values were ex-
traordinarily high, ranging from 1 in 6,000 to 1 in 16. Because of
the awesome amount of carcinogens found in cigarette smoke
and the fact that carcinogens combine their individual actions in
an additive or even multiplicative fashion, it is not surprising
that the actual risk for lung cancer is as high as one in ten.
Hence, cancer is in a cigarette.

Among the worst offenders are the nitrosamines. Strictly regulated by federal agencies, their concentrations in beer, bacon,
and baby bottle nipples must not exceed 5 to 10 parts per billion. A typical person ingests about one microgram a day, while
the smokers' intake tops this by 17 times for each pack of
cigarettes smoked. In 1976, a rocket fuel manufacturer in the
Baltimore area was emitting dimethylnitrosamine into the surrounding air, exposing the local inhabitants to an estimated 14
micrograms of the carcinogen per day. The plant was promptly
shut down. However eagerly the government tries to protect us
from outdoor pollution and the carcinogenic risk of consumer
products, it blatantly suspends control if the offending chemical
is in, or comes from, a cigarette. Hence, hypocrisy is in a cigarette.

Sending the Wrong Message

But there is still more in a cigarette than addiction, poison,
pollution, disease, and hypocrisy. A half century of aggressive
promotion and sophisticated advertising that featured alluring
role models from theater, film and sport, has invested the cigarette
with an enticing imagery. Imagery which captivates and seduces
a growing youngster. The youngster, indispensable for being re-
cruited into the future army of smokers, does not start to smoke

cigarettes for the nicotine, but for the false promises they hold. Hence, deceit is in a cigarette.

In summary, no drug ever ingested by humans can rival the long-term debilitating effects of tobacco; the carnage perpetuated by its purveyors; the merciless irreversibility of destiny once the victim contracts lung cancer or emphysema; the militant denial on the part of those who, with the support of stockholders and the sanction of governments, legally push their lethal merchandise across borders and continents killing every year two and one-half to three million people worldwide. All things added together: death is in a cigarette.

"A number of respected scientists do not believe a causal relationship between smoking and illness has been established."

Cigarette Smoking May Not Be Harmful

Horace R. Kornegay

Horace R. Kornegay practices law in Greensboro, North Carolina, and is a former president of the Tobacco Institute. In the following viewpoint, he argues that the case against smoking is built on statistics that are not valid. One by one, Kornegay presents the most prominent research studies on tobacco and then contends that they are not totally valid.

As you read, consider the following questions:

1. How does Kornegay argue against the laboratory "proof" that smoking causes cancer?
2. How does the author refute the link between heart disease and smoking?
3. Do you agree with the author that the claim of "300,000 excess deaths" being caused by smoking is merely propaganda? Why or why not?

Horace R. Kornegay, "The Cigarette Controversy," *Engage/Social Action*, September 1980. Reprinted with permission.

For many adults, cigarette smoking is one of life's pleasures. Does it cause illness—even death? No one knows.

The case against smoking is based almost entirely on inferences from statistics. The "conventional wisdom" about smoking came from judgments expressed by committees of doctors in England and the United States. In our country, antismoking organizations pressured the government to endorse these judgments. Never before (or since) had a committee "discovered" a single "cause" for so many diseases.

A number of respected scientists do not believe a causal relationship between smoking and illness has been established. Others believe that it has.

If smoking does cause disease, why, after years of intensive research, has it not been shown *how* this occurs? And why has no ingredient in smoke been identified as the causal factor?

Smoking: Health Statistics

Statistics are said to show that among the 60 million Americans who are smokers, some may fall victim sooner, or in greater number, than other people to three major types of ailments— cancer, diseases of the heart and circulatory system, and the pulmonary illnesses, emphysema and chronic bronchitis.

These happen to be our greatest medical problems, coming to the forefront as the major infectious diseases of the past were "conquered" through scientific research. There have been other coincidental trends, among them the growth in popularity of cigarettes.

Scientists call these heart and lung problems "degenerative" ailments, for they seem to develop very slowly, through some kind of distortion or breakdown of body mechanisms. Though each illness is very different, all three—and more—are blamed by some sources primarily on one factor—cigarettes.

Laboratory Work

We hear about laboratory "proof" that smoking causes cancer. Mice have been painted, hamsters swabbed, and rats injected with "tars" condensed from tobacco smoke in laboratories but not found in the smoke itself. Rabbits have been fed nicotine. Dogs have been forced to "smoke" through holes cut in their windpipes. Subsequent "changes" in various cells of these animals have been cited as evidence that cigarettes cause diseases, though production with smoke of human-type lung cancer—or heart disease or emphysema—has *never been verified* in laboratory experiments.

It is no wonder that an American Cancer Society official has said that "a clever enough researcher can make almost anything induce cancer in animals, *but his findings may have no relevance to human exposure."*

Somehow it's possible, the argument goes, that direct exposure to tobacco smoke can damage cells in the respiratory tract. The human heart is not exposed to smoke, and so there is even greater guessing about how it might be affected.

The Problems of Guesswork

Simply blaming cigarettes for heart disease doesn't help. In some countries not even statistics fit that notion. The government's National Heart and Lung Institute points out that we've learned so much about how to treat heart ailments that we overlook how little we know about their *causes*. "We tend to obscure our ignorance," the Institute says, "by making it seem that a problem has been solved when it has, in fact, been only half solved."

Emphysema, which makes breathing difficult, is a kind of lung disease typically found in older persons. Doctors ponder whether, among other things, it might be caused by inhaling some substance or whether it might result from some blood circulation difficulty. In any event, and despite speculation that smoking has something to do with it, the official view of the government institute responsible for lung research remains candid: "We do not know the cause of pulmonary emphysema, how to stop its progress even if detected early, or how to prevent heart disease caused by emphysema."

Unproven Causes

There *is* a cigarette controversy. The *causal theory*—that cigarette smoking causes or is the cause of the various diseases with which it is reported to be related statistically—is just that, a theory.

That the cause or causes of lung cancer and other diseases has *not* been scientifically proved is supported in the almost 4,000 printed pages of testimony and evidence presented on the cigarette labeling bills of 1982 and 1983 by research workers, government officials, voluntary health association representatives and behavioral experts.

The Tobacco Institute, *The Cigarette Controversy: Why More Research Is Needed,* February 1984.

Those who consider smoking a menace, rather than an enjoyment, have acted as prosecutors, trying to convince the public they have an airtight case. But isn't the "jury" entitled to some serious doubts? For example:

• Statistics do not explain why the majority of smokers never develop the diseases "associated" with smoking.

- Smoking cannot be the *sole* cause of *illness, because in every* case nonsmokers are afflicted too. For example, a study published in the [1979] *Journal of the National Cancer Institute* reported that the incidence of lung cancer among nonsmokers doubled in the [1970s].
- Research suggests that because a patient tells a doctor he or she smokes, that patient is more apt to be diagnosed with an ailment "associated" in the familiar statistics with smoking.
- At the same time that increases in lung cancer have been reported, new techniques and equipment have made it possible to identify more cases with certainty.
- Too many conflicting reports are ignored in the antismoking messages from "authorities." For instance, the American Heart Association warns about tobacco but doesn't remind us that in Japan, where the smoking rate is much *higher* among men than in the United States, the heart disease death rate is far *lower*. Or that the US rate has been *falling* for the past fifteen years in the face of *increasing* smoking.
- We are told that more people have been smoking at younger ages, which suggests to some that illnesses associated with smoking should appear sooner. Yet the peak age for lung cancer stays right around sixty and, if anything, may be moving to *older* ages.

Such observations, needless to say, do not *exonerate* cigarettes. Yet, drawing conclusions *against* cigarettes is equally unjustified.

Deceptive Propaganda

No doubt you have heard or read that smoking is responsible for "300,000 excess deaths" in this country each year. Let's look at how this "fact" developed:

In 1964, the assistant surgeon general said that such an estimate would involve "making so many assumptions," that it might be "misleading." Yet a year later, a former advertising executive who just doesn't like smoking announced that cigarettes cause 125,000 to 300,000 deaths a year.

Another government official agreed, claiming smoking was responsible for *at least* 125,000 premature deaths a year. He acknowledged getting the figure from the advertising man.

So the advertising man was asked in a Congressional hearing where *he* got *his* estimate. His reply: From the government! The government man tried to justify it. He took some arbitrary percentages of the annual deaths from various ailments, including several *which were not even claimed by the Surgeon General to be causally related to smoking!*

Later the Surgeon General himself undertook to explain the 300,000 figure. He did this by:
- Taking as his basis the unsupported estimate above.

- Adding to it another unsupported 102,000 deaths—"from diseases where the relationship to cigarette smoke, while not so obvious, is nevertheless clearly indicated."
- Adding to *this* another unsupported but "reasonable estimate" of 60,000 excess deaths from smoking *women*, who had not been included in the earlier estimates.

Nobody took the trouble to expose this silly game, or to point out that the "authorities" considered *nothing but smoking* in comparing the longevity of one group of persons with another. But scientists, quietly studying twins, made a significant contribution. Let us see what happens, they reasoned, to people with *identical genetics* and different smoking habits.

Experiment Failures

Experiments using air pollutants, such as sulfur oxides and oxides of nitrogen, have produced emphysema in laboratory animals. Yet many animal experiments have failed to induce emphysema with long-term exposure to cigarette smoke.

The Tobacco Institute, *Cigarette Smoking and Chronic Obstructive Lung Diseases: The Major Gaps in Knowledge,* 1984.

By 1970 a study appeared of Swedish identical twin pairs with differing smoking habits, including cases where one twin didn't smoke at all. There was no association between smoking and higher overall mortality. Later similar findings were reported among Danish twins. But tobacco's foes still repeat that number—300,000. A simple, rounded, large, impressive—and meaningless—statistic.

Many Contrasts

Smoking and health statistics have been built up by comparing smokers and nonsmokers. But when large numbers of people are sorted into two groups this way, are there *no other differences* between them? Differences which might account for contrasts in health patterns?

There are, indeed, say authorities who have studied such things. Some of them are surprising.

Smokers generally are more communicative. They are more creative, more energetic, drink more coffee and liquor, marry more often, prefer spicier and saltier food. They take part in more sports and change jobs more often. *They are more likely to have parents with heart disease and high blood pressure!*

These and other findings, accumulating in the medical literature, raise the question of whether smokers may have higher illness rates *because of the kind of people they happen to be.*

Science has learned that a blueprint of our constitutional, physical and chemical makeup is laid down at the moment of conception. This is genetics and, as the saying goes, we cannot choose our grandfathers. The blueprint is still fuzzy—we do *not* know, for example, the extent to which our genes may map our actual behavior and choice of lifestyle, and how these in turn may affect our relative well-being.

The Nonsmoker

Some persons who believe smoking is harmful to the smoker have also jumped to the conclusion that tobacco smoke harms the nonsmoker.

Scientists have conducted many experiments to test this hypothesis, carefully analyzing "smoke-filled rooms" and looking for "pollutants" under extreme conditions rarely, if ever, found in a normal social situation. Result: The preponderance of evidence simply does not support the health effect theory. As the scientific journal which published a controversial study by California researchers earlier [in 1980], editorialized: "Generally speaking, the evidence that passive smoking in a general environment has health effects remains sparse, incomplete and sometimes unconvincing."

Yet some persons would like government bodies to adopt new laws or regulations to curb our right to make our own personal decisions about smoking.

In this case, the solution seems clear: Personal courtesy, thoughtfulness, and tolerance by both smokers and nonsmokers; a few simple, voluntary practices in special situations, and respect for individual freedom of choice.

Needed: Objective Research

It is human nature to want to assume some things we don't really *know*. Certainly that has been the case among many people who have had something to say about smoking and health.

But that is not the spirit of science. True scientists make assumptions *only* for the purpose of *testing* them, proving or disproving them.

In that spirit, notwithstanding the easy answers some people claim to have, scientists throughout the world continue to seek the *truth about smoking.*

"Indirect, or secondhand, smoking causes death not only by lung cancer, but even more by heart attack."

Secondary Smoke Is Harmful to Nonsmokers

Lawrence K. Altman

While there has been concern for years that cigarettes harm smokers, there is now also concern about the effects of tobacco smoke on nonsmokers. In the following viewpoint, Lawrence K. Altman states that secondary, or passive, smoke harms people who inhale fumes from smokers. He cites cardiologists and other researchers who claim that secondary smoke increases a nonsmoker's risk of cancer and heart disease. Altman is a writer for *The New York Times*.

As you read, consider the following questions:

1. What does Altman say is the effect of passive smoke on the arteries?
2. How does passive smoke affect children, according to the author?
3. According to Altman, what do the newer studies on passive smoke prove?

After years of questioning the potential health hazards of secondhand cigarette smoke, a growing number of scientists and health officials are becoming persuaded that the dangers are real, broader than once believed and parallel those of direct smoke.

It has long been established that smoking harms the health of those who do the smoking. Now new epidemiological studies and reviews are strengthening the evidence that it also harms the health of other people nearby who inhale the toxic fumes generated by the smoker, particularly from the burning end of the cigarette. Such indirect, or secondhand, smoking causes death not only by lung cancer, but even more by heart attack, the studies show. The studies on passive smoking, as it is often called, also strengthen the link between parental smoking and respiratory damage in children.

In reports and in interviews, more than a dozen experts said there was little question that passive smoking is an important health hazard.

What has swayed many scientists is a remarkable consistency in findings from different types of studies in several countries with improved methods over those used in the first such studies a few years ago. The new findings confirm and advance two landmark reports in 1986 from the Surgeon General, who concluded that passive smoking caused lung cancer, and from the National Research Council, which said passive smoking is associated with lung cancer.

A Leading Cause of Death

"The links between passive smoking and health problems are now as solid as any finding in epidemiology," said Dr. Cedric F. Garland, an expert in the epidemiology of smoking at the University of California at San Diego. . . .

The newer understanding of the health hazards of passive smoking were underscored in a report at a world conference on lung health in Boston in May 1990. Dr. Stanton A. Glantz of the University of California at San Francisco estimated that passive smoke killed 50,000 Americans a year, two-thirds of whom died of heart disease.

Passive smoking ranks behind direct smoking and alcohol as the third leading preventable cause of death, Dr. Glantz said in what experts called an unusually thorough review of all 11 epidemiological studies published on the subject.

About 400,000 Americans die from breathing their own smoke each year, the Surgeon General's 1989 report said. About 100,000 die from alcohol, according to a report in 1987 from the National Institute on Alcohol Abuse and Alcoholism.

Donald Shopland of the National Cancer Institute, who has

helped prepare the Surgeon General's reports on smoking since 1964, said "there's no question" now that passive smoking is also a cause of heart disease.

Steve Kelley. Reprinted with permission.

The evidence for the health hazards of passive smoking is largely statistical and epidemiological, techniques that have often pointed the way for scientists to confirm the findings from laboratory research.

Animal Experiments

Dr. Mark L. Witten of the University of Arizona reported what he said was the first documented damage to animals from passive smoking. In experiments begun when he was at the Massachusetts General Hospital in Boston, Dr. Witten exposed rabbits to sidestream smoke for 15 minutes a day for 20 days in amounts comparable to those received by children of smoking parents.

The animals developed lung damage resembling an asthmatic reaction. Cells in the airways of the rabbits degenerated and their lungs became more permeable, posing a significant risk for the development of serious lung disease by creating an easier entry point for microbes, pollutants and toxins.

The new findings on passive smoking parallel recent changes in laws and rules that limit smoking in public places. In recent years, all but four states (Missouri, North Carolina, Tennessee and Wyoming) have passed comprehensive laws limiting smoking in places like restaurants, schools, stores, hospitals and theaters, according to Action for Smoking and Health, an advocacy group. In 1990, airlines banned smoking on all flights of less than six hours.

Only a decade ago many scientists were skeptical over the initial links between passive smoking and lung cancer.

Dr. Garland, the San Diego expert, said: "We were out on a limb when we started, but now we have the kind of replication one would want to see play a role in public policy.". . .

Mainstream and Sidestream Smoke

Cigarette smoke consists of more than 4,700 compounds, including 43 carcinogens, the E.P.A. [Environmental Protection Agency] says. Major differences exist in the components of mainstream and sidestream smoke that largely reflect the degree of combustion. Mainstream smoke is inhaled from smoking and consists of large particles deposited in the larger airways of [the] lung.

Sidestream smoke is generated from the burning end of cigarettes, cigars and pipes during the smoldering between puffs. Sidestream smoke may come from someone else's tobacco or from one's own, and is the major source of environmental tobacco smoke. Sidestream smoke is a mixture of irritating gases and carcinogenic tar particles that reach deeper into the lungs because they are small.

Scientists say that because of incomplete combustion from the lower temperatures of a smoldering cigarette, sidestream smoke is dirtier and chemically different from mainstream smoke.

Effects on the Heart

Dr. Henry D. McIntosh, a former president of the American College of Cardiology, said he agreed with Dr. Glantz's review that found a 30 percent increase in risk of death from heart attacks among nonsmokers living with smokers. The risk correlated with the amount of the spouse's smoking; the heavier a smoker, the greater the risk.

Researchers have found that passive smoking makes platelets, the tiny fragments in the blood that help it clot, stickier. The findings were made on 10 healthy nonsmokers who sat for 20 minutes in an open hospital corridor beside smokers.

Platelets can form clots on plaques in fat-clogged arteries to cause heart attacks, and they may also play a role in promoting arteriosclerosis, the underlying cause of most heart attacks.

Researchers have also shown from animal and human studies

that chemicals in sidestream smoke may injure cells on the inside lining of the arteries and thus promote development of plaque and arteriosclerosis.

Dr. Glantz's review, which was done in collaboration with Dr. William W. Parmley, chief of cardiology at the University of California at San Francisco and a former president of the American College of Cardiology, highlighted the interplay between such processes. Although platelets do not normally stick to the inside lining of arteries, such sticking is easier when cells in the lining have been damaged. Under such conditions, the platelets can release substances that cause further damage to the artery.

Researchers have also shown that passive smoking adversely affects heart function, decreasing the ability of people with and without heart disease to exercise. "You don't get oxygen to the heart as well," Dr. Glantz said.

Passive smoking increases the demands on the heart during exercise and reduces the heart's capacity to speed up. For people with heart disease, the decreased function can precipitate the chest pains from angina.

The decreased heart function may reflect impeded enzyme activity within cells, an effect that has been documented with passive smoke in animals, Dr. Glantz said.

Blood tests of adolescent children whose parents smoked showed changes that increase their risk of heart disease, according to studies by Dr. William B. Moskowitz's team at the Medical College of Virginia in Richmond. The children, exposed to passive smoke since birth, had increased amounts of cholesterol and lower levels of HDL, a protein in blood that is believed to protect against heart attacks. The researchers found that the greater the exposure to passive smoke, the greater were the biochemical changes.

Studies on Lung Cancer

The effects of passive smoking on heart disease were not part of the E.P.A. study, which relied on the agency's carcinogenic assessment guidelines to evaluate lung cancer and respiratory illness.

The E.P.A. reviewed 24 epidemiological studies of passive smoking and lung cancer, 11 more than in the Surgeon General's report in 1986. The newer studies confirm those in the first 13 studies. "The evidence is remarkably consistent, even with different methods, and is persuasive," said one E.P.A. official who asked not to be identified.

A pioneering report linking passive smoking and lung cancer came in 1981 from a 14-year Japanese study by Dr. Takeshi Hirayama. His research methods were criticized at first, but critical review, corrections and revisions have "failed to discredit the findings," a draft of the E.P.A. report said.

Lawrence Garfinkel, an epidemiologist who is vice president of the American Cancer Society, said that he was at first skeptical of Dr. Hirayama's report but that he was convinced from later studies, including his own, that there was about a 30 percent increased risk of developing lung cancer from passive smoking. . . .

Other Types of Cancer

Dr. Glantz estimated that one-third of the 50,000 deaths from passive smoking were from cancer. In addition to lung cancer, researchers have linked cancer of the cervix to both mainstream and sidestream smoke.

Mainstream smoke, but not sidestream, has been linked to cancers of the mouth, throat, voice box, esophagus, urinary bladder, kidney and pancreas.

Sidestream smoke, but not mainstream smoke, has been linked to cancers of the brain, thyroid, and breast. Several groups are trying to do other studies to determine whether such findings are spurious and whether sidestream smoke can cause cancers not caused by mainstream smoke.

The American Academy of Pediatrics estimates that 9 million to 12 million American children under the age of 5 may be exposed to passive smoke.

The E.P.A. focused on the nearly 30 epidemiologic studies on passive smoking and respiratory disorders published since the 1986 reports.

Passive Smoke and Childhood Illness

The newer studies strengthed earlier conclusions that passive smoke increases the risk for serious early childhood respiratory illness, particularly bronchitis and pneumonia in infancy. Increased coughing was reported from birth to the mid-teen-age years among 13 newer studies of passive smoking and respiratory symptoms.

Researchers say that young children may develop symptoms after exposure to passive smoke for only a few months. The E.P.A. said passive smoke may be a particular problem because of an infant's immature immunologic and respiratory systems.

The E.P.A. also found that passive smoke can lead to middle ear infections and other conditions in young children. The agency has said that asthmatic children are particularly at risk and that lung problems as children can extend to adulthood.

"No one has shown that casual exposure to tobacco smoke is harmful."

Secondary Smoke Is Not Harmful to Nonsmokers

Jacob Sullum

In the following viewpoint, Jacob Sullum argues that because there has been too little research on the effects of cigarettes on nonsmokers, it is impossible to determine whether secondary smoke is harmful. Sullum states that only six out of twenty-five studies have found that secondary smoke increases the risk of disease in nonsmokers. Sullum is an associate editor of *Reason*, a magazine of libertarian political and social opinion.

As you read, consider the following questions:

1. According to Sullum, what is the difference between breathing environmental tobacco smoke and smoking?
2. Why is Sullum dissatisfied with the studies done on the consequences of secondary smoke exposure?
3. What does the author feel is the best solution to the smoker versus nonsmoker disputes?

From "Smoke and Mirrors" by Jacob Sullum. Reprinted, with permission, from the February 1991 issue of *Reason* magazine. Copyright © 1991 by the Reason Foundation, 2716 Ocean Park Blvd., Suite 1062, Santa Monica, CA 90405.

The idea that tobacco smoke is not just an annoyance, but a hazard as well, rests on evidence concerning the effects of "involuntary smoking." The term itself is misleading, since it implies both that a nonsmoker's exposure is analogous to a smoker's and that the nonsmoker has no choice in the matter. It conjures up the image of a person being tied down and compelled to smoke a pack of Camels.

Yet breathing environmental tobacco smoke (ETS) is quite different from smoking. The chemicals in the smoke are diluted by the surrounding air, and a bystander neither inhales them as deeply nor retains them as long as a smoker. This distinction is often lost in the warnings of antismoking activists.

"We know that tobacco smoke causes disease and can kill you," Scott Ballin [of the Coalition on Smoking OR Health] says. "It makes sense that a person who doesn't smoke cigarettes, who's sitting next to a smoker and inhaling the smoke, is also at some risk." But many substances that are toxic at certain concentrations—vitamin A, for example—are benign or even healthy at others. So this "common-sense" approach will not do.

A Lack of Evidence

The actual evidence on environmental tobacco smoke is considerably less solid than antismoking activists make it out to be but more convincing than the tobacco industry might like you to think. To put the question into perspective, consider that there have been thousands of studies on the effects of smoking. By contrast, only 25 have looked at the consequences of ETS exposure.

Of these, six have found that exposure to ETS can increase the risk of disease in nonsmokers—primarily lung cancer in the spouses of smokers. The results of the other studies were either negative or statistically insignificant. (The Environmental Protection Agency has attempted to derive significant findings from these data, but it's not clear whether the aggregated studies' populations were comparable.) In 1986, then-Surgeon General C. Everett Koop concluded that "involuntary smoking is a cause of disease, including lung cancer, in healthy nonsmokers."

Yet the detailed discussion in the surgeon general's report has a more cautious tone, citing shortcomings in the research. The studies may not have controlled for all the relevant variables. Socioeconomic status and indoor pollutants, for example, are both associated with lung cancer. Furthermore, some of the subjects may have been misidentified as nonsmokers, since the researchers relied on questionnaires to classify them. Because the spouses of smokers are more likely to be smokers themselves, misidentification of even a small percentage of the subjects would have been enough to skew the results.

The only study to find an increased risk for children raised in homes with smokers was reported in *The New England Journal of Medicine* in 1990. The study compared the childhood exposure of 191 lung-cancer patients to that of 191 people without lung cancer who had never smoked. Yet although the lungcancer patients were classified as "nonsmokers," they explicitly included former smokers.

A Low Risk for Nonsmokers

Even if we take the link between lung cancer and spousal smoking to be established, we should keep the possible risk in perspective. Being married to a smoker may raise your likelihood of developing lung cancer, but this likelihood for nonsmokers is very small to begin with.

Where Are the Victims?

It must be said that the EPA, by pretending a proven link between secondhand smoke and cancer deaths, is not picking on an innocent victim. It's a scientific cinch that direct smoking can cause cancer, and the autopsy reports—with names of victims—have accumulated a vast body of proof.

No such hard and conclusive proof is available for passive smoke. To encourage total removal of smoking from public areas and workplaces, the EPA needn't stir up another radon scare.

Leonard E. Larsen, *The Washington Times*, December 13, 1990.

It's also important to recognize what the research does not show. Beware of claims that ETS kills thousands of Americans each year. At the Seventh World Conference on Tobacco and Health in 1990, for example, a researcher estimated that secondary smoke each year causes 34,900 additional deaths from heart disease and 12,600 additional deaths from cancer in the United States.

Yet a link between ETS and heart disease has never been demonstrated. In Koop's words: "Further studies on the relationship between involuntary smoking and cardiovascular disease are needed in order to determine whether involuntary smoking increases the risk of cardiovascular disease." An international symposium at McGill University reached a similar conclusion in November 1989. Furthermore, estimates of additional cancer deaths are purely hypothetical, since none of the ETS studies have measured actual exposure to secondary smoke. Even if they had, it isn't clear that the results would be representative of the average American's exposure or that the dose-response relationships derived from the studies would apply to the general population. Koop again: ". . . more data on the dose and distribution of ETS exposure in the population are needed in order to accurately estimate the magnitude of risk." So the additional-death figures are about as reliable as Mitch Snyder's estimate of the homeless population.

A Matter of Choice

Although almost all of the evidence on the effects of secondary smoke relates to long-term exposure in the home, the research has been used to justify laws restricting or banning smoking in businesses. At least 44 states and hundreds of cities and counties have adopted such laws. Yet there is very little reason to believe that ETS exposure in the workplace is hazardous. And despite the impression given by antismoking activists, there is *no evidence* that casual, short-term exposure such as that encountered in a restaurant or on an airplane poses a risk to nonsmokers.

In any case, nonsmokers can always choose not to patronize those businesses that allow smoking. While the owner of the property has a right to establish rules for smoking, the customer has a right to go elsewhere. In addition to revealing the fallacy of "involuntary" exposure to smoke, consumer choice is crucial to the economic argument against government-imposed smoking regulations.

Restaurateurs, retailers, airlines, and innkeepers stay in business by accommodating their customers. If there is a demand for smoke-free dining, shopping, flying, or lodging, someone can make money by providing it. On the other hand, smokers also eat, buy things, go places, and stay in hotels, so businesses have an economic incentive to take their desires into account as well.

Smoking Policies in Business

Similarly, businesses must compete for employees, and one way to attract and keep them is by providing them with the sort of work environment they want. In a free market, the smoking policies established by businesses will therefore reflect the preferences of consumers and employees.

Ahron Leichtman [president of Citizens Against Tobacco Smoke] accepts this argument, at least in part. "The marketplace does work," he says. But he argues that the tobacco industry has "brainwashed" restaurateurs into thinking they will lose business if they ban smoking and blinded them to the fact that they are already losing business by permitting smoking. Thus, he says, restaurateurs in Beverly Hills were deluded when they complained that they lost customers to competitors in Los Angeles after the city council enacted a restaurant smoking ban in 1987. (Los Angeles and San Francisco have considered similar ordinances.)

In addition to tricking restaurateurs into acting against their own interests, Leichtman says, the tobacco industry pressures businesses to allow smoking by threatening "economic boycotts." He cites Philip Morris's attempts to rally smokers against businesses that ban smoking. But aren't nonsmokers equally free to protest?

The Health Police

The war against smoking is turning into a jihad against people who smoke. Smokers are being exiled from public and private places and are facing discrimination in employment. . . .

Although the Public Health Service has been reticent about publicizing the fact, every study cited in support of the statement that "cigarette smoking causes cancer" reveals that a smoker is thoroughly unlikely to get cancer—only that he is statistically more likely to get it than a nonsmoker. No one can say precisely how much more likely. This is true of all supposed "carcinogens."

B. Bruce-Briggs, *Fortune*, April 25, 1988.

Maybe, Leichtman says, but they don't. "Very few people actually speak up about tobacco smoke, because they are just too plain timid," he says. "They don't want to be ostracized for doing so. The bottom line is they just don't complain." But given that nonsmokers outnumber smokers by nearly three to one, it's far more plausible that they don't complain because smoke simply doesn't bother them as much or as often as it bothers Leichtman.

Air Rights

Not every nonsmoker, after all, is an antismoker. Many nonsmokers would prefer a smoke-free environment if the government provided it to them without charge, at the expense of businesspeople and smokers. Relatively few, however, would be willing to pay for the privilege through higher prices or the effort (and perhaps embarrassment) of complaining or taking their business elsewhere.

"I'm the sort of guy who would pay a surcharge, if I had to, for a nonsmoking environment," concedes Leichtman, who says he's allergic to tobacco smoke. "I shouldn't have to." Why not? Ultimately, Leichtman retreats to the public-protection argument. "The owner of this building would not be permitted to have asbestos fibers falling from the ceiling. . . . It stands to rea-

76

son that the air should be relatively safe."

But tobacco smoke differs from asbestos fibers and other pollutants in several crucial ways. It is the by-product of an activity that some customers (or employees) wish to engage in, and its presence is conspicuous and well known. By entering a business that allows smoking, you consent to be exposed to tobacco smoke, just as you consent to be subjected to loud music by entering a dance club or attending a rock concert.

While loud music is not his cup of tea, Leichtman concedes that government has no business banning it. But he insists that tobacco smoke is different. He's right: Even relatively brief exposure to loud music is known to damage hearing, but no one has shown that casual exposure to tobacco smoke is harmful.

Find Out What the Rules Are

Clearly, though, the spread of antismoking ordinances throughout the nation is not merely the product of complaints by a few supersensitive individuals. Tobacco smoke in confined spaces has always been annoying, but tolerance for it has waned in this country with the spread of information about the dangers of smoking and the associated decline in the percentage of the population that smokes. This shift has changed the assumptions underlying relations between smokers and nonsmokers.

It's no longer safe to assume, in a home or a business, that the owner will not object if you light a cigarette. The onus is now on the smoker to find out what the rules are. It's still reasonable to expect diners to understand that they run the risk of exposure to tobacco smoke when they eat out. But as smoking becomes less and less common, restaurateurs may have to post signs to that effect in order to secure informed consent.

Customers should recognize that smoking policy is not simply an either/or proposition. Restaurateurs, for example, may choose from a wide range of ground rules, including a complete ban on smoking, separate seating, qualified permission (say, if no one objects), and prohibition (or tolerance) of complaints about smoke. Generally, of course, they will try to accommodate both smokers and nonsmokers.

The Final Say

None of this, however, changes the basic principle that the owner has the final say. Too often, confrontations between smokers and nonsmokers are based on irreconcilable assumptions: Smokers feel they have every right to enjoy their cigarettes, while annoyed bystanders are equally certain they are entitled to a smoke-free environment. The only way to make sense of these conflicting claims is by reference to property rights. Otherwise, the majority will simply impose a solution, which is what the antismoking movement advocates.

If you don't smoke, this prospect may not trouble you very much. You may be glad to be rid of tobacco smoke on airplanes and in restaurants, in stores and hotels, no matter how this state of affairs came about. For that matter, you may not care if you never see a tobacco ad again or if the cost of cigarettes goes up. Furthermore, you may be a clean-living, sensible person who can't imagine how any of your habits could possibly offend others enough to prompt government interference. But you never know.

As James M. Buchanan has noted, using the state's power to control your neighbor's annoying habits is a risky business. "Let those who would use the political process to impose their preferences on the behavior of others be wary of the threat to their own liberties," he writes. "The liberties of some cannot readily be restricted without limiting the liberties of all."

"The nonsmoker would be better off if the smoker . . . did not exist."

Public Smoking Should Be Restricted

Robert E. Goodin

Robert E. Goodin is a professorial fellow in philosophy at the Australian National University in Canberra and an associate editor of *Ethics*, a philosophical journal. In the following viewpoint, Goodin measures both the harms and benefits that smokers and nonsmokers endure and argues that nonsmokers have an essential right to breathe smoke-free air. He says nonsmokers cannot be expected to avoid places where there might be smoking, like public transportation, public buildings, and the workplace.

As you read, consider the following questions:

1. In Goodin's "gas bomber" analogy, how does he prove that nonsmokers have a right to smoke-free air?
2. According to the author, which group suffers more: smokers who cannot smoke in public, or nonsmokers who must breathe passive smoke? How does Goodin reach his conclusion?
3. After reading Goodin's viewpoint, do you think the nuisance of cigarette smoke is reason enough to regulate public smoking?

There are three classes of negative effects on others arising from a person's smoking. Two are clearly harms. The third is of only a slightly different character.

First, there is the well-established harm to the fetus inflicted by the mother's smoking. . . .

Second, there is the harm to others arising from "passive smoking," that is the inhalation of "sidestream" smoke from the burning tip of a lit cigarette and of smoke exhaled by a nearby smoker. . . .

Both of those are "real harms"—real health hazards imposed on one person by another's smoking nearby. Third, there are the mere disamenities that nonsmokers experience when breathing others' smoke. As the Royal College of Physicians argues, whether or not passive smoking damages health, "there is already sufficient evidence as to the discomfort and annoyance that breathing other people's smoke can cause. Non-smokers at work and play, in transport and in public places, should have the right not to be so exposed."

Emitting offensive odors, when done by a factory, is subject to public regulation. In Malaysia, it is illegal to carry the evil-smelling durian fruit on public transportation. Many nonsmokers (especially ex-smokers) find the smell of burning tobacco similarly offensive, and it might therefore be banned on similar grounds. Here, even John Stuart Mill can be enlisted in support: "There are many acts which, being directly injurious only to the agents themselves, ought not to be legally interdicted, but which, if done publicly, are a violation of good manners, and coming thus within the category of offences against others, may rightfully be prohibited." Primary among the examples Mill has in mind here are "offences against decency"—sin, blasphemy, and such like. But he goes on to say that the moral case against offensive behavior in public is "equally strong" even where (as is presumably the case with smoking) the "actions [are] not in themselves condemnable, nor supposed to be so."

Is Offensiveness Harmful?

"Offense," of course, is not quite harm, though it may be the first cousin to it. That makes it a notoriously tricky notion to fit into the essentially harm-based rationales central to standard moral and legal justifications for social regulation. In such schemes, "harmless immoralities" are ordinarily deemed permissible—especially when they touch upon values of free speech and expression—whether or not others are offended by them. (Certainly we have grievous qualms about letting the notion of "offense" range so widely as to ban sexually explicit plays, politically pointed protest, or interracial marriage in the deep South. We are nonetheless comfortable in regulating, as "offensive nuisances," smelly or noisy factories. They may be "mere nuisances," posing no real harms to health, but showing that they are a nuisance is more than enough to justify us in restricting what they may do and where they may do it. . . .

Verdict: Clear the Air

In 1976 Donna Shimp, who had worked for the New Jersey Bell Telephone Company for fifteen years, sued the company for not providing her with a healthful working environment. Allergic to cigarette smoke, Mrs. Shimp charged that the smoke in her work area caused her to suffer continuous irritation of her nose, throat, and eyes. In fact, she was made so ill that she had to stop working.

At the trial, Mrs. Shimp demonstrated that she had frequently requested either better ventilation or restricted smoking, but nothing was done. The judge ruled in her favor. He commented that the telephone company prohibited smoking near some of its sophisticated electronic equipment. "If such rules are established for machines," he said, "I see no reason why they should not be held in force for humans."

Gilda Berger, *Smoking Not Allowed*, 1987.

So too, perhaps, with smoking. After all, nonsmokers are in an increasingly large majority among the population, outnumbering smokers three to one.

Insofar as they find smoking similarly a public nuisance, we might appeal to similar standards to justify its regulation as we do to justify regulation of smelly factories. Showing "real harm" to health is always a stronger argument for regulation, of course; and there is evidence of that, too. . . . The point here is just that that might not be strictly necessary. The nuisance argument might in itself suffice.

The argument for restricting smoking in enclosed public spaces is characteristically couched in terms of the rights of nonsmokers to clean air. The issue has been joined . . . from the other side, too. The tobacco industry's United Kingdom pressure group, the Tobacco Advisory Council, maintains that smokers also enjoy a right to smoke, and that "neither group [smokers or nonsmokers] has any absolute right to dictate to the other."

I take it that the rights-based argument can be settled, presumptively at least, in favor of the nonsmoker. In the old adage, your freedom stops at the end of my nose; and in the case of environmental tobacco smoke, your smoke obviously transgresses the privacy of my nasal passages. Norman Daniels said, "Just as my bodily integrity is violated by a punch in the nose, so too is it threatened by toxins and carcinogens others place in the environment. . . . Just as I have a rights claim against those who would punch me in the nose, so too I have one against those who would batter my lungs." The surgeon general has rightly concluded, "The right of smokers to smoke ends where their behavior affects the health and well-being of others; . . . the choice to smoke cannot interfere with the non-smoker's right to breathe air free of tobacco smoke."

In this way, we can break down the apparent symmetry between the loss that would be suffered by the smoker, denied the pleasures of tobacco to spare the nonsmoker, and those that would be suffered by the nonsmoker, denied the pleasures of clean air to indulge the smoker. "Each interferes with the other," it is true. But the nonsmoker "merely wishes to breathe unpolluted air and, in the pursuit thereof, and unlike the smoker, does not reduce the amenity of others" in so doing. "The conflict of interest does not arise from *reciprocal* effects and does not imply equal culpability. The conflict arises from the damage inflicted by one of the parties on the other," E. J. Mishan said. The symmetry suggested by the "right to smoke versus the right to clean air" formulation is thus illusory. . . . The smoker would be neither better nor worse off if the nonsmoker did not exist, whereas the nonsmoker would be better off if the smoker (qua smoker) did not exist.

In Defense of Smoke-Free Air

At root, the grounds for assigning priority to the right to breathe clean air are simply that everyone—smoker and nonsmoker alike—needs this right in order to flourish. The point is effectively evoked by a fanciful example offered by James Repace: "Suppose that individual nonsmokers, in defense of their asserted right to breathe tobacco-smoke-free indoor air, were to release a gas into indoor spaces where they were forced to breathe tobacco smoke. Suppose further that when sucked through the burning cone of a cigarette, pipe, or cigar this gas decomposed into irritating byproducts which cause moderate to intense discomfort to the smoker, much the way ambient tobacco smoke affects the nonsmoker. Would smokers feel that they had the inalienable right to gas-free air?" If so, they must concede that nonsmokers have a right to smoke-free air, a right which takes priority over their right to smoke.

Some might say that the analogy is not a perfect one. For example, it might be argued that, unlike the antismoker gas bomber, the smoker is not intentionally harming anyone. The gas bomber actually intends to discomfort anyone who lights up a cigarette in the room. The discomfort caused to others by smokers' smoking is regarded, even by smokers themselves, as an unfortunate by-product of their smoking; they would happily remove that side effect if they could do so, without undue cost or discomfort to themselves. To this claim, the antismoker gas bomber might reply that he does not intend to harm anyone, either. Smokers will be discomforted by his gas only if they smoke. If they refrain from smoking, they will not be harmed in the slightest. Furthermore, the gas bomber might continue, if they do smoke then nonsmokers would have been analogously discomforted. The gas bomb can thus be construed as an act of self-defense which, though preemptive, has the endearing property of harming potential aggressors only if and when they turn into actual ones.

Some such argument might establish a presumptive priority of the right to clean air over the right to smoke. Like all presumptions, however, this one can always be overcome—in this case, in either of two ways. One is to show that nonsmokers have voluntarily consented to others' smoking. The other is to show, through a calculation of costs and benefits, that the losses to smokers who are stopped from smoking would far exceed the losses to nonsmokers who are exposed to environmental tobacco smoke. Each of these possibilities will be considered, and rejected, in turn.

Everyone Has to Breathe

In the case of the smoker, it could (wrongly, as we have seen) be argued that the risks were somehow voluntarily incurred. In the case of the passive smoker, that argument would be far harder to sustain. Passive smokers do not themselves light up. They merely breathe. You can voluntarily choose to do something only if you can, realistically, choose not to do it; and no one can choose not to breathe. Since passive smoking—or, more technically, "exposure to environmental tobacco smoke"—"generally occurs as an unavoidable consequence of being in proximity to smokers, particularly in enclosed indoor environments," the surgeon general prefers simply to define passive smoking as "involuntary smoking" [according to the U.S. Department of Health and Human Services.]

Smokers might sometimes have sought and been granted the permission of all nonsmokers in the vicinity for them to light up. Assuming that that consent was given freely (i.e., that it was not a tyrannical boss 'asking' permission of a secretary) and that it was based on full information about the hazards of passive smoking, nonsmokers' exposure to environmental tobacco smoke would indeed then be voluntary. Given the dangers of duress and of fraudulent claims that rights have been waived, we may prefer to treat the right to clean air as if it were as in-

83

alienable as the right to life itself. But in any case, this whole voluntary waiver scenario is plausible only among moderately small groups of people.

Among larger and more anonymous groups, the only sense in which passive smoking might be thought to be voluntary would be insofar as people voluntarily enter environments they knew were or would become smoky. Thus, it might be argued that if people do not want to breathe other people's smoke, they should not go into notoriously smoky places like English pubs.

There is, of course, the question of why nonsmokers should banish themselves rather than smokers controlling themselves. In any case, there is a range of places it is unreasonable to expect people to avoid going. One is to work. Another is onto public transportation. Another is into public buildings. Another, perhaps, is to public entertainments (restaurants, theaters, and such like). If people cannot reasonably be expected to avoid going to work, and getting there by public transportation, then the Humean doctrine ("no consent without the possibility of withholding consent") would imply that they have not voluntarily consented to the risks of passive smoking in those places, either.

Costs and Benefits

Even if we suppose that the issue is properly couched in terms of rights—and especially if we do not—a calculation of the costs and benefits to all interested parties under all policy options is nonetheless relevant. Some rights violations matter more than others, after all. It would be a violation of bodily integrity for someone else to force smoke into your lungs. It would equally be a violation of bodily integrity for someone else to brush against your arm, yet few courts would take cognizance of that invasion. Technically, it might count as a case of assault, but the law does not deal in trifles, as the saying goes. Neither should public policy.

When deciding which rights violations matter most, we tend to employ a rough-and-ready utilitarian calculus of a sort, taking into account both costs to the violated and benefits to the violator. In that calculus, the former weighs particularly heavily. If rights holders have suffered serious harm, then rights violators have wronged them, almost regardless of whatever benefits the rights violators themselves stood to gain (or losses to avert). Thus, insofar as the case against passive smoking can be made in terms of increased lung cancer and other potentially grave illnesses, the deontological case is once again quickly closed. But insofar as the stakes are more modest—offensive odors and watery eyes—we would have to take seriously into account costs and benefits to both parties, on the model of nuisance law, for example.

84

Dealing in straight utilitarian terms, the case against passive smoking is necessarily less strong than that against direct smoking. That is simply because the passive smoker gets only a small fraction of the dose of poisonous substances that is received by the active smoker. A smoker's chances of lung cancer are increased by 980 percent, a passive smoker's by only 34 percent; and so on. Since the costs of passive smoking are necessarily lower than those of active smoking, there is more of a chance that the benefits there might outweigh the costs, in a utilitarian calculus. . . .

However much smokers might want to smoke, it is not in their interests to do so. We are doing them a favor—conferring upon them an objective health benefit—by stopping them from smoking, even for a little while. . . .

Who Will Suffer Most?

We must take account of the severity of the characteristic reactions involved: of smokers forced to suffer withdrawal for the period of time they would be constrained from smoking, on the one hand; of nonsmokers forced to suffer environmental tobacco smoke for the period of time they would be closeted with it, on the other. Of course, variable physiology on both sides means that some people will suffer more than others. Not all smokers would suffer withdrawal during a two-hour flight; not all nonsmokers would mind the smoke all that much. But most smokers would probably suffer some withdrawal symptoms over the course of a whole day at work, and surveys show that most nonsmokers suffer at least eye, nose, and throat irritation from being subjected to day-long smoking in an enclosed office. . . .

What decisively favors regulation of smoking in enclosed spaces, is the magnitude of the possible suffering by each party. At worst, the smoker prevented from smoking suffers discomfort. The nonsmoker exposed to environmental tobacco smoke for a prolonged period might, at worst, suffer lung cancer or other debilitating diseases. That is not the most common outcome, by a long stretch. But in light of other less risky airborne contaminants that the Environmental Protection Agency does regulate, it certainly is a common enough outcome to take seriously in framing policies.

The second crucial element . . . is the number of people affected, on both sides. Nonsmokers now outnumber smokers in the United States by a ratio of almost three to one. That is not a big enough differential to decide matters all by itself, perhaps. But conjoined with the above argument—that smokers will lose something less than three times what nonsmokers will gain from a ban—this fact does prove decisive. Numbers conspire with intensity in arguing for restricting passive smoking.

> "If I own a restaurant and choose to permit smoking, you have no right to come in and force someone not to smoke."

Public Smoking Should Not Be Restricted

Tibor Machan

Tibor Machan teaches philosophy at Auburn University in Alabama. He is a senior editor for *Reason* magazine and the author of *Public Realms and Private Rights*. In the following viewpoint, Machan argues that smoking regulations imposed on private establishments are a violation of individual rights. Machan says government intervention isn't necessary to solve the problems of public smoking. In a free society, he says, people are free to do wrong or to take risks, as long as no one else's rights are violated.

As you read, consider the following questions:

1. What two freedoms do smoking prohibitions overlook, according to Machan?
2. How does the public smoking debate compare to that concerning prayer in schools, in the author's view?
3. Why does the author oppose smoking restrictions governing private property?

Tibor Machan, "Coping with Smoking," *Freeman*, April 1989. Reprinted with permission.

Various legislative bodies are enacting laws forbidding business proprietors from permitting smoking on their private property—in offices, cinemas, aircraft, stores, and other places. Such policies are touted as a means to combat a harmful habit and to foster public health. But there are serious problems with this approach to the problems of smoking.

Owners of private establishments are being prevented—mostly by city ordinances—from deciding who will be permitted to smoke on their premises. But such government-mandated prohibitions ignore the rights of those who don't mind smoking as well as those who wish to live in a tolerant society. Since smokers now are in the minority, some believe this is the time to descend on them in full force. Their critics are willing to ignore individual rights to freedom of association and private property.

Of course, the issue often is presented in a way that makes it appear that smokers are the ones who violate individual rights. They are said to be assaulting the rest of us with their smoking. But is this really the case? And are the laws really designed to protect the rights of individuals against the intrusions of smokers?

No doubt, smokers can be annoying. Their smoke even may be harmful to those around them. One need not dispute these contentions still to be concerned with their rights.

Government Restrictions

In most cases, anti-smoking ordinances aren't limited to public places such as municipal courts. If the government confined itself to protecting the rights of nonsmokers in bona fide public areas, there would be nothing wrong with the current trend in legislation.

Instead of such a limited approach, however, government has embarked upon the full regimentation of people's choices concerning smoking. The government, under the leadership of public health officials, has decided to bully smokers, regardless of whether they violate anyone's rights or merely indulge with the consent of others. This is where government-mandated smoking bans have reached a dangerous phase.

There are many risks that people suffer willingly. And in a society that respects individual rights this has to be accepted. Boxers, football players, nurses, doctors, and many other people expose themselves to risks of harm that come from others' behavior. What is central, however, is that when this exposure is voluntary, in a free society it may not be interfered with. The sovereignty of persons may not be sacrificed even for the sake of their physical health.

Individuals' property rights are supposed to be protected by the Fifth Amendment. Not unless property is taken for public use—for the sake of a legitimate state activity—is it properly subject to government seizure. By treating the offices, work spaces, and lobbies of private firms as if they were public property, a grave injustice is done to the owners.

N.Y. Begins Citing Smoking Law Violators
"Hey, Sarge - We've got ourselves the Kingpin... a CIGAR SMOKER!!!"

When private property comes under government control, practices may be prohibited simply because those who engage in them are in the minority or waver from preferred government policy. Members of minority groups can easily lose their sphere of autonomy.

There is no need, however, to resort to government intervention to manage the public problems engendered by smoking. There are many cases of annoying and even harmful practices that can be isolated and kept from intruding on others. And they do not involve violating anyone's right to freedom of association and private property.

Respect Individual Rights

The smoking issue can be handled quite simply. In my house, shop, or factory, I should be the one who decides whether there will be smoking. This is what it means to respect my individual rights. Just as I may print anything I want on my printing press, or allow anyone to say whatever he or she wants in my lecture hall, so I should be free to decide whether people may smoke in my facilities.

Those displeased by my decision need not come to my facilities to work, play, or whatever. If the concern is great and the opportunity to work in a given place is highly valued, negotiations or contract talks can ensue in behalf of separating smokers from nonsmokers. In many cases all that's needed is to bring the problem to light. Maybe the firm's insurance costs will be high where there is smoking, or maybe a change in policy will come about because customers and workers are gradually leaving.

In some cases it may go so far as to involve tort litigation. Exposing employees to serious dangers that are not part of the job description and of which they were not warned may be actionable. But what the company does initially at least must be its decision. And the onus of proof in these cases must be on those who claim to have suffered unjustified harm. Government legislation and regulation often subvert this carefully conceived process, just because some people are impatient with how others run their own lives and properties.

Smoking in a Free Society

Consider the somewhat analogous case of freedom of religion. If I own and run a private school, I decide whether students may pray. In state schools, of course, the state decides. And a sound system of government won't get on the side of either the prayers or the non-prayers. Similarly, the state should say nothing about the ultimate benefits or harms of smoking. This is no different from the well-respected view that the state shouldn't get on the side of a particular religion or even a scientific theory.

It is important to note that for many people, smoking is not categorically, universally bad. For some people it may be O.K. to smoke, just as it could be O.K. to have a couple of drinks or to run five miles a day. For others, smoking is clearly harmful to their health. In either case, health may not be the highest good for many people. All things considered, even those whose health suffers may wish to smoke. In a free society, people are free to do what is wrong, so long as they don't violate the rights of others.

But, some will cry out, here's the rub: smoking can adversely affect others, and there is reason for those who could be harmed to stay away from smokers.

Freedom of Association

But this doesn't mean that we should force someone who doesn't mind smoking to stay away from smokers. If I own a restaurant and choose to permit smoking, you have no right to come in and force someone not to smoke. You must deal with me first and I might accommodate you or I might not, depending on my values and choices. In a free society this should be the general policy. If you believe that I subject you to harm that you were not warned of, you can sue me. But this is a private dispute, not a matter for public policy.

Some want no smoking near them and ought to be free to associate with others who do not smoke. They should eat in restaurants, work in businesses, and play in clubs where smoking isn't allowed. Others like to smoke and should be free to join the like-minded to carry on their various activities. And some who don't smoke may not mind others smoking nearby. They, too, should be free to seek the appropriate company in the appropriate settings.

A free, pluralistic society can accommodate all these people. It isn't necessary to appoint the government as the caretaker of our health and the overseer of our interpersonal negotiations concerning how we best get along with each other. Only when there are decisive grounds for deeming an action as violating someone's rights should government enter the picture and prohibit it.

Evaluating Sources of Information

When historians study and interpret past events, they use two kinds of sources: primary and secondary. Primary sources are eyewitness accounts. For example, an interview with a research scientist who studies the effects of passive smoke on nonsmokers would be a primary source. A magazine article that cited the scientist's statistics would be a secondary source. Primary and secondary sources may be decades or even hundreds of years old, and often historians find that the sources offer conflicting and contradictory information. To fully evaluate documents and assess their accuracy, historians analyze the credibility of the documents' authors and, in the case of secondary sources, analyze the credibility of the information the authors used.

Historians are not the only people who encounter conflicting information, however. Anyone who reads a daily newspaper, watches television, or just talks to different people will encounter many different views. Writers and speakers use sources of information to support their own statements. Thus, critical thinkers, just like historians, must question the writer's or speaker's sources of information as well as the writer or speaker.

While there are many criteria that can be applied to assess the accuracy of a primary or secondary source, for this activity you will be asked to apply three. For each source listed on the following page, ask yourself the following questions: First, did the person actually see or participate in the event he or she is reporting? This will help you determine the credibility of the information—an eyewitness to an event is an extremely valuable source. Second, does the person have a vested interest in the report? Assessing the person's social status, professional affiliations, nationality, and religious or political beliefs will be helpful in considering this question. By evaluating this you will be able to determine how objective the person's report may be. Third, how qualified is the author to be making the statements he or she is making? Consider what the person's profession is and how he or she might know about the event. Someone who has spent years being involved with or studying the issue may be able to offer more information than someone who simply is offering an uneducated opinion; for example, a politician or layperson.

Keeping the above criteria in mind, imagine you are writing a paper on passive cigarette smoke. You decide to cite an equal number of primary and secondary sources. Listed below are several sources that may be useful for your research. *Place a P next to those descriptions you believe are primary sources. Place an S next to those descriptions you believe are secondary sources.* Next, based on the above criteria, *rank the primary sources, assigning the number (1) to what appears to be the most valuable, (2) to the source likely to be the second-most valuable, and so on, until all the primary sources are ranked. Then rank the secondary sources, again using the above criteria.*

P or S		Rank in Importance
_____	1. A television interview with a smoker who criticizes a restaurant's no-smoking policy.	_____
_____	2. An article in an American Heart Association newsletter describing the results of a university's passive-smoking study.	_____
_____	3. Viewpoint three in this chapter.	_____
_____	4. A radio news report of a demonstration by antismoking groups.	_____
_____	5. A magazine editorial arguing that smokers have the right to smoke in public areas.	_____
_____	6 A television report outlining the increase in public-smoking laws in some states.	_____
_____	7. A newspaper article quoting a scientist who describes the dangers of passive smoke to a congressional committee.	_____
_____	8. A pamphlet published by a smokers' rights group stating that passive smoke is not harmful.	_____
_____	9. A researcher's study on the relationship between tobacco smoke and cancer, published in a medical journal.	_____
_____	10. A *Wall Street Journal* article that describes changes in the tobacco industry.	_____
_____	11. An editorial in favor of public-smoking restrictions.	_____
_____	12. Viewpoint four in this chapter.	_____

Periodical Bibliography

The following articles have been selected to supplement the diverse views presented in this chapter.

Joseph E. Brown — "Scared Smokeless," *Reader's Digest*, May 1989.

Alexander Cockburn — "The Other Drug War," *The Wall Street Journal*, September 27, 1990.

Geoffrey Cowley — "Secondhand Smoke," *Newsweek*, June 11, 1990.

James Drummond — "Hazardous to Whose Health?" *Forbes*, December 11, 1989.

Carolyn Gloeckner — "Where There's Smoke, There's Disease," *Current Health*, November 1990.

Harry V. Jaffa — "The Anti-Anti-Smoking Brigade," *National Review*, November 5, 1990.

Jonathan Kapstein — "Europe Tries to Clear the Air," *Business Week*, February 12, 1990.

Florence King — "I'd Rather Smoke than Kiss," *National Review*, July 9, 1990.

Morton Mintz — "No Ifs, Ands, or Butts," *The Washington Monthly*, July/August 1990.

William B. Moskowitz — "Passive Smoking, Active Risks," *American Health*, June 1990.

Kristine Napier — "Alcohol and Tobacco: A Deadly Duo," *Priorities*, Spring 1990.

John Schwartz — "Catching Hell for Smoking," *Newsweek*, April 23, 1990.

R. Emmett Tyrrell Jr. — "Zealots Against Science," *The American Spectator*, July 1990.

Nora Underwood — "Taking on Tobacco," *Maclean's*, April 9, 1990.

Ernest van den Haag — "The Smokescreen of Addiction," *National Review*, November 5, 1990.

3 CHAPTER

How Harmful Is Alcohol?

**Chemical
Dependency**

Chapter Preface

In the fight against America's drug problem, the prime objective has been restricting illegal drugs such as cocaine and marijuana. But many people would argue that the most damaging drug to our society is a legal one—alcohol. Former National Council on Alcoholism director Thomas Seessel asks, "Why do we continue to pussyfoot around alcohol while we raise no end of hell about marijuana, cocaine, and other illegal drugs?"

Experts say that by whatever standard the drug problem is measured—number of users, availability, ties to crime and violence, or costs to society in health and deaths—alcohol is number one. According to the National Clearinghouse for Alcohol and Drug Information, alcoholism costs the United States $116 billion annually in reduced worker productivity, indirect mortality, treatment, lost employment, and other factors. The cost society pays in dollars for alcohol abuse is almost double the figure for all other drug addictions combined.

But many other experts view alcohol as a problem that is lessening as society becomes more aware of its dangers and responds by cutting use. Liquor industry statistics show a drop in per capita consumption of alcohol since 1980. Howard Shaffer, director of Harvard Medical School's Center for Addiction Studies, says, "There has clearly been a change of lifestyle. It is a new temperance movement, the new sobriety." Allen Haveson, a spokesperson for the National Council on Alcoholism, agrees. "A large number of Americans have adopted a moderate lifestyle. They have begun to moderate or stop drinking."

How harmful is alcohol? The authors in the following chapter examine this question.

"[Alcoholism] is a disease that kills its victims and its victims' victims."

Alcoholism Is a Disease

Kathleen Whalen FitzGerald

For decades some experts have maintained that alcoholism is an inherited disease. In the following viewpoint, Kathleen Whalen FitzGerald agrees that alcoholism is genetically transmitted. She argues that alcoholism should be treated as a disease and not as a character flaw. FitzGerald is a recovering alcoholic and author of *Alcoholism: The Genetic Inheritance*, from which this viewpoint is excerpted.

As you read, consider the following questions:

1. Which studies does FitzGerald cite as evidence that alcoholism is an inherited disease?
2. Why does the author object to the term "alcoholic personality"?
3. According to FitzGerald, how is the use of alcohol a cultural norm in society?

Excerpts reprinted, with permission, from *Alcoholism: The Genetic Inheritance* by Kathleen Whalen FitzGerald, © 1988 by Kathleen W. FitzGerald.

For over thirty years, the American Medical Association has recognized alcoholism as a disease with identifiable and progressive symptoms that, if untreated, lead to mental damage, physical incapacity, and early death. Yet we still do not treat alcoholism as a disease, but as a sin, a social stigma, a moral aberration.

The life of the alcoholic is generally cut short by ten to twelve years; yet alcoholism is an "ism" like names of doctrines or theories or styles: fascism, imperialism, cubism, Thomism, realism, heroism. What other possibly fatal disease is an "ism"? Cancerism? Diabetesism? AIDSism? Alcoholism is not a theory or doctrine or style. It is a disease that kills its victims and its victims' victims.

As long as we cling to the name alcoholism, we relegate the disease to the dark chambers of sin and shame and preclude its acceptance as an illness. The name, likewise, resonates as an "ism," an abstract, theoretical entity that deflects from the reality of a disease that can be treated and healed. . . .

A Hereditary Disease

It always has been commonly accepted that alcoholism runs in families. But unlike red hair, or a talent for art, which are recognized as hereditary, the explanation offered has been that children raised in alcoholic homes somehow learn it; and in some perverted, guilty way, want it, court it, and deserve it. At best, when inheritance is admitted, it is an inherited weakness of moral fiber that is adjudged to be the cause.

Indeed, alcoholism [or Jellinek's disease, from Dr. E.M. Jellinek, author of *The Disease Concept of Alcoholism*] does run in families. It has been scientifically proven so. We know that it is transmitted *genetically*; not through the mind or the environment but through the body chemistry. And like all inherited traits, it manifests itself where it will, among rich and poor, without respect of person, without the volition of parents or children. . . .

The origins of Jellinek's disease are laid at the time of conception and come through that same mystery of creation that brings a shape of the nose, a unique smile, an ear for music, and the myriad other dynamics handed down from one generation to another in the hidden secrets of the cell.

Goodwin's Adoption Studies

In 1973, Donald W. Goodwin, a psychiatrist and researcher in the field of alcoholism, conducted a landmark study using case records of thirty-year-old Danish males who had been adopted at six weeks of age by nonalcoholic families. He found that:

1. Those who had been born of alcoholic fathers were three times more likely to develop alcoholism than those from nonalcoholic fathers; and

97

2. The sons of alcoholic fathers developed alcoholism at an earlier age.

In a second study in 1974, Goodwin compared sons of alcoholics who had been raised by the alcoholic parent and their brothers who had been adopted by nonalcoholic families. He found that the sons who were raised in the nonalcoholic environment were just as likely to become alcoholic as those who remained with their natural family.

Chuck Asay, by permission of the *Colorado Springs Gazette-Telegraph*.

Goodwin also found in a comparison of children born of alcoholic parents with those born of nonalcoholic parents that both groups were "virtually indistinguishable" with regard to psychiatric problems such as depression, anxiety neurosis, personality disturbance, psychopathology, criminality, and drug abuse. Mental problems do not cause alcoholism.

These studies by Goodwin have been replicated with the same results, putting to rest any remaining "nature versus nurture" debate. Nature won. . . .

The "Alcoholic Personality"

Jellinek's disease is, by definition, a physical, biochemical, degenerative, addictive illness. It is a primary disease that causes other diseases.

It does not have its origins in the mind, therefore it is not a mental illness, although it results in mental problems. Likewise, it does not have its origins in the soul, although it leads to spiritual bankruptcy. And more importantly, it does not have its origins in a strange or perverted personality, although it twists the personality and creates a stranger.

In an attempt to explain alcoholism, we chose the broad term "alcoholic personality." It means that alcoholics, even before they began drinking, were somehow different from the rest—perhaps too loud or too quiet, a little offbeat, unable to fit in. . . .

The problem with the term "alcoholic personality" is that it uses the *effects* that the disease produces to describe its *cause*. There is simply no such thing as the "alcoholic personality.". . .

The Myth Destroyed

The myth of the "alcoholic personality" has been destroyed by a 1983 study published by George Vaillant, M.D., of the Harvard University Medical School. The study followed 660 young men from 1940 until 1980, from adolescence into late middle age. These men were drawn from two distinct social/ economic groups: 204 were sophomores at Harvard University; 456 were junior high school boys from the inner-city of Boston.

A significant element of this study and one that makes it so valuable in terms of understanding the "natural history" of Jellinek's disease is that the research did not begin at the end when the disease was full-blown and work its way backward to when the men were boys and had not yet begun to drink. It began at the beginning when the subjects were young and no one knew or suspected who, if any, would develop Jellinek's disease.

After forty years of extensive research, it was clearly shown that there were *no significant personality characteristics to predict those who would contract Jellinek's disease and those who would not.*

Dr. Vaillant stated that in their youth, future alcoholics were as psychologically stable as those who would not develop problems with drinking. He likewise stated that it was difficult to comprehend that the personality did not develop the alcoholism; the alcoholism developed the "alcoholic personality."

The Disease's Lineage

The one consistent predictor of alcoholism, Vaillant found, was the factor of an alcoholic parent. Those boys with an alcoholic parent were *five times* more likely to develop alcoholism than were those boys with no alcoholic parents, despite the stability (or lack of it) in the family. Jellinek's disease, because it springs from a skewed body chemistry, is clearly inherited.

It may be passed from mother to son, from father to daughter, from grandparent to grandchild, even skipping a generation or two. This hereditary component may be obscured by the fact that a parent or grandparent "never touched the stuff." Whatever reason (religious, medical, social) stopped the former generation from drinking also stopped it from testing its vulnerability to alcohol.

In other words, because there was no apparent alcoholism in one's ancestral line does not rule out the fact that, as in other genetically transmitted diseases, the abstinent ancestors may well have passed on to their children and to their children's children their vulnerability to alcohol. As these vulnerable children, who may have no knowledge that they are "sitting ducks" for alcoholism, test out their vulnerability, they kick off the disease. . . .

The "Institution" of Alcoholism

Over twenty-five years ago, Dr. Jellinek addressed the issue of whether alcoholism was a self-inflicted condition. In refuting that theory, he wrote, ". . . in our culture, drinking is a custom to which society attaches an astonishingly great importance" and added that it comes close to being an institution in our society.

Secondly, he comments, alcohol addiction is insidious because "the changes toward a pathological process are imperceptible . . . since it develops within the context of an activity that belongs to the 'normal' and even valued behaviors of a society."

One of the basic cultural norms of American society is the use of alcohol. It is a value to learn "how to drink," because our family gatherings, our business transactions, our recreational and sporting events demand that one knows how to drink.

In a memorable scene from *The Catcher in the Rye*, Holden Caulfield and his friends, in New York on holiday from prep school, laugh at a group of women from the Midwest who order gin and tonic in a restaurant. Everyone knows you don't drink gin and tonic in the winter.

The cultural values of our society are quite specific as to what, when, and how we drink. It is unfortunate that these same cultural values do not accommodate those whose body chemistries punish them for accepting these values.

100

"The idea that alcoholism is a disease is a harmful myth."

Alcoholism Is Not a Disease

Herbert Fingarette

Some experts take issue with classifying alcoholism as a disease and argue that alcoholism is voluntary behavior that is within the alcoholic's control. In the following viewpoint, Herbert Fingarette agrees with this view and states his belief that the role of genes and heredity in alcoholism is limited. Fingarette is a philosophy professor at the University of California at Santa Barbara, and author of *Heavy Drinking: The Myth of Alcoholism as a Disease.*

As you read, consider the following questions:

1. According to Fingarette, what factors cause alcoholics to drink?
2. How does the author view alcohol treatment programs?
3. Which legal cases does Fingarette cite in arguing that alcoholism is not a disease?

The alcoholic is a tragic figure and deserves our compassion. But the idea that alcoholism is a disease is a harmful myth.

The slogan "alcoholism is a disease" sounds scientific. But the public has not been told of the accumulated scientific evidence that by now clearly undermines almost all that slogan suggests, as well as the burgeoning treatment industry based on it.

Foremost is the idea that alcoholics, the victims of the supposed disease, suffer "loss of control" over drinking. In my book, *Heavy Drinking*, I described some of the many experiments and clinical reports, published in the mainstream research literature, that have demonstrated consistently that alcoholics can and do have a great deal of control over their drinking.

One of the most persistent of such myths propagated by the advocates of the disease concept of alcoholism is that if a sober alcoholic takes a first drink, the effect is to cause a physical inability to stop. This is unquestionably false. One sees this clearly in studies where alcoholics have been deceived about what they are drinking. Those who were in reality drinking alcohol, but were led to believe their beverage was non-alcoholic, made no effort to drink a lot of it. Certainly none drank uncontrollably, even after they had alcohol in their system.

Alcoholics Can Stop Drinking

The point is that it is not the chemical effect of alcohol that triggers the drinking. It is things like the particular social setting, the stresses of job or family, the belief that they are "alcoholics" and "have" to drink.

Ironically, the so-called "treatment programs" for the "disease of alcoholism" provide overwhelming proof that alcoholics do have control. Almost all treatment methods of dealing with this so-called disease, whether they are "medical" or of the Alcoholics Anonymous type, immediately confront the alcoholic with this proposition: To enter this program you must take responsibility for the way you're living. You can and you must stop drinking at once, and you must remain abstinent voluntarily. What's more, the patients do it. Because now they want to. Of course this would be impossible if the drinking were actually caused by some physical or other uncontrollable process in the alcoholic's body.

Still, one might ask: Regardless of the inconsistency, isn't the bottom line that these treatments are effective? The truth, unfortunately, is that they are not. They are largely waste. Yet we are paying out over a billion dollars a year—financed largely by taxes and higher insurance premiums for all—in order to support a proliferation of public and private alcoholism clinics that are known to be largely failures.

A shocking accusation? Yet at least half a dozen independent studies, by leading scientific authorities here and abroad, as well as the 1983 comprehensive report to the U.S. Congress, tell us again and again that these programs contribute little or nothing to the improvement of their patients. The programs, of course, report that a substantial proportion of their patients leave the program much improved. Are they lying? Not at all.

Don't Reward Heavy Drinking

What the public is not told is that the rates of improvement for similar persons who do not go through treatment is about the same. The programs contribute nothing additional. What counts is motivation plus things like educational level, job status, and family status.

Offensive Analogy

Alcohol may be, metaphorically, a poison—but that doesn't make alcoholism a disease. To urge that it be so regarded by the law and by society is to commit the sin of offensive analogy. . . .

Alcoholics should be able to confess that they—like all of the rest of us in various ways—are weak. That won't make them feel as blameless as a diabetes victim. But it should give them heart to know that guts, spirit, and determination can defeat weakness—whereas they are powerless against disease.

Mona Charen, *The Conservative Chronicle*, May 11, 1988.

Another of the prevalent ideas fostered by the advocates of the disease concept of alcoholism is that it is genetically caused—which is a harmful half-truth. The full truth, reported in the data of the geneticists themselves, is that the role of genes seems real but quite limited. For example, the major genetic study by Dr. Robert Cloninger and his associates concluded: "Major changes in social attitudes about drinking styles can change dramatically the prevalence of alcohol abuse regardless of genetic predisposition." In short, you can't blame it on the genes; your life is in your own hands.

The unspoken but real significance of the "disease" notion is not medical but economic and political. Once the "disease" label is accepted widely as applying to some human problem, it becomes a license for health professionals to assume authority and to expand their practice.

Sometimes that is justified. Not here, though. It has become a legal basis for arguing that heavy drinkers should be excused from legal and moral responsibilities for any misdeeds. It has been used to justify providing them increasingly with special government and insurance benefits. We are told this is compassion. And it would be, if the money spent for "treatment" got results. It would be compassion if it encouraged alcohol abusers to stop, whereas in reality the benefits are *rewards* for heavy drinking, and the excuses *encourage* evasion of responsibility.

Court Rulings: No Disease

Why is there such resistance to public challenge of this doctrine? I do not ascribe malicious motives to the alcoholism treatment personnel if I point out that when tens of thousands of careers and billions of dollars are at stake, it is contrary to human nature to expect disinterested openness to new evidence. And those many alcoholics who have been emotionally indoctrinated join in resisting bitterly the public exposure of a doctrine to which they have a kind of religious commitment.

Fortunately, there are islands of objectivity in this sea of propaganda. In two landmark cases, one of them in 1988, the U.S. Supreme Court dispassionately reviewed the arguments on both sides of the issue as presented by leading exponents.

In the earlier 1968 case of *Powell*, the court rejected the criminal defense that alcoholism is a disease and hence that it ought to excuse the alcoholic for crimes committed while intoxicated.

In an April 1988 case, the Supreme Court agreed with what I have been reporting—and relied directly on my research. The court concluded that among the authorities there does not exist a consensus that alcoholism is a disease. Still further, said the court, there does exist a substantial body of medical evidence that alcoholic drinking is not involuntary, even where a genetic factor might exist. And, finally, the court concluded that it is therefore a reasonable rule to hold alcoholics responsible for their drinking and its effects.

Self-Motivation Is Primary

In reporting this evidence to the public, my objective has not been to heap blame on alcoholics. Far from it. We ought to have compassion for these people who have gradually, unwittingly, over years got themselves increasingly tangled up in a tragically destructive way of life. But help begins by confronting the alcoholic with the truth, not with the evasion that it is a "disease" that has taken over the alcoholic's will.

We should offer them our best counsel, and our moral support. But they must also face the fact that no one can do the job for them. They have to take their lives in their hands and change the way they live. Many alcoholics do responsibly fight their way to a better way of life. This is where the evidence now points, and where hope lies.

"Fetal-alcohol exposure is the most common-known cause of mental retardation in this country. "

Drinking During Pregnancy Causes Fetal Alcohol Syndrome

Elisabeth Rosenthal

Since the mid-1980s there has been increasing publicity about pregnant women who drink and Fetal Alcohol Syndrome (FAS). In the following viewpoint, Elisabeth Rosenthal maintains that alcohol can cause permanent physical and mental damage to a developing fetus. Rosenthal believes that doctors should tell their pregnant and breast-feeding patients to abstain completely from alcohol. Rosenthal is an emergency-room physician in New York City.

As you read, consider the following questions:

1. Why is it difficult to diagnose FAS quickly after birth, according to Rosenthal?
2. Into which ethnic groups are alcohol-affected babies most likely to be born, according to studies cited by the author?
3. What does Rosenthal say are the difficulties that alcohol-affected children face in school?

At the Human and Behavior Genetics Laboratory at Emory University, in Atlanta, a videotape recording shows a smiling 8-year-old girl peering from behind thick glasses at two clear plastic boxes topped by red bows, each containing a chocolate-chip cookie. The game, a psychologist explains, is to open both boxes and remove the cookies—and no eating until both cookies are out. The girl's 35-year-old mother observes.

The child seems to understand and, with the eagerness of a race horse at the gate, lunges at the boxes. For an endless few minutes, she pulls intently at the ribbons and tugs doggedly at the bows, clearly not up to this most elementary task. Finally, the mother comes to the rescue by untying one box and, with the second still sealed, the grinning child pops a cookie in her mouth.

"Ugh. This is too painful to watch," exclaims Dr. Claire D. Coles, the center's director of Clinical and Developmental Research, as she puts the tape on pause. "Look at that nice little girl. Her face is dysmorphic. She's too small for her age. And her fine motor coordination is awful.

"What's worse, look at the mother. She's also mildly dysmorphic. She spent her childhood in special-ed classes. The whole family suffers from prenatal alcohol exposure. All three kids, the mother, her brother."

In the last decade it has become unquestionably clear that alcohol is a potent teratogen, which can cause irreversible damage to the body and brain of the developing fetus. Experts like Dr. Coles now believe that women who are pregnant or contemplating pregnancy should not drink—at all.

Fetal alcohol syndrome and its more subtle variant, fetal alcohol effect, are umbrella terms used to describe the condition affecting the scarred offspring of drinking mothers. Victims with the full-blown syndrome, whose mothers generally drank heavily throughout pregnancy, often suffer physical malformations and mental retardation. Even those less fully affected, sometimes the progeny of women who drank only intermittently, may end up with lifelong learning disabilities and behavioral problems.

Staggering Estimates

No one knows exactly how many individuals are afflicted with fetal alcohol damage, but the estimates are staggering. The Centers for Disease Control estimate that more than 8,000 alcohol-damaged babies are born each year, or 2.7 babies for every 1,000 live births. Others feel that these figures are low. On some Indian reservations, 25 percent of all children are reportedly afflicted. . . .

Some experts believe fetal-alcohol exposure is the most common-known cause of mental retardation in this country. Dr.

Robert J. Sokol, dean of the School of Medicine at Wayne State University in Detroit and director of Wayne State's Alcohol Research Center, estimates that 1 out of 10 retarded adults in residential care has fetal alcohol syndrome. . . .

David Seavey, © 1988, *USA Today*. Reprinted with permission.

In screening for alcohol-related injuries, an expert in birth defects, or dysmorphologist, examines the suspect child for the unusual facial characteristics, small head and body size, poor mental capabilities and abnormal behavior patterns that typify alcohol-related birth defects. In infancy, the evaluation is usually prompted by knowledge of a mother's drinking, or because a newborn develops the shakes or seizures typical of alcohol withdrawal. But at this stage the symptoms are easily overlooked. Only 20 percent of those with the full syndrome have marked facial abnormalities, and those with the effect look fine.

"Except when a child is grossly dysmorphic," the syndrome is not diagnosed, says Dr. Sterling K. Claren, Aldrich Professor of Pediatrics at the University of Washington School of Medicine in Seattle. As for fetal alcohol effect, he adds, it "really cannot be diagnosed in newborns."

Most Cases Undiagnosed

Many children with the full syndrome come to expert attention only after they fail to gain weight and meet developmental landmarks. Sometimes a physician notices an abundance of physical complaints—crossed eyes, heart murmurs or recurrent ear infections—that suggest congenital malformation. Some are not recognized until years later, when they begin having trouble at school. Some are not recognized at all. Dr. José F. Cordero of the Centers for Disease Control's Division of Birth Defects and Developmental Disabilities believes that as many as two-thirds of cases of the full syndrome remain undiagnosed, with the figure for those less severely affected even higher.

Dr. Coles and her staff, as part of their study, crisscross Atlanta, turning their trained eyes on the progeny of alcoholic pregnancies to look for signs of damage. On a day in November 1989, she visited a ramshackle housing project to examine a one-month-old boy whose mother is an alcohol and cocaine abuser. She put the baby through a series of tests: shaking rattles near his ear, tweaking a toe with a rubber band, recording his cry.

The boy has no physical signs of fetal alcohol syndrome, she later explains, but his behavior is worrisome. "He is too irritable, too distractable," she said. "Kids at 30 days should be calm and able to focus on a rattle." But, she added, "If you weren't trained you might not recognize this as a substance-abuse baby."

Anne Cutcliffe's adopted daughter had seen various doctors before she was referred to Dr. Coles for an evaluation at age 2. "I guess I recall when I got her at 9 months, she was not an attractive child," said Mrs. Cutcliffe, who lives in Atlanta and has five older children. "She only weighed 10½ pounds and her eyes were crossed. All she could do was turn from her stomach to her back. I guess it proves love is blind, because I never did see all those things that other people saw." The girl's biological mother was an alcoholic.

Alcohol's Effect on Mother and Fetus

As many as 86 percent of women drink at least once during pregnancy, according to the Public Health Service, and experts estimate that between 20 and 35 percent of pregnant women drink regularly. In a 1989 study of 2,278 highly educated women (39 percent had postgraduate degrees), 30 percent consumed more than one drink a week during pregnancy; only 11 percent smoked.

Alcohol freely crosses the placenta, and the fetus's blood-alcohol level will equal that of the mother's. A study in *The New England Journal of Medicine* showed that women have lower levels than men of the stomach enzyme that neutralizes alcohol, leaving them particularly vulnerable to high levels of alcohol in the bloodstream. The mother's blood alcohol must reach a certain level—the toxic threshold—before the fetus is at risk. Binge drinking seems to be particularly risky. While a drink each night might never push a mother's blood level above the danger threshold, a night of drinking in honor of a birthday might well raise the level enough to endanger the fetus.

Lower I.Q. Scores

Even moderate drinking by women in the first month or two of pregnancy, often before they realize they are pregnant, can impair the child's intellectual ability upon reaching school age, a study indicates. . . .

The most recently published finding from the research involved 53 mothers who had on average three drinks or more a day in the first month or so of pregnancy. Their children were found at age 4 to score substantially lower on intelligence tests than other children. Specifically, the average score on I.Q. tests for these children was 105, 5 points below the average for all children in the study.

Daniel Goleman, *The New York Times*, February 16, 1989.

The type of damage produced by drinking depends on the fetus's stage of development. The first trimester of pregnancy is devoted to the organization of the fetus's bones and organs, while the second and third trimesters center on growth and maturation. The brain develops throughout the nine-month period. "So we'd predict physical malformations from heavy drinking in the first trimester and growth retardation from drinking in the third," says Dr. Claren. "But brain damage can occur at any time." In addition, the toxic threshold for brain damage seems to be much lower than for damage to other organs.

There is a rough correlation between the amount a mother imbibes during pregnancy and the severity of the baby's defects, but scientists are struggling to understand the many other factors that come into play. One major mystery is why so many drinking women frequently have apparently normal babies. Even in hopeless alcoholics, the chance of having a baby with the full-blown syndrome is only 35 percent.

The fetus may be more vulnerable on certain days of preg-

109

nancy. "Two drinks may be above the threshold on day 33 and on day 39, below," Dr. Claren said.

Women may also differ in their genetic susceptibility to having children with the syndrome, a tendency which some believe may follow ethnic and racial lines. Dr. Sokol has found that black women are seven times more likely to have fetal-alcohol-affected children than white women with similar drinking habits. (Pregnant or not, studies have found that black and Hispanic women are more likely to be abstinent than white women. And a woman's alcohol consumption tends to rise with her level of education and income.) The Centers for Disease Control data show that the syndrome is 30 times more commonly reported in Native Americans than it is in whites, and six times more common in blacks.

Dr. Coles believes these figures may be "partly an artifact of reporting. Researchers don't go into nice private hospitals and start looking for alcohol-damaged babies." At least one study found that women of lower socioeconomic status are diagnosed correctly more often.

Although experts stress that there is no evidence in human beings that a rare single drink does damage, most say that with so much still unknown the only prudent course for the pregnant mother is abstinence. "Pregnancy is a time when women should be conservative with their bodies," says Dr. Claren. "Women think three or four times before they take an aspirin. They quit smoking. Then they turn around and have a drink? Some obstetricians advise women not to drink. Many others make up some dose of liquor which they think is O.K. To me that's crazy." Experts recommend that women who are breast-feeding also abstain, because brain maturation continues after birth. . . .

Limitations in Alcohol-Affected Children

Two research groups, Dr. Coles's in Atlanta and Dr. Ann Streissguth's in Seattle, have followed alcohol-affected children for 6 and 14 years respectively. They find that some of the traits that are only hinted at in newborns blossom in early childhood, creating potentially disastrous school experiences. In Dr. Coles's group, children at age 6 showed poorer memory, shorter attention spans, lower I.Q.'s, diminished achievement levels and other learning disabilities when compared to normal children. Dr. Streissguth's group also reported attention deficits and other behavior problems at this age.

These shortcomings may add up to a limited ability to learn and to learn from experience. These kids "have a unique flavor among the learning disabled," observes Dr. Claren. "They seem to be really untrainable." Anne Cutcliffe remembers her daughter, at 6, making such slow progress in reading that her teachers decided she should repeat the first grade. When she started first grade a second time, after the four-month summer vacation, she had lost even the small progress she'd made the year before and had to start again at the most basic level.

Education and Treatment

Most children with the full syndrome will be found, with formal psychological testing, to be "developmentally delayed" and will qualify for special education. But some will limp along in regular classes. Even those who qualify for special education are often put into classes that don't meet their needs.

Most treatment programs for the mildly mentally handicapped were designed for patients like those with Down's syndrome, who are quiet, good workers and enjoy repetitive tasks. Parents and health professionals describe the alcohol-affected in very different terms: impulsive, unable to learn from mistakes, undisciplined, showing poor judgment, distractable, uninhibited. "We have to shift gears" to meet the needs of alcohol-affected kids, says Dr. Streissguth. She has applied for Federal funding to develop special therapeutic programs designed for them.

The flip side of the alcohol-affected personality is a winning one: outgoing, loving, physical, trusting. But together they lead to trouble. "She'll walk up to anyone on the street and stare at them and make conversation," says Anne Cutcliffe of her daughter. "Immediately she's buddies. It doesn't matter who." And Dr. Streissguth agrees that as young adults those with the syndrome often take sociability and physicality to unwelcome extremes: "They talk too loud or they stand too close. They seem not to pick up on normal social cues."

"Reports on FAS have generated needless worry among occasional or moderate [pregnant] drinkers."

Drinking During Pregnancy May Not Cause Fetal Alcohol Syndrome

Stanton Peele

Stanton Peele is a psychologist and health researcher at Mathematica Policy Research in Princeton, New Jersey. In the following viewpoint, Peele argues that alcohol consumed in low-to-moderate amounts during pregnancy is not harmful, and that the dangers ascribed to these quantities are exaggerated. He believes the campaign against pregnancy and alcohol ignores America's larger problem of poor prenatal care. Peele is the author of *The Diseasing of America: Addiction Treatment Out of Control.*

As you read, consider the following questions:

1. Why are attacks against alcohol immune from criticism, according to Peele?
2. What kind of guilt does the author believe a mother may feel if her child has behavioral problems?
3. According to Peele, what factors are responsible for low birth weight?

Stanton Peele, "The New Thalidomide." Reprinted, with permission, from the July 1990 issue of *Reason* magazine. Copyright © 1990 by the Reason Foundation, 2716 Ocean Park Blvd., Suite 1062, Santa Monica, CA 90405.

A growing number of pregnant women in the United States avoid alcohol as if it were thalidomide. The pronouncements of government officials, journalists, and other professional alarmists have convinced them that drinking any amount of alcohol during pregnancy endangers the fetus. This new conventional wisdom is embodied in the federal warning that now appears on every bottle of wine, beer, and liquor manufactured for sale in this country: "According to the Surgeon General, women should not drink alcoholic beverages during pregnancy because of the risk of birth defects."

The horrible effects of fetal alcohol syndrome—which include mental retardation, cardiac defects, and facial deformities—were publicized throughout the 1980s. More recently, *The Broken Cord*, Michael Dorris's account of his experiences in raising an adopted Native American child suffering from FAS, has renewed the storm of anxiety about alcohol consumption during pregnancy. Dorris's book warns people that the danger of drinking by pregnant women has been vastly underestimated. The news media have been eager to amplify that view.

Blurring Important Distinctions

The success of the campaign against drinking during pregnancy demonstrates that any attacks on alcohol, no matter how far-fetched, misleading, or counterproductive, are nowadays immune from criticism. By blurring important distinctions, reports on FAS have generated needless worry among occasional or moderate drinkers while distracting attention from the real problems of prenatal care.

People have long recognized that heavy alcohol consumption is a risky behavior for pregnant women. But U.S. researchers first used the term *fetal alcohol syndrome* in the early 1970s to describe severe abnormalities in the newborn children of alcoholic mothers, including brain damage and readily observable physical deformities.

Such children are quite rare, however, even among heavy drinkers. In their 1984 book *Alcohol and the Fetus*, based on a comprehensive survey of the research, Dr. Henry Rosett and Lyn Weiner of Boston University reported that studies find FAS occurs in only 2 percent to 10 percent of children born to alcohol abusers. Furthermore, they reported that in every one of the 400 FAS cases described in the scientific literature, the mother "was a chronic alcoholic who drank heavily during pregnancy."

The infrequency of FAS has prompted researchers to expand their focus beyond the severe birth defects sometimes caused by heavy drinking. Hence "fetal alcohol effect," which refers to more subtle impairment that might ordinarily escape attention. Closely tied to the rather vague notion of fetal alcohol effect is

113

the suggestion that light or moderate drinking might also be dangerous. Warnings about FAS, fetal alcohol effect, and the alleged risks of any drinking during pregnancy get tossed together in the news media.

No Threat

If taking alcohol during pregnancy were a real threat, many other societies would be in trouble. Some of us may want to believe that the behavior of the French and Italians may be a bit odd according to our standards, but no study reports that they suffer a greater amount of fetal effects from their use of alcohol during pregnancy—and some evidence suggests that in France, at least, they suffer fewer effects.

Morris E. Chafetz, *The Wall Street Journal*, March 5, 1990.

A February 1990 article by Dr. Elisabeth Rosenthal in *The New York Times Magazine*, "When a Pregnant Woman Drinks," begins with a horrific tale of an FAS victim. In this case, not only did the 8-year-old girl have FAS, but so did her siblings and her mother. Immediately following this extreme example, the article describes how Dr. Claire Coles, an FAS expert, has begun to "see the survivors of drinking pregnancies everywhere." For example, upon visiting a reform school Coles observed, "My God, half these kids look alcohol affected." The bait-and-switch juxtaposition of Coles's observation with the severe FAS case creates the false impression that such alcohol-related birth defects are common. *Alcohol affected,* the term used by Coles, is generally applied to infants who have problems that fall short of FAS, such as irritability, attention deficits, hyperactivity, or developmental delays. The condition cannot be discerned simply by looking at a child. But for those who see fetal alcohol effect "everywhere," even criminal behavior may be the result of a mother's drinking. (Attorneys representing condemned California murderer Robert Alton Harris offered such an argument.)

Promoting Hysteria

Increasingly, problems such as delinquency and learning disabilities are being attributed to maternal drinking. Combined with warnings about moderate alcohol consumption, this tendency is likely to cause irrational guilt among many parents. The mother of a child who gets into trouble or has difficulty in school will start to wonder if this has anything to do with the wine she occasionally drank during her pregnancy.

Weiner, co-author of *Alcohol and the Fetus*, has described the anxiety caused by exaggeration of the danger from drinking during pregnancy: "Women are worrying about wine vinegar in their salad dressing and getting hysterical about the risk of eating rum cake, and they think they need an abortion after they hear the scare stories."

What grounds, if any, are there for such alarm? Rosenthal's article is accompanied by a subhead that warns, "New Studies Show that Even Moderate Consumption Can Be Harmful to the Unborn Child." But the article cites only *one* study to support this claim: In 1988, a University of Pittsburgh researcher found "minor anomalies" in children of mothers who consumed less than one drink a day during pregnancy.

Rosenthal has latched onto one highly unusual finding in a sea of contradictory evidence, ignoring a host of studies that have found no effect from consumption of two drinks a day or less. In 1984 Rosett and Weiner concluded that "the recommendation that all women should abstain from drinking during pregnancy is not based on scientific evidence." The overwhelming majority of studies since then have also failed to find evidence that moderate drinking harms the fetus. In fact, Dr. Jack Mendelson, a distinguished alcohol researcher at Harvard Medical School, has declared, "It is possible that some doses of alcohol, low or moderate, may improve the probability for healthy pregnancies and healthy offspring."

Complications: Race and Class

Given the rush to condemn any drinking during pregnancy despite the dearth of research evidence to support such a policy, you might guess that fetal alcohol effect, if not FAS itself, is a widespread phenomenon. But the Centers for Disease Control estimate that 8,000 "alcohol-damaged babies" are born each year, which works out to a rate of 2.7 for every 1,000 live births (0.27 percent).

Yet *New York Times* health columnist Jane Brody offered a much higher figure in 1986, when she announced, "An estimated 50,000 babies born last year suffered from prenatal alcohol exposure." (Brody, by the way, does not think it's enough merely to abstain from alcohol during pregnancy: "Even drinking *before* pregnancy [as little as one drink a day] may have an untoward result," she reported.)

Rosenthal does not offer her own estimate, but she says the CDC figure seems low, apparently because "on some Indian reservations, 25 percent of all children are reportedly afflicted." But as she later notes, "The CDC data show that the syndrome is 30 times more commonly reported in Native Americans than it is in whites, and six times more common in blacks." These figures indicate that alcohol-related damage among babies of white, middle-class women is actually less common than 2.7 cases per 1,000, since all groups are averaged together in producing the overall rate.

Indeed, it's not clear what the middle-class women who read the *Times* can learn from the experience of grossly dysfunctional families such as the one described at the beginning of Rosenthal's article or from reports about Native American children such as the mentally retarded boy in *The Broken Cord*. For one thing, styles of drinking vary widely across racial and socioeconomic groups.

=====

Child I.Q.: The Real Factors

Women's drinking and birth defects are big news. *The New York Times* ran a front page story and a Sunday magazine piece promoting the proposition that "as little as one drink" during pregnancy can lead to intellectual and physical defects. But the research upon which these broad generalizations are based shows no such thing.

In one set of these studies, the authors clearly state that their data could not be interpreted below a *three* drink per day level. They noted, moreover, that the "strongest predictors of child I.Q." were other factors: "maternal education, mother-infant interactions, paternal education, race and birth order." Is it the occasional glass of wine or social factors, like education and poverty, that should have been highlighted? . . .

Alcohol abuse is one of the major public health hazards today—to the drinkers, their families and innocent bystanders. Indeed, it is reported to have accounted for more than 100,000 deaths in 1987 in the U.S. alone. But modest occasional drinking, during pregnancy or at other times, has not been shown to be a threat to an otherwise healthy person.

Jeanne Mager Stellman and Joan E. Bertin, *The New York Times*, June 4, 1990.

=====

White, middle-class women are more likely to drink than black women (and low-income women generally), but they tend to drink moderately. Black women are more likely to abstain, but those who don't are more likely to drink heavily. The fact that FAS rates are much higher among low-income minorities therefore contradicts the hypothesis that moderate drinking during pregnancy is damaging and that higher rates of abstinence would reduce FAS.

And a 1982 study by Boston University researcher Ralph Hingson suggests that other factors in the lives of poor, ghetto-dwelling women contribute to birth defects that have been ascribed solely to alcohol. After studying a sample of 1,700 women in Boston City Hospital, Hingson concluded that "neither level of drinking prior to pregnancy nor during pregnancy was significantly related to infant growth measures, congenital abnormality, or [other] features compatible with fetal alcohol syndrome."

Rather, a combination of factors—including smoking, malnutrition, and poor health care—seems to be responsible for low birth weight and other problems often attributed to drinking. "The results underline the difficulty in isolating and proclaiming single factors as the cause of abnormal fetal development," Hingson and his colleagues wrote.

A Misdirected Crusade

So the crusade against drinking during pregnancy is misdirected in several ways. It focuses on moderate rather than heavy drinking, on middle-class rather than low-income mothers, and on alcohol consumption rather than the set of behaviors that increases the risk of birth defects. The women most likely to give birth to damaged babies—the ones who abuse alcohol and drugs, smoke, and neglect their health—are not affected by messages tailored to the middle class.

The error in strategy is especially troubling given the nation's relatively poor performance in prenatal care. The number of birth defects in the United States has doubled in the last 25 years. While the U.S. neonatal death rate dropped in the 1980s, it still compares unfavorably with those of European nations, Japan, Australia, Singapore, Bermuda, and even Guam. Shrill warnings about low levels of drinking during pregnancy may make health experts feel virtuous, but they won't improve those figures one bit. Developing comprehensive community programs for high-risk mothers would help, but this requires more than Sunday-supplement alarmism.

"Drinking before your 21st birthday is now against the law in all 50 states, and nearly every high school student in the country violates it."

Drinking Threatens America's Youth

David Olinger

Some people believe alcohol abuse, rather than marijuana or other illicit drug use, is the number one problem among young adults today. In the following viewpoint, David Olinger agrees with this view and asserts that almost every high school student in America drinks to excess. To support his view, Olinger cites a report identifying drunken driving as the leading killer among teens. Olinger is a staff writer for the *St. Petersburg Times*, a Florida daily newspaper.

As you read, consider the following questions:

1. Why do you think many parents are relieved if their children use only alcohol and no other drugs, as Olinger states?
2. According to the author, how do some teenagers illegally obtain alcohol?
3. What does Olinger believe is the best argument for enforcing the drinking-age law?

David Olinger, "Children at the Crossroads," *St. Petersburg Times*, June 25, 1989. Reprinted with permission.

No crime kills more children in America. Each year, it is blamed in the deaths of more than 4,000 teen-agers.

Yet no crime is more rampant, no law more widely disregarded. In Florida, one of every three children commits this crime by the age of 12. Parents commonly violate this law without even knowing it. Police officers, upon finding a houseful of youthful offenders, will seize the evidence but may file no charges and call no parents.

Businesses large and small benefit from widespread violation of this law. Distillers and advertisers profit. So do convenience stores, cocktail lounges and limousine rental companies, unless they get caught at it repcatedly. So do young entrepreneurs who make and sell phony drivers' licenses.

The crime? Drinking in America before your 21st birthday. In Florida, it's a second-degree misdemeanor, punishable by up to two months in jail and a $500 fine. A father who gives his 19-year-old son a beer is committing a crime, and the son commits a crime by drinking it.

Number One Drug Problem

But the law's just a bluff. In reality, six of seven Florida high school students break it. As long as they don't drink, drive and hurt somebody, they risk only a $100 fine, and then only if they're unlucky enough to buy a six-pack in front of a state liquor investigator.

And as long as the kids don't turn to other drugs, many parents will be relieved that they're just drinking.

State Education Commissioner Betty Castor says that's a serious mistake. In a survey of 13,800 students, her department found that many children tried alcohol before they finished fourth grade. Three of four middle school students reported alcohol was easy to get. One of four high school students admitted to drinking in cars.

Among children, Castor said, "Alcohol is the No. 1 drug problem in our state."

They called themselves CHIPS, a name borrowed from the television show that glamorized the California Highway Patrol.

But this acronym glamorized something else. It stood for Clearwater High Intoxicated Party Society.

CHIPS was run by "a group of about eight to 10 guys," said one high school senior who partook of the service. It sponsored weekend parties at homes of high school students whose parents were away. It supplied the beer kegs, provided football players as bouncers and charged an admission fee to cover expenses and any damages to the party site. A big party might draw 200 kids and gross $600.

"It worked out good, you know. People didn't have to worry

about getting the alcohol," the senior said.

CHIPS faded away, but there were successor organizations. In 1989 it was called CPD—Clearwater Party Department. Its leaders even used Clearwater Police Department stickers to advertise its existence. Not every high school class has a similar club, but most have weekend drinking parties. Half the high school students in the nation drink weekly. Two of five admit to binge drinking—five or more drinks in a night within the last two weeks.

Easy to Get

Getting alcohol is easy, they say. Any teen-ager can get it any night.

To understand just how easy, I talked to a dozen young people who have repeatedly violated Florida's minimum drinking age law. In most cases I agreed not to use their full names.

How many ways have they found to get alcohol?

Let me recite a few. You can drink your parents' supply. You can get an older friend to buy it. You can ask an older brother or sister to "lose" a driver's license and give it to you. You can go to a store that doesn't check IDs or buy a fake driver's license. You can go to a night club that admits 18-year-olds and sneak drinks. If you're young and female, wear makeup and a miniskirt, a 19-year-old said, "You'll get in."

Children Drink at Earlier Ages

While cocaine may come, and marijuana may go, alcohol remains the "gateway drug of choice," say clinicians, who report that kids are drinking more, at a younger age, than earlier generations of elementary school students.

Confirmation of their fears came in October 1990 with the release of *The Troubled Journey*, a national survey of 47,000 public and private school students by Search Institute of Minneapolis.

It found that 9 to 16 percent of sixth, seventh and eighth-graders had consumed five or more drinks, consecutively—on one or more occasions—in the preceding two weeks.

San Diego Union, December 2, 1990.

Tracey Barry was a straight-A student at Countryside High in Clearwater. She edited its student newspaper. In 1989 she enrolled as a freshman at prestigious Vassar College.

She started drinking at the age of 15—"I have three older brothers," she explained—and lost interest in it at 17.

In the meantime, she met a lot of high school students who drank socially at weekend parties, and a few who would get drunk twice in a weekend.

"The more you can drink, it's almost a status kind of thing. 'I can drink you under the table. I can shotgun five beers.' You're very macho and very cool and very tough if you can drink a lot," Tracey said.

To "shotgun" a beer, you tap a hole in the bottom and drink it without stopping.

Tracey knew it was illegal for a teen-ager to drink of course. She also noticed that wherever she looked, the adult world communicated positive messages about alcohol. It was associated with sensuality, relaxation, celebration. On soap operas, if people have a problem, they get a drink. Cocktail lounges advertise "happy hours." Weddings have open bars. In wine cooler ads the men and women are all beautiful and beautifully dressed, and all have a drink in hand.

"Everywhere you go, there's that statement attached that if alcohol is there, you're going to have fun," she said.

Almost any weekend there were high school drinking parties. Police raids were common—she saw "a dozen or more"—but criminal charges were not.

"Even from parties I've been to where the police quote, 'bust the party,' I've never seen them arrest someone or call their parents. They confiscate stuff."

And the kids, she said, "will get in their cars and drive off to another party."

Clearwater Police Department policy is to charge teens caught drinking at weekend parties, but "Of course, officer discretion is allowed," said Capt. J.D. Eastridge, its patrol commander. "When you consider that we have one or two officers responding to a situation like that—it's a difficult situation, sure."

Less discretion is allowed at the Division of Alcoholic Beverages and Tobacco, a state agency that enforces liquor laws at licensed establishments. Its agents charge every youth they catch drinking. . . .

Failure to Curb Teen Drinking

It would be easy to conclude that a nationwide effort to outlaw teen drinking has failed. Drinking before your 21st birthday is now against the law in all 50 states, and nearly every high school student in the country violates it. Prohibition was more effective in the 1920s than the drinking-age laws are today.

And why shouldn't 18-year-olds be permitted to drink? Legally they can vote, get married, have children, own property, be prosecuted as adults, enlist in the Army, go to college, serve drinks in a bar and buy guns. But they can't buy a beer for three more years.

The best argument for enforcing a law that few obey is simply this: It apparently discourages drinking just enough to save hundreds of young lives each year.

As the legal drinking age has been raised to 21 nationally, the number of teens killed in car crashes has declined. In 1982, alcohol-related traffic accidents killed 5,380 youths aged 15 to 20 in the United States. By 1987, the death toll had dropped to 4,204.

In 1982, one of three teen drivers involved in fatal accidents was drunk. In 1988 it was down to one of five, and "that's a pretty big drop," said a National Highway Traffic Safety Administration researcher.

Drunk Driving: Main Killer Among Teens

Still, the numbers are grim. "Drinking and driving continues to be the No. 1 killer of teen-agers," the National Commission Against Drunk Driving reported in 1988. Statistically, your risk of dying in an alcohol-related crash doubles if you're under 21, even though legally you can't drink at all.

Nationally, six drunken teen drivers will kill somebody on a typical day. In Florida, such tragedies occur about twice a week. Always, the circle of pain ripples out from the immediate victims to families and friends.

Seventeen-year-old Mark Puterman went for his last drive just five days before he would have graduated from high school in 1988. He was a popular kid and a decent student. Five colleges had accepted him. His parents never knew he drank.

He told them he was going to a party that night, and agreed to be home by 12:30 a.m. Instead he went to the Victory Cafe, a restaurant and bar north of Tampa, to drink with teen-age friends. He almost made it home. Just 1½ miles away, he slammed his mother's Volkswagen into a utility pole and died.

A blood alcohol test showed Mark was drunk.

One Mother's Anger

His mother, Grace Puterman, entered a grief counseling program called Life Center with her husband. She still finds it terribly painful to talk about Mark. "Raw," was the word she used.

His death affects every day of her life. It disturbs her now to watch children's sports heroes advertise beer on TV. She gets angry now when she sees how available alcohol is to children, and how rarely the places that sell it to them get punished. She wishes now that teen-agers would face a real penalty for drinking illegally, like a suspended driver's license. If she sees them sipping beer in a restaurant now, she goes to the manager to demand an ID check. She wishes more parents would.

"I don't want anybody to suffer the way we have," she said. "He was our only son."

"Evidence is mounting that alcohol consumption among young people is dropping."

Drinking Is Declining Among America's Youth

Marj Charlier and Gerardo M. Gonzalez

Liquor industry statistics show that in every year since 1980, Americans' consumption of liquor has dropped. In Part I of the following viewpoint, Marj Charlier maintains that this decline is greatest among young people below age twenty-one. Charlier argues there is an increasing trend among underage university students to abstain from alcohol. In Part II, Gerardo M. Gonzalez agrees that drinking by college students has decreased in recent years. Gonzalez cites statistics from his annual surveys to show that student alcohol use has decreased. Charlier is a staff reporter for the *Wall Street Journal*, a daily business newspaper, and Gonzalez is an associate professor of counselor education at the University of Florida in Gainesville.

As you read, consider the following questions:

1. What paradox does Charlier see among many liquor manufacturers?
2. Do you agree with Charlier's belief that teenage drinking rates are declining? Why or why not?
3. What reasons does Gonzalez offer for the reduction in student alcohol use?

I

At the University of Texas in Austin, a new student fad has taken hold: sobriety.

In spring 1990, a fraternity banned alcohol during the campus's annual spring fling for high school students. All 28 of the school's fraternities decided to go dry for fall's "rush week," the annual debauchery when they recruit new members. And a non-alcoholic bar has sprouted along Austin's Sixth Street of honky tonks.

These events may put a dent in the university's reputation as a party school, but "it's just not acceptable to drink and drive," says Larry Dubinski, a Zeta Beta Tau senior and a member of the Interfraternity Council at the university. "And people don't drink as much anymore."

What's happening in Austin isn't an aberration. Across the country, evidence is mounting that alcohol consumption among young people is dropping. And that has put the makers of beer and booze in an awkward position. Many have taken steps recently to discourage alcohol abuse, especially among the young. But at the same time, they all market ferociously to young people, their biggest customers, who are just starting to develop brand loyalties.

Unmistakable Signs of Change

So far, widespread abstinence doesn't seem a serious threat. But the signs of change are unmistakable. Non-alcoholic after-prom and after-graduation parties are spreading—there's even an annual convention now where students go to learn how to organize such parties. And teenagers are starting to like the looks of a dry world. Lance Rizzo, an 18-year-old from Humble, Texas, who just graduated from high school, quit drinking about 18 months ago. "Hangovers, the lost money, the car wrecks are not part of my life anymore," he says. Is he ridiculed by his peers for his teetotalling? "Absolutely not," he says. "It seems to be what's in."

Statistics show consumption is falling faster among young adults than in the general population. The percentage of 18- to 24-year-olds who drink vodka fell to 21.9% in 1990 from 32.2% in 1984, according to Simmons Market Research Bureau. Consumption by people of all ages declined less sharply, to 22.1% from 26%, Simmons says. Even beer, typically the drink of choice among the young, is slipping: In 1989, 46.7% of the 18- to-24 age group drank beer, down from 56.3% in 1984. Among the population as a whole, beer consumption eased only 1.6 percentage points.

It isn't easy to pinpoint the roots of this sobering trend. Certainly, the federally mandated 21-year-old minimum drinking age has had a big impact on consumption by the under-21 set. But the most populous states have had 21-year-old minimums for at least three years, yet consumption continues to drop. And drinking also has declined in the 25-to-34 bracket.

Health awareness has had an impact: The fitness boom may be waning, but many people are counting calories. And some states passed laws in the past 10 years making the hosts of private parties as liable as bartenders for serving drunks. "We're in a society right now where people tend to get sued a lot," says Mr. Dubinski of the University of Texas fraternity group. In 1988 the fraternity council adopted a rule requiring fraternities to provide free taxis or designated drivers at parties where alcohol is served.

Meanwhile, campaigns to stop underage drinking and to moderate drinking by party-prone 21- to 34-year-olds have gathered steam. From January to June 1990, Students Against Driving Drunk received 400,000 requests for its parent-student contracts, which stipulate that the kids won't try to drive when they're drunk. In just 10 years, Mothers Against Drunk Driving has gathered 2.8 million members. Nearly 80% of all high schools in the U.S. have SADD chapters, and 400 communities have MADD chapters.

Alcohol-related automobile deaths among 15- to 19-year-olds plunged to 2,170 in 1988 from a peak of 6,281 in 1982, partly because "kids began to see that death is related to alcohol and drug use," says Robert Anastos, the founder and president of SADD. "They figured out that you don't have to drink and drive."

II

In an effort to assess recent changes in college students' drinking patterns, I started in 1981 to collect data among students who visited Daytona Beach, Florida during their spring breaks. Approximately 300,000 college students from throughout the United States visit Daytona Beach during spring break each year. Each year since 1981 I have set up an exhibit booth during spring break at Daytona Beach's College Expo. College Expo is the nation's largest consumer fair for young adults, featuring product samples and demonstrations, entertainment, and various other promotional programs. Dozens of national and regional companies participate in College Expo, setting up exhibits that feature their products. The exhibits are free and open to the public. Thousands of college students who come to Daytona Beach during spring break visit College Expo to participate in the activities sponsored by the companies and take advantage of many free product samples distributed at the exhibits.

Student Alcohol Survey

The exhibit booth used for this study was titled "The BACCHUS College of Alcohol Knowledge." It featured a questionnaire consisting of ten questions on the effects of alcoholic beverages to which each student could answer "True," "False," or "Don't know";

125

a section on demographic information; and a section on drinking habits. Based on the responses to the drinking habits section of the questionnaire, a Quantity-Frequency (QF) index was computed to provide information on the number of drinks (beer, wine or distilled spirits) that a student usually consumed during a month. Students completed the entire questionnaire in about ten minutes. Each day during the week of College Expo in 1981, 1982, 1983, 1984, 1985 and 1986 the exhibit was open between 1:00 p.m. and 6:00 p.m. The exhibit was staffed by student volunteers from the University of Florida, who encouraged other students passing by to stop and complete the BACCHUS Alcohol Knowledge Test and receive a free party planning kit. Each year hundreds of students stopped by the exhibit and completed the questionnaire. Their responses were anonymous and no attempt was made to identify the respondent.

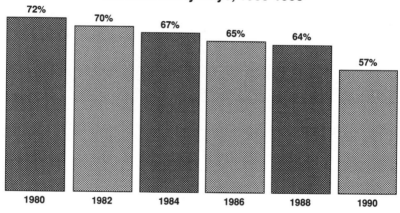

Seniors Who Used Alcohol in the Last Thirty Days, 1980-1990

72% — 1980
70% — 1982
67% — 1984
65% — 1986
64% — 1988
57% — 1990

Drug Abuse Update, Spring 1991.

There were 1,881 usable questionnaires collected in 1981, 1199 in 1982, 1233 in 1983, 1660 in 1984, 1581 in 1985 and 1334 in 1986. The vast majority of the respondents each year indicated that they currently drank alcoholic beverages. Overall, 88% of the males and 86% of the females said they were drinkers. However, there was a consistent trend between 1981 and 1986 toward reduced consumption by both male and female drinkers as measured by the Quantity-Frequency (QF) scale. Male student drinkers showed a decrease from an average consumption of fifty-three drinks (12 oz. of beer, 5 oz. of wine or 1-1/2 oz. of liquor) per month in 1981 to an average consumption of forty-six drinks per month in 1986. Female student drinkers consumption decreased from an average of thirty-nine drinks per month in 1981 to twenty-nine drinks per month in 1986. . . .

Consumption Is Down

The findings of this study lend support to the concern expressed by college administrators and researchers that raising the drinking age does not necessarily reduce alcohol consumption by college students. It may well be possible, as some college administrators fear, that the raise in the drinking age will force student drinking underground and will only change where and how they drink—possibly for the worse. However, it is important to note that regardless of changes in drinking age laws, consumption of alcoholic beverages by college students has significantly decreased in recent years. Interestingly, the trends toward reduced consumption of alcohol by college students since 1981 to some extent parallel alcohol consumption trends found among the population at large. It is also interesting that since 1980 consumption rates for other drugs of abuse, including marijuana, have been decreasing for both high school and college students.

One might speculate that the reduction in the use of alcohol and other drugs in recent years may be due to the increasing attention these problems have received in the media, school programs, and parent and community groups. For example, the number of colleges reporting that they have formed a task force or committee focusing on alcohol education and prevention nearly doubled between 1981 and 1985. The number of colleges reporting that they have designated a specific time period, such as alcohol awareness week, for focusing on alcohol education and prevention efforts showed an almost five-fold increase during the same period.

Research is needed to see whether, in fact, some of the positive changes in consumption rates reported on the college campus can be attributed to the significant increase in alcohol education and prevention efforts. There is some evidence that classroom-type, extended alcohol education programs can have a significant impact in the reduction of alcohol-related problems among college students.

Recognizing Deceptive Arguments

People who feel strongly about an issue use many techniques to persuade others to agree with them. Some of these techniques appeal to the intellect, some to the emotions. Many of them distract the reader or listener from the real issues.

A few common examples of argumentation tactics are listed below. Most of them can be used either to advance an argument in an honest, reasonable way or to deceive or distract from the real issues. It is important for a critical reader to recognize these tactics in order to rationally evaluate an author's ideas.

a. *scare tactics*—the threat that if you don't do or don't believe this, something terrible will happen.

b. *personal attack*—criticizing an opponent *personally* instead of rationally debating his or her ideas.

c. *generalization*—using statistics or facts to generalize about a population, place, or thing.

d. *testimonial*—quoting or paraphrasing an authority or celebrity to support one's own viewpoint.

e. *slanter*— the attempt to persuade through inflammatory and exaggerated language instead of through reason

f. *bandwagon*—the idea that "everybody" does this or believes this.

The following activity can help you sharpen your skills in recognizing deceptive reasoning. The statements below are derived from the viewpoints in this chapter. *Beside each one, mark the letter of the type of deceptive appeal being used. More than one type of tactic may be applicable. If you believe the statement is not any of the listed appeals, write N.*

1. Pregnant women should not drink because their babies will be born severely retarded and physically malformed.

2. Dr. Allan is simply a prudish moralizer who hates everyone who drinks alcohol.

3. Babies born with FAS are rare, so all pregnant women should feel safe about drinking.

4. Dr. Louis Sullivan, head of the Department of Health and Human Services, says heavy drinking in the first trimester of pregnancy can cause physical deformities in babies.

5. Since nearly all doctors now believe that alcoholism is a disease, those who do not are simply quacks.

6. If Americans continue abusing drugs and alcohol at such high rates, then their and their children's lives will be ruined.

7. Why shouldn't I drink? Every high school student in America is doing it.

8. The president of A & Z Brewing claims to discourage alcohol abuse, but he is really a scheming profiteer who advertises beer to young people.

9. President George Bush says drinking and driving is one of the most serious threats to Americans.

10. The life spans of all alcoholics are cut short by ten to twelve years.

11. If alcoholics want to recover, they should look at their own sinfulness, immorality, and selfish desires as the cause of their problems.

12. You must stop drinking at once, and you must remain abstinent, or else you will risk certain death.

13. Private alcoholism treatment centers are failures. They care only about making money and nothing for the alcoholic's well-being.

Periodical Bibliography

The following articles have been selected to supplement the diverse views presented in this chapter.

James Alsdurf — "Alcoholism: Is It a Sin After All?" *Christianity Today*, February 3, 1989.

Robert Bazell — "The Drink Link," *The New Republic*, May 7, 1990.

Geoffrey Cowley — "The Gene and the Bottle," *Newsweek*, April 30, 1990.

Current Health 2 — "Alcohol in the Life of a Teen," October 1990.

Shifra Diamond — "Drinking Habits May Be All in the Family," *Mademoiselle*, August 1990.

David Gelman — "Roots of Addiction," *Newsweek*, February 20, 1989.

William Madsen — "Thin Thinking About Heavy Drinking," *The Public Interest*, Spring 1989.

Sara Nelson — "A Nation Under the Influence," *Seventeen*, March 1990.

Stanton Peele — "Second Thoughts About a Gene for Alcoholism," *The Atlantic*, August 1990.

Andrew Purvis — "DNA and the Desire to Drink," *Time*, April 30, 1990.

Scott Russell Sanders — "Under the Influence," *Harper's Magazine*, November 1989.

Scholastic Update (teacher's edition) — "Alcohol: America's No. 1 Addiction," November 16, 1990.

Jonathan Schwartz — "The Usual," *Gentlemen's Quarterly*, December 1989.

U.S. News & World Report — "Genes with a Don't-Drink Label," April 30, 1990.

Richard E. Vatz and Lee S. Weinberg — "Confusion over Alcoholism," *USA Today*, September 1989.

Should Drug Laws Be Reformed?

Chemical Dependency

Chapter Preface

Bootlegging, speakeasies, bathtub gin, flappers, and Al Capone are familiar images from the era of Prohibition, so-called because of the constitutional amendment that prohibited the sale and manufacture of alcoholic beverages from 1920 to 1933. During that period, the demand for banned alcohol was met by members of organized crime who smuggled it into the U.S. or manufactured it illicitly. Escalating violent crime and the inability to enforce the laws against alcohol use finally led to Prohibition's repeal.

Today, crack houses, boarder babies (drug-addicted babies deserted at birth), Uzi machine guns, gangs, and drive-by shootings are images of another social predicament that many people compare to the Prohibition era. Some experts suggest that the way to end these drug-related problems is to follow the example of 1933 and legalize illegal drugs. For instance, Nobel prize-winning economist Milton Friedman contends that repealing laws against the manufacture, sale, and use of drugs would reduce violent crimes like theft and murder as it did when Congress repealed the prohibition against alcohol. Friedman maintains that legalization would also eliminate the immense profits earned by international drug cartels, street-drug dealers, and corrupt officials.

Opponents of legalization, most notably, President George Bush and William J. Bennett, the former director of the Office of National Drug Control Policy, believe repealing drug laws is not the answer. As Bennett states, "After the repeal of Prohibition . . . consumption of alcohol soared by 350 percent." He argues that legalization would likewise dramatically increase the number of drug users and addicts and would undoubtedly increase violent crime. He urges the maintenance and enforcement of strict laws against drugs.

In many ways the drug problem of the 1990s resembles the alcohol problem of the 1920s. But the hypothesis that legalizing illegal drugs can alleviate drug-related crime and violence remains to be tested. The authors in this chapter debate the implications of changing the nation's drug laws.

"Once the drug war is considered in rational terms, the solution becomes obvious: declare peace. Legalize the stuff."

Illegal Drugs Should Be Legalized

Richard J. Dennis

Richard J. Dennis is president of *New Perspectives Quarterly*, a publication of the Center for the Study of Democratic Institutions, a Los Angeles organization that investigates social, political, and global issues. He is also the chairperson of the advisory board of the Drug Policy Foundation in Washington, D.C. In the following viewpoint, Dennis contends that the war on drugs has failed to reduce chemical dependency or crime. He advocates legalizing certain drugs such as marijuana and cocaine to reduce the social and economic costs of drug abuse.

As you read, consider the following questions:

1. According to Dennis, what are some of the wrong ways to discuss the problem of illegal drugs?
2. What results does the author expect from the legalization of illicit drugs?
3. Why does Dennis promote legalization of drugs and how will legalization solve that illegal drug problem?

Reprinted, with permission, from "The Economics of Legalizing Drugs," by Richard J. Dennis, *The Atlantic*, November 1990. Copyright © 1990 by Richard J. Dennis as first published in *The Atlantic*.

Americans have grown so hysterical about the drug problem that few public figures dare appear soft on drugs or say anything dispassionate about the situation. In a 1989 poll 54 percent of Americans cited drugs as the nation's greatest threat. Four percent named unemployment. It is time, long past time, to take a clear-eyed look at illegal drugs and ask what government and law enforcement can really be expected to do.

Drug illegality has the same effect as a regressive tax: its chief aim is to save relatively wealthy potential users of drugs like marijuana and cocaine from self-destruction, at tremendous cost to the residents of inner cities. For this reason alone, people interested in policies that help America's poor should embrace drug legalization. It would dethrone drug dealers in the ghettos and release inner-city residents from their status as hostages.

Once the drug war is considered in rational terms, the solution becomes obvious: declare peace. Legalize the stuff. Tax it and regulate its distribution, as liquor is now taxed and regulated. Educate those who will listen. Help those who need help.

Arguments for the benefits of drug legalization have appeared frequently in the press, most of them making the point that crime and other social hazards might be reduced as a result. . . .

Wrong Ways to Discuss Drugs

The drug problem is not a moral issue. There's a streak of puritanism in the national soul, true, but most Americans are not morally opposed to substances that alter one's mind and mood. That issue was resolved in 1933, with the repeal of Prohibition. There is no question that drugs used to excess are harmful; so is alcohol. Americans seem to have no moral difficulty with the notion that adults should be allowed to use alcohol as they see fit, as long as others are not harmed.

The drug problem is not the country's most important health issue. The use of heroin and cocaine can result in addiction and death; so can the use of alcohol and tobacco. In fact, some researchers estimate the yearly per capita mortality rate of tobacco among smokers at more than a hundred times that of cocaine among cocaine users. If the drug-policy director is worried about the effect on public health of substance abuse, he should spend most of his time talking about cigarettes and whiskey.

The drug problem is not entirely a societal issue—at least not in the sense that it is portrayed as one by politicians and the media. Drug dealing is a chance for people without legitimate opportunity. The problem of the underclass will never be solved by attacking it with force of arms.

So what is the problem? The heart of it is money. What most Americans want is less crime and less profit for inner-city thugs and Colombian drug lords. Less self-destruction by drug users would be nice, but what people increasingly demand is an end to the foreign and domestic terrorism—financed by vast amounts of our own money—associated with the illegal drug trade.

Legalization

This, as it happens, is a problem that can be solved in quick and pragmatic fashion, by legalizing the sale of most drugs to adults. Virtually overnight crime and corruption would be reduced. The drug cartels would be shattered. Public resources could be diverted to meaningful education and treatment programs.

Chuck Asay, by permission of the *Colorado Springs Gazette-Telegraph*.

The alternative—driving up drug prices and increasing public costs with an accelerated drug war—inevitably will fail to solve anything. Instead of making holy war on the drug barons, the President's plan subsidizes them. . . .

The appropriate standard in deciding if a drug should be made legal for adults ought to be whether it is more likely than alcohol to cause harm to an innocent party. If not, banning it cannot be justified while alcohol remains legal. For example, a sensible legalization plan would allow users of marijuana to buy it legally. Small dealers could sell it legally but would be regulated, as beer dealers are now in states where beer is sold in grocery stores.

Their suppliers would be licensed and regulated. Selling marijuana to minors would be criminal.

Users of cocaine should be able to buy it through centers akin to state liquor stores. It is critical to remove the black-market profit from cocaine in order to destabilize organized crime and impoverish pushers. Selling cocaine to minors would be criminal, as it is now, but infractions could be better policed if effort were concentrated on them. Any black market that might remain would be in sales of crack or sales to minors, transactions that are now estimated to account for 20 percent of drug sales.

Cocaine runs the spectrum from coca leaf to powder to smokable crack; it's the way people take it that makes the difference. Crack's effects on individual behavior and its addictive potential place it in a category apart from other forms of cocaine. The actual degree of harm it does to those who use it is still to be discovered, but for the sake of argument let's assume that it presents a clear danger to people who come in contact with the users. A crack user, therefore, should be subject to a civil fine, and mandatory treatment after multiple violations. Small dealers should have their supplies seized and be subject to moderate punishment for repeat offenses. Major dealers, however, should be subject to the kinds of sentences that are now given. And any adult convicted of selling crack to children should face the harshest prison sentence our criminal-justice system can mete out.

The same rules should apply to any drug that presents a substantial threat to others. . . .

As for heroin, the advent of methadone clinics shows that society has realized that addicts require maintenance. But there is little practical difference between methadone and heroin, and methadone clinics don't get people off methadone. Heroin addicts should receive what they require, so that they don't have to steal to support their habit. This would make heroin unprofitable for its pushers. And providing addicts with access to uninfected needles would help stop the spread of AIDS and help lure them into treatment programs.

The Drug War Costs

The major argument against legalization, and one that deserves to be taken seriously, is a possible increase in drug use and addiction. But it can be shown that if reasonable costs are assigned to all aspects of the drug problem, the benefits of drug peace would be large enough to offset even a doubling in the number of addicts.

Any numerical cost-benefit analysis of drug legalization versus the current drug war rests on assumptions that are difficult to substantiate. The figures for the costs of drug use must be estimates, and so the following analysis is by necessity illustrative rather than definitive. But the numbers used in the analysis below are at least of the right magnitude; most are based on government data. These assumptions, moreover, give the benefit of the doubt to the drug warriors and shortchange proponents of drug legalization.

Tragedy into Disaster

Drugs are a tragedy for addicts. But criminalizing their use converts that tragedy into a disaster for society, for users and nonusers alike. Our experience with the prohibition of drugs is a replay of our experience with the prohibition of alcoholic beverages.

Milton Friedman, *New Dimensions*, June 1990.

The statistical assumptions that form the basis of this cost-benefit analysis are as follows:

• *The social cost of all drug use at all levels can be estimated by assuming that America now has two million illicit-drug addicts.* Slightly more than one million addicts use cocaine (including crack) about four times a week; 500,000 addicts use heroin at about the same rate. This means that there are about 1.5 million hardcore addicts. Some experts argue that the figures for addiction should be higher. An estimate of the social cost of drug use should also take into account casual use, even if the social cost of it is arguable; 10 million people, at most, use cocaine and other dangerous drugs monthly. To ensure a fair estimate of social cost, let's assume that America now has two million drug addicts.

• *Legalization would result in an immediate and permanent 25 percent increase in the number of addicts and the costs associated with them.* This projection is derived by estimating the number of people who would try hard drugs if they were legalized and then estimating how many of them would end up addicted. In past years—during a time when marijuana was more or less decriminalized—approximately 60 million Americans tried marijuana and almost 30 million tried cocaine, America's most popular hard drug. (It is fair to assume that nearly all of those who tried cocaine also tried marijuana and that those who haven't tried marijuana in the past twenty-five years will not decide to try decriminalized cocaine.) This leaves 30 million people who have tried marijuana but not cocaine, and who might be at risk to try legal, inexpensive cocaine.

In a 1985 survey of people who voluntarily stopped using cocaine, 21 percent claimed they did so because they feared for their health, 12 percent because they were pressured by friends and family, and 12 percent because the drug was too expensive.

137

The reasons of the other half of those surveyed were unspecified, but for the purpose of this exercise we will assume that they stopped for the same reasons in the same proportions as the other respondents. (Interestingly, the survey did not mention users who said they had stopped because cocaine is illegal or out of fear of law enforcement.) It seems reasonable to assume that many people would decide not to use legalized drugs for the same reasons that these experimenters quit. Therefore, of the 30 million people estimated to be at risk of trying legal cocaine, only about a quarter might actually try it—the quarter that is price-sensitive, because the price of cocaine, once the drug was legalized, would plummet. This leaves us with approximately 7.5 million new cocaine users. How many of them could we expect to become cocaine addicts? The estimate that there are now one million cocaine addicts suggests a one-in-thirty chance of addiction through experimentation. Thus from the 7.5 million new users we could expect about 250,000 new addicts, or an increase of 25 percent over the number of cocaine addicts that we now have. We can assume about the same increase in the number of users of other hard drugs.

Those who argue that wide availability must mean significantly higher usage overlook the fact that there is no economic incentive for dealers to push dirt-cheap drugs. Legalization might thus lead to less rather than more drug use, particularly by children and teenagers. Also, the public evinces little interest in trying legalized drugs. In 1989, at the direction of this author, the polling firm Targeting Systems Inc., in Arlington, Virginia, asked a nationwide sample of 600 adults, "If cocaine were legalized, would you personally consider purchasing it or not?" Only one percent said they would. . . .

Drug Peace

If we choose drug peace as opposed to drug war, we'll save $10 billion a year in federal law enforcement, $10 billion a year in new state and local prosecution, about $8 billion a year in other law-enforcement costs (80 percent of the current $10 billion a year), about $6 billion a year in the value of stolen property associated with drug use (80 percent of the current $7.5 billion), and $3.75 billion a year by eliminating the need to match the Colombians' drug profits dollar for dollar. We'll also benefit from taxes of $12.5 billion. These social gains amount to $50.25 billion.

If use rises 25 percent, instead of declining by that amount, it will result in a social cost of $25 billion (50 percent of $50 billion). Therefore, the net social gain of drug peace is $25.25 billion. If legalization resulted in an immediate and permanent increase in use of more than 25 percent, the benefits of drug peace would narrow. But additional tax revenue would partly make up for the shrinkage. For example, if the increase in use was 50 percent instead of 25 percent, that would add another $12.5 billion in social costs per year but would contribute another $2.5 billion in tax revenue. . . .

Some Objections Considered

• *Crack is our No. 1 drug problem. Legalizing other drugs while crack remains illegal won't solve the problem.* Although crack has captured the lion's share of public attention, marijuana has always commanded the bulk of law-enforcement interest. Despite de facto urban decriminalization, more than a third of all drug arrests occur in connection with marijuana—mostly for mere possession. Three fourths of all violations of drug laws relate to marijuana, and two thirds of all people charged with violation of federal marijuana laws are sentenced to prison (state figures are not available).

Crack appears to account for about 10 percent of the total dollar volume of the drug trade, according to National Institute on Drug Abuse estimates of the number of regular crack users. Legalizing other drugs would free up most of their law-enforcement resources currently focused on less dangerous substances and their users. It's true that as long as crack remains illegal, there will be a black market and associated crime. But we would still reap most of the benefits of legalization outlined above.

• *Legalization would result in a huge loss in productivity and in higher health-care costs.* In truth, productivity lost to drugs is minor compared with productivity lost to alcohol and cigarettes, which remain legal. Hundreds of variables affect a person's job performance, ranging from the consumption of whiskey and cigarettes to obesity and family problems. On a purely statistical level it can be demonstrated that marital status affects productivity, yet we do not allow employers to dismiss workers on the basis of that factor.

If legal drug use resulted in higher social costs, the government could levy a tax on the sale of drugs in some rough proportion to the monetary value of those costs—as it does now for alcohol and cigarettes. This wouldn't provide the government with a financial stake in addiction. Rather, the government would be making sure that users of socially costly items paid those social costs. Funds from the tax on decriminalized drugs could be used for anti-drug advertising, which could be made more effective by a total ban on drug advertising. A government that licenses the sale of drugs must actively educate its citizens about their dangers, as Holland does in discouraging young people from using marijuana.

• *Drug legalization implies approval.* One of the glories of

American life is that many things that are not condoned by society at large, such as atheism, offensive speech, and heavy-metal music, are legal. The well-publicized death of Len Bias and other harrowing stories have carried the message far and wide that drugs are dangerous. In arguing that legalization would persuade people that drug use is safe, drug warriors underestimate our intelligence.

No Restrictions

• *Any restriction on total legalization would lead to continuing, substantial corruption.* Under the plan proposed here, restrictions would continue on the sale of crack and on the sale of all drugs to children. Even if black-market corruption continued in those areas, we would experience an immediate 80 percent reduction in corruption overall.

• *Legalization is too unpredictable and sweeping an action to be undertaken all at once. It would be better to establish several test areas first, and evaluate the results.* The results of such a trial would probably not further the case of either side. If use went up in the test area, it could be argued that this was caused by an influx of people from areas where drugs were still illegal; if use went down, it could be argued that the area chosen was unrepresentative. . . .

• *Legalizing drugs would ensure that America's inner cities remain places of hopelessness and despair.* If drugs disappeared tomorrow from America's ghettos, the ghettos would remain places of hopelessness and despair. But legalization would put most drug dealers out of business and remove the main source of financing for violent gangs. At the least, legalization would spare the inner cities from drug-driven terrorism.

• *Marijuana in itself may be relatively harmless, but it is a "gateway drug." Legalization would lead its users to more harmful and addictive drugs.* While government studies show some correlation between marijuana use and cocaine addiction, they also show that tobacco and alcohol use correlate with drug addiction. Moreover, keeping marijuana illegal forces buyers into an illegal market, where they are likely to be offered other drugs. Finally, 60 million Americans have tried marijuana, and there are one million cocaine addicts. If marijuana is a gateway drug, the gate is narrow. . . .

Drug use in the United States can be seen as a symptom of recent cultural changes that have led to an erosion of traditional values and an inability to replace them. There are those who are willing to pay the price to try to save people from themselves. But there are surely just as many who would pay to preserve a person's right to be wrong. To the pragmatist, the choice is clear: legalization is the best bet.

"There are some excellent reasons why marijuana, cocaine, heroin, and other drugs are now controlled, and why they ought to remain so."

Illegal Drugs Should Remain Illegal

James A. Inciardi and Duane C. McBride

James A. Inciardi and Duane C. McBride maintain that legalizing drugs would result in a dramatic increase in crime and an even greater number of drug addicts. In the following viewpoint, the authors believe illegal drugs must remain illegal and that the war on drugs is necessary to decrease chemical dependency throughout the U.S. Inciardi is a professor and the director of the division of criminal justice at the University of Delaware. He has worked extensively in the field of drug policy and written many articles and books on the subject. McBride is a professor in the department of behavioral sciences and the school of business at Andrews University in Berrien Springs, Michigan.

As you read, consider the following questions:
1. What are the authors' objections to legalizing drugs?
2. Why do Inciardi and McBride argue that drugs should continue to be illegal?
3. What methods do the authors recommend to eliminate the drug problem?

From James A. Inciardi and Duane C. McBride, *The Drug Legalization Debate*, pp. 45-65 passim, 74-75, © 1991 by Sage Publications, Inc. Reprinted by permission of Sage Publications, Inc.

Ever since the passage of the Harrison Act in 1914, American drug policy has had its critics.

The basis of the negative assessments has been the restrictive laws designed to control the possession and distribution of narcotics and other "dangerous drugs," the mechanisms of drug law enforcement and the apparent lack of success in reducing both the *supply of* and the *demand for* illicit drugs.

Arguments for Legalization

Concerns over the perceived failure of American drug policy [have] spirited a national debate over whether contemporary drug control approaches ought to be abandoned, and replaced with the decriminalization, if not the outright legalization, of most or all illicit drugs. . . .

The arguments posed by the supporters of legalization seem all too logical. *First,* they argue, the drug laws have created evils far worse than the drugs themselves—corruption, violence, street crime, and disrespect for the law. *Second,* legislation passed to control drugs has failed to reduce demand. *Third,* you cannot have illegal that which a significant segment of the population in any society is committed to doing. You simply cannot arrest, prosecute, and punish such large numbers of people, particularly in a democracy. And specifically in this behalf, in a liberal democracy, the government must not interfere with personal behavior if liberty is to be maintained. And *fourth,* they add, if marijuana, cocaine, heroin, and other drugs were legalized, a number of very positive things would happen:

(1) drug prices would fall

(2) users could obtain their drugs at low, government-regulated prices and would no longer be financially forced to engage in prostitution and street crime to support their habits

(3) the fact that the levels of drug-related crime would significantly decline would result in less crowded courts, jails, and prisons, and would free law enforcement personnel to focus their energies on the "real criminals" in society

(4) drug production, distribution, and sale would be removed from the criminal arena; no longer would it be within the province of organized crime, and therefore, such criminal syndicates as the Medellín Cartel and the Jamaican posses would be decapitalized, and the violence associated with drug distribution rivalries would be eliminated

(5) government corruption and intimidation by traffickers as well as drug-based foreign policies would be effectively reduced, if not eliminated entirely

(6) the often draconian measures undertaken by police to enforce the drug laws would be curtailed, thus restoring to the American public many of its hard-won civil liberties

To these contentions can be added the argument that legalization in any form or structure would have only a minimal impact on current drug-use levels. Apparently, there is the assumption that given the existing levels of access to most illegal drugs, current levels of use closely match demand. Thus there would be no additional health, safety, behavioral, and/or other problems accompanying legalization. And, finally, a few protagonists of legalization make one concluding point. Through government regulation of drugs, the billions of dollars spent annually on drug enforcement could be better utilized. Moreover, by taxing government-regulated drugs, revenues would be collected that could be used for preventing drug abuse and treating those harmed by drugs.

Mike Ramirez/Copley News Service. Reprinted with permission.

The argument for legalization seems to boil down to the basic belief that America's prohibitions against marijuana, cocaine, heroin, and other drugs impose far too large a cost in terms of tax dollars, crime, and infringements on civil rights and individual liberties. And while the overall argument may be well intended and appear quite logical, it is highly questionable in its historical, sociocultural, and empirical underpinnings and demonstrably naive in its understanding of the negative consequences of a legalized drug market. . . .

Considerable evidence exists to suggest that the legalization of drugs would create behavioral and public health problems to a degree that would far outweigh the current consequences of the drug prohibition. There are some excellent reasons why marijuana, cocaine, heroin, and other drugs are now controlled, and why they ought to remain so. What follows is a brief look at a few of these drugs.

Marijuana. There is considerable misinformation about marijuana. To the millions of adolescents and young adults who were introduced to the drug during the social revolution of the 1960s and early 1970s, marijuana was a harmless herb of ecstasy. As the "new social drug" and a "natural organic product," it was deemed to be far less harmful than either alcohol or tobacco. More recent research suggests, however, that marijuana smoking is a practice that combines the hazardous features of both tobacco and alcohol with a number of pitfalls of its own. Moreover, there are many disturbing questions about marijuana's effect on the vital systems of the body, on the brain and mind, on immunity and resistance, and on sex and reproduction.

[For example,] one of the more serious difficulties with marijuana use relates to lung damage. The most recent findings in this behalf should put to rest the rather tiresome argument by marijuana devotees that smoking just a few "joints" daily is less harmful than regularly smoking several times as many cigarettes. Researchers at the University of California at Los Angeles reported early in 1988 that the respiratory burden in smoke particulates and absorption of carbon monoxide from smoking just one marijuana joint is some four times greater than from smoking a single tobacco cigarette. Specifically, it was found that one "toke" of marijuana delivers three times more tar to the mouth and lungs than one puff of a filter-tipped cigarette; that marijuana deposits four times more tar in the throat and lungs and increases carbon monoxide levels in the blood fourfold to fivefold. . . .

Behavioral Aspects of Marijuana Use

Aside from the health consequences of marijuana use, recent research on the behavioral aspects of the drug suggests that it severely affects the social perceptions of heavy users. Findings from the Center for Psychological Studies in New York City, for example, indicated that adults who smoked marijuana daily believed the drug helped them to function better—improving their self-awareness and relationships with others. In reality, however, marijuana had served to be a "buffer," so to speak, enabling users to tolerate problems rather than face them and make changes that might increase the quality of their social functioning and satisfaction with life. The study found that the research

144

subjects used marijuana to avoid dealing with their difficulties, and the avoidance inevitably made their problems worse—on the job, at home, and in family and sexual relationships.

Cocaine. Lured by the Lorelei of orgasmic pleasure, millions of Americans use cocaine each year—a snort in each nostril and the user is up and away for 20 minutes or so. Alert, witty, and with it, the user has no hangover, no lung cancer, and no holes in the arms or burned-out cells in the brain. The cocaine high is an immediate, intensively vivid, and sensation-enhancing experience. Moreover, it has the reputation for being a spectacular aphrodisiac: It is believed to create sexual desire, to heighten it, to increase sexual endurance, and to cure frigidity and impotence. . . .

A Utopian Idea

Legalization is an idea, however, whose time has not yet come. Not only because this seductive Utopian idea would backfire (which it would), but because legalization of marijuana, cocaine, crack, and heroin is an idea at war with America's concept of the good society.

Patrick Buchanan, *New Dimensions,* June 1990.

Yet the pleasure and feelings of power that cocaine engenders make its use a rather unwise recreational pursuit. In very small and occasional doses it is no more harmful than equally moderate doses of alcohol, but there is a side to cocaine that can be very destructive. That euphoric lift, with its feelings of pleasure, confidence, and being on top of things, that comes from but a few brief snorts is short-lived and invariably followed by a letdown. More specifically, when the elation and grandiose feelings begin to wane, a corresponding deep depression is often felt, which is in such marked contrast to users' previous states that they are strongly motivated to repeat the dose and restore the euphoria. This leads to chronic, compulsive use. And when chronic users try to stop using cocaine, they are typically plunged into a severe depression from which only more cocaine can arouse them. Most clinicians estimate that approximately 10% of those who begin to use cocaine "recreationally" will go on to serious, heavy, chronic, compulsive use. To this can be added what is known as the "cocaine psychosis."

As dose and duration of cocaine use increase, the development of cocaine-related psychopathology is not uncommon. Cocaine psychosis is generally preceded by a transitional period characterized by increased suspiciousness, compulsive behavior, fault finding, and eventually paranoia. When the psychotic state is reached, individuals may experience visual and/or auditory hallucinations, with persecutory voices commonly heard. Many believe that they are being followed by police, or that family, friends, and others are plotting against them. Moreover, everyday events tend to be misinterpreted in ways that support delusional beliefs. When coupled with the irritability and hyperactivity that the stimulant nature of cocaine tends to generate in almost all of its users, the cocaine-induced paranoia may lead to violent behavior as a means of "self-defense" against imagined persecutors. . . .

Not to be forgotten are the physiological consequences of cocaine use. Since the drug is an extremely potent central nervous system stimulant, its physical effects include increased temperature, heart rate, and blood pressure. In addition to the many thousands of cocaine-related hospital emergency visits that occur each year, there has been a steady increase in the annual number of cocaine-induced deaths in the United States, from only 53 in 1976 to almost 1,000 a decade later. And while these numbers may seem infinitesimal when compared with the magnitude of alcohol- and tobacco-related deaths, it should be remembered that at present only a small segment of the American population uses cocaine.

Crack and Heroin

Crack. Given the considerable media attention that crack has received since the summer of 1986, it would appear that only a minimal description of the drug is warranted here. Briefly, *crack*-cocaine is likely best described as a "fast-food" variety of cocaine. It is a pebble-sized crystalline form of cocaine base, and has become extremely popular because it is inexpensive and easy to produce. Moreover, since crack is smoked rather than snorted, it is more rapidly absorbed than cocaine—reportedly crossing the blood-brain barrier within six seconds—creating an almost instantaneous high.

Crack's low price (as little as $3 per rock in some locales) has made it an attractive drug of abuse for those with limited funds, particularly adolescents. Its rapid absorption initiates a faster onset of dependence than is typical with cocaine, resulting in higher rates of addiction, binge use, and psychoses. The consequences include higher levels of cocaine-related violence and all the same manifestations of personal, familial, and occupational neglect that are associated with other forms of drug dependence.

Heroin. A derivative of morphine, heroin is a highly addictive narcotic, and the drug historically most associated with both addiction and street crime. Although heroin overdose is not uncommon, unlike alcohol, cocaine, tobacco, and many prescription drugs, the direct physiological damage caused by heroin use tends to be minimal. And it is for this reason that the protagonists of drug legalization include heroin in their arguments. By making heroin readily available to users, they argue, many problems could be sharply reduced if not totally eliminated, including the crime associated with supporting a heroin habit; the overdoses resulting from problematic levels of heroin purity and potency; the HIV (human immunodeficiency virus) and hepatitis infections brought about by needle-sharing; and the personal, social, and occupational dislocations resulting from the drug-induced criminal life-style.

The belief that the legalization of heroin would eliminate crime, overdose, infections, and life dislocations is for the most part delusional, for it is likely that the heroin use life-style would change little for most American addicts, regardless of the legal status of the drug. And there is ample evidence to support this argument—in the biographies and autobiographies of narcotics addicts, in the clinical and ethnographic assessments of heroin addiction, and in the treatment literature.

And to this can be added the many thousands of conversations conducted by the authors with heroin users during the past two decades.

The point is this: Heroin is a highly addicting drug. For the addict, it becomes life consuming: It becomes mother, father, spouse, lover, counselor, confidant, and confessor. Because heroin is a short-acting drug, with its effects lasting at best four to six hours, it must be taken regularly and repeatedly. Because there is a more rapid onset when taken intravenously, most heroin users inject the drug. Because heroin has a depressant effect, a portion of the user's day is spent in a semistupefied state. Collectively, these attributes result in a user more concerned with drug-taking than health, family, work, or anything else. . . .

Drugs and Street Crime

For the better part of the current century there has been a concerted belief in what has become known as the "enslavement theory of addiction"—the conviction that because of the high prices of heroin and cocaine on the drug black market, users are forced to commit crimes in order to support their drug habits. In this regard, supporters of drug legalization argue that if the criminal penalties attached to heroin and cocaine possession and sale were removed, three things would occur: The black market would disappear, the prices of heroin and cocaine would decline significantly, and users would no longer have to engage in street crime in order to support their desired levels of drug intake. Yet there has never been any solid empirical evidence to support the contentions of this enslavement theory.

From the 1920s through the close of the 1960s, hundreds of

studies of the relationship between crime and addiction were conducted. Invariably, when one analysis would support enslavement theory, the next would affirm the view that addicts were criminals first, and that their drug use was but one more manifestation of their deviant lifestyles. In retrospect, the difficulty lay in the way the studies had been conducted, with biases and deficiencies in research designs that rendered their findings to be of little value.

Research since the middle of the 1970s with active drug users in the streets of New York, Miami, Baltimore, and elsewhere, on the other hand, has demonstrated that enslavement theory has little basis in reality, and that the contentions of the legalization proponents in this behalf are mistaken. All of these studies of the criminal careers of heroin and other drug users have convincingly documented that while drug use tends to intensify and perpetuate criminal behavior, it usually does not initiate criminal careers. In fact, the evidence suggests that among the majority of street drug users who are involved in crime, their criminal careers were well established prior to the onset of either narcotics or cocaine use. . . .

Legalization Would Destroy the Ghettos

A timeless feature of cities has been concentrated poverty. Concentrations of poverty appear in all metropolitan areas and are greatest in inner cities. Moreover, poverty in American cities tends to be more concentrated among the members of minority groups than among whites. As such, minority group membership and living in the ghetto tend to go hand-in-hand across the American urban landscape. Numerous explanations for this situation have been offered: that cities tend to attract the poor, many of whom cannot or will not help themselves and, therefore, create and sustain the conditions of their own degradation; that in great part many of the poor adapt to their impoverished conditions by creating a set of attitudes and behaviors that tend to perpetuate poverty—the so-called "culture of poverty" thesis; that the cause of poverty is not with the poor but with the systematic limitation of opportunity imposed by the wider society; that attempts by the urban poor to improve their economic power are hindered by "ghetto colonialization"—the ownership of ghetto businesses by persons from outside the ghetto; and that the wider society encourages the persistence of poverty because it has positive functions, providing (a) an underclass to do the "dirty work" of society, (b) a pool of low-wage laborers, (c) a place where less qualified members of the professions can practice, (d) a population that can be exploited by businesses and served by social agencies, and (e) a reference point to justify the norms and behavior patterns of the wider society. And there are other reasons for urban poverty and its persistence that have been put forth. Whatever the reasons, it seems to be generally agreed that part of the problem lies in the wider society—that the American social structure has economically disenfranchised significant portions of its urban inner cities.

Urban ghettos are not particularly pleasant places in which to live. There are vice, crime, and littered streets. There is the desolation of people separated culturally, socially, and politically from the mainstream. There are the disadvantages of a tangle of economic, family, and other problems—delinquency, teenage pregnancy, unemployment, child neglect, poor housing, substandard schools, inadequate health care, and limited opportunities. There are many modes of adaptation to ghetto life. A common one is drug use, perhaps the main cause of the higher drug use rates in inner cities. And it is for this reason that the legalization of drugs would be a nightmare.

The social fabric of the ghetto is already tattered, and drugs are further shredding what is left of the fragile ghetto family. A great number of inner-city families are headed by women, and for reasons that are not all that clear, women seem to be more disposed to become dependent on crack than men. In New York City since 1986, this led to a 225% increase in child neglect and abuse cases involving drugs, and a dramatic rise in the number of infants abandoned in city hospitals and those born addicted or with syphilis, as well as a surge in children beaten or killed by drug-addicted parents.

Within this context, the legalization of drugs would be an elitist and racist policy supporting the neocolonialist views of underclass population control. In a large sense, since legalization would increase the levels of drug dependence in the ghetto, it represents a program of social management and control that would serve to legitimate the chemical destruction of an urban generation and culture. . . .

Reducing Supply and Demand

If not legalization in the light of a problematic "war" on drugs, what then?

It is eminently sensible to strengthen the supply-side programs aimed at keeping heroin, cocaine, marijuana, and other illegal drugs out of the country. However, the emphasis of federal policy has been a bit lopsided. Between 1981 and the passage of the Anti-Drug Abuse Act of 1986, federal funding for drug treatment was cut by 40%. The results included sharp reductions in the available number of treatment slots, overcrowded treatment centers, and the turning away of tens of thousands of drug abusers seeking help. Then, of the $1.7 billion authorized by the 1986 legislation, almost 80% was earmarked for enforcement efforts. Moreover, much of the $363 million Congress targeted for state education and treatment programs became bogged down by the red tape of an entrenched bureaucratic process.

The difficulty lies in the fact that allocating resources for warring on drugs is always more of a political rather than a commonsense process. Arrests and seizures are easy to count, making for attractive press releases and useful political fodder. And in recent years the figures were indeed dramatic. Reporting on the number of persons in treatment is far less impressive to a constituency. But the tragedy of it all is that the waiting time for treatment entry in some cities is up to a year.

No Quick-Fix Approaches

In the final analysis, drug abuse is a complicated and intractable problem that cannot be solved with quick-fix approaches tended to by politically appointed boards. Deploying more patrol boats in the Caribbean or diverting additional high-technology military hardware will not guarantee an end to or even a slowing of the war. Intercepting drugs at the borders or cutting off illegal drugs at their sources are praiseworthy goals, but they are likely impossible ones. And pressuring source countries into compliance with U.S. objectives is also an elusive task, even when there is willingness.

Thus, if total elimination of the supply of drugs is impossible, then more attention must be focused on the demand side of the equation. For after all, without drug users there would be no drug problem. The weapons here are treatment and education, initiatives that seem to be both working and failing—working for some but failing for others.

On the treatment side, many drug users seeking help are unable to find it, for, as noted earlier, treatment resources fail to match the demand. This problem is easily solved by a financial restructuring of the war on drugs. For the many thousands of users in need of help but unwilling to enter treatment programs, compulsory treatment may be in order.

On the education side, it is already clear that American youths are beginning to turn away from drugs. Moreover, surveys by the University of Michigan's Institute for Social Research suggest that this trend will continue. But all of these positive indicators relate only to mainstream American teenagers. Crack-cocaine is now tragically abundant in inner-city neighborhoods throughout the country. The antidrug messages from government, schools, parent groups, sports figures, and the entertainment media are either not reaching, or have little meaning to, ghetto youth. Like the situation with treatment, the bottom line involves a restructuring of ideas, resources, and goals.

"Prohibition is a good idea that doesn't work."

Illegal Drug Use Should Be Decriminalized

Arnold Trebach

In the following viewpoint, Arnold Trebach argues that the solution to the drug problem is decriminalization. Decriminalization would continue to make drugs illegal but the police and government would tolerate moderate, recreational use. Trebach maintains that funds marked for drug enforcement could then be spent on drug treatment and urban development. Trebach is a professor of criminal justice at American University in Washington, D.C. and the director of the privately funded Drug Policy Center.

As you read, consider the following questions:

1. Why does Trebach believe the war on drugs is unnecessary?
2. According to the author, what lessons should the U.S. learn from the Netherlands and Great Britain?
3. According to the author, what social problems result from the war on drugs?

Excerpted, with permission, from "Why Not Decriminalize?" by Arnold Trebach, *New Perspectives Quarterly*, Summer 1989.

Approximately one-fourth of the US population uses an illegal drug at least once a year. When our government talks about a war on drugs, it is talking about a war on 25 percent of the American people.

Two of the most reliable sources for this data are federally issued from the National Institute on Drug Abuse. They are the Drug Abuse Warning Network (DAWN), which is a survey of about half to three-quarters of the medical examiners and emergency rooms in the country—and the Household Survey.

These studies show that approximately 50-60 million people use illegal drugs in the US. The most prominent drug is marijuana, with between 18-35 million regular users. There are approximately five million heroin users, five-to-ten million cocaine users and several million users of various other drugs. . . .

Prohibition Doesn't Work

The record is very clear: We have tried prohibition, many other countries have tried it, and the record around the world, with few exceptions, is dismal. Prohibition is a good idea that doesn't work.

In the US today, all I see are the perverse results of prohibition. Under President Ronald Reagan, we went from a prison population of 329,821— people serving a sentence of one year or more for drug-related and other crimes—at the end of 1980 to 627,402 at the end of 1988. The prison population rose 90.2 percent in eight years—the greatest rise in modern history, and this does not include jail populations, juveniles or patients in drug-treatment facilities. The prison numbers only include people serving hard time. Do our government officials want to run the numbers up to a million before they stop and take a look at their policy?

In Iran, there is a story of the roving executioner of the revolution, Ayatollah Khalkhali. Khalkhali had a power that many people here dream of. If he found you with drugs, he put you up against a wall and shot you. According to wire reports, within a seven-week period, he killed 176 people. Khalkhali was photographed standing amidst stacks of opium bags and drug products. Yet, he was criticized because drug use was still rampant. His defensive response was, "If we wanted to kill everybody who had five grams of heroin, we would have to kill five thousand people." And then he added this classic phrase: "And this would be difficult." Despite all his power, drug use was rampant.

I have been radicalized by recent events—traumatized and radicalized. I am scared that if we keep it up we will fill the prisons with young people, especially blacks and Hispanics and we will continue to allow people to die from AIDS, saying, "You use drugs, you deserve to die, because we don't want to give a wrong message to anybody." This lack of civility and safety is going to

spread through our society like it did in Rome before its fall.
Drugs are a societal problem, but they also offer a societal benefit. People use drugs because it makes them feel better, and something that makes millions of people feel better can't be all bad.

Defining Drug Abuse

There will always be large numbers of people taking a lot of
mind-altering substances, both legal and illegal. This reality becomes a disastrous situation when we say we really mean prohibition and we're really going to enforce it. What we should be
worried about is drug abuse, which I define as the use of a
chemical substance, a mind-altering substance, legal or illegal,
in a manner that adversely affects one's physical health, work
performance, or loving relationships. By this standard, simply
taking an illegal drug is not drug abuse.

We need to recognize that the line between illegal and legal
drugs is a historical accident based primarily upon emotion rather
than science. All drugs—including alcohol, tobacco, heroin, cocaine, PCP, marijuana—are dangerous. At the same time, all can
be used in relatively nonharmful ways by many people. The difficulty arises when people find they can't get along without
these chemical crutches. . . .

Evaluate Options

The past 20 years have demonstrated that a drug policy shaped
by exaggerated rhetoric designed to arouse fear has only led to
our current disaster. Unless we are willing to honestly evaluate
our options, including various legalization strategies, we will run
a still greater risk: we may never find the best solution for our
drug problems.

Ethan Nadelmann, *The Drug Legalization Debate*, 1991.

I have come to the conclusion that it is the active enforcement
of prohibition that makes the drug problem in the US a disaster.
We can continue to make drugs illegal, but we should enforce
the drug laws like we enforce our sex laws. We show good sense
in the enforcement of sex laws, generally. For example, we have
sodomy laws on the books but we don't enforce them. If one
looks at the current sex laws they will be appalled. There is absolutely no way to enforce those laws and have anybody out of
jail except infants. Basically, the sex laws are on the books for
the purposes of moral suasion. We should treat the drug laws
the same way.

Square the circle. We cannot do it through prohibition because
the financial temptations of drugs are too great. So, we should

begin to seriously look at the alternative: decriminalization.

I support a compromise combination of the English and the Dutch systems: For starters, all drugs could remain illegal. We must develop a set of written guidelines on how to uniformly enforce these laws. The Dutch are best on this; they are very proud of their guidelines for arrest and prosecution, worked up by their cops, prosecutors and judges. A perfect example: for possession and small sales, generally speaking, no action is taken.

Under controlled circumstances in Amsterdam, kids can come into what are called youth clubs and can get "soft drugs": marijuana and hashish. And yet, even though kids can get all the pot they want right off the menus of coffee houses, less than one percent of the population uses marijuana daily.

In addition, the Dutch say to people in trouble with drugs: "You are a member of the Dutch family. We want you to work and go to school." I would be much harder. I would say, "If you are going to take drugs, fine, we'll try to get it to you without much hassle, but we don't want you sitting around just getting high and doing nothing. If you are just getting high and nodding off, you're a loser, you should be doing something productive, you should be a good husband, a good wife, a good worker, a good student."

Britain is more aggressive on this point. The British attitude is: "We don't want to give you drugs if you are not functioning well." The test is whether the addict can function in the world.

Many Treatment Facilities

The most advanced place I know of regarding addicts is Liverpool, England. Liverpool has a wide array of treatment facilities. If addicts need detoxification or drug-free treatment, they can get help in Liverpool. Health officials there make sure that injecting addicts take part in a needle exchange program, receive instructions on injecting, and get general health care.

In addition to providing boxes of clean needles, the addict receives boxes of condoms and instructions on safe sex. The result is that 14 percent of the injecting addicts in the Liverpool area are using condoms, while only 7 percent of the British population is. These statistics show that the injecting addicts of Liverpool are being more conscientious about safe sex than the British population as a whole.

Furthermore, of stunning significance is the fact that AIDS is virtually unknown among addicts who have presented themselves for treatment at Liverpool clinics. A study of approximately 2,000 injecting addicts found that not one of them tested positive either for AIDS or the HIV [human immunodeficiency virus], though there have been reports of a few such positive tests recently.

The police in Liverpool are very supportive of these maintenance programs. They admit that much of what the addict does is illegal, but they are comfortable with the compromises that have been made.

Social Programs

If we combine the Dutch and British strategies with neighborhood, family and employment help, we will begin to see a change. Amsterdam has a population of roughly 670,000. In Washington, DC, the population is roughly 622,000. Amsterdam has a lot of drug trade in the street. In 1988, the city had approximately 40 murders, one-third of them connected with the drug trade. In 1988, Washington, DC had 372—60-80 percent connected with the drug trade.

Decriminalization

Alcohol and tobacco cause many more deaths in users than do drugs. Decriminalization would not prevent us from treating drugs as we now treat alcohol and tobacco: prohibiting sales of drugs to minors, outlawing the advertising of drugs and similar measures. Such measures could be enforced, while outright prohibition cannot be. Moreover, if even a small fraction of the money we now spend on trying to enforce drug prohibition was devoted to treatment and rehabilitation, in an atmosphere of compassion, not punishment, the reduction in drug usage and in the harm done to the users could be dramatic.

Milton Friedman, *New Dimensions*, June 1990.

I could see people able to get drugs relatively easily. I could see people smoking in front of a cop and not getting arrested. I could see people in trouble with drugs being able to come in and get clean needles or treatment. I could see 40, 50, 60 murders occurring annually in Washington, DC, one-third connected with the drug trade. Then, the drug trade would be tolerable. It would not be a drug-free situation, but then again, I don't believe it ever will be.

Eventually, we must consider *full* legalization along the line of the alcohol model. This would not be a lawless situation. Indeed, the task of the future is to design new boundaries for the civil and criminal laws controlling drugs. That task is very complicated but it is possible. The mission of creating a drug-free society, on the other hand, is both impossible and destructive.

"Law enforcement is not a political option or a policy question; it's a moral imperative. "

Law Enforcement Efforts Should Be Increased

William J. Bennett

In the following viewpoint, William J. Bennett argues that stricter enforcement of existing laws against using, possessing, dealing, and trafficking in drugs can reduce dependency on illegal drugs. Bennett is a senior editor at the *National Review*, a conservative weekly newsmagazine. He is also the former director of the Office of National Drug Control Policy.

As you read, consider the following questions:

1. According to the author, how will enforcing drug laws reduce chemical dependency?
2. How do other urban problems, like unemployment, poverty, and lack of education relate to the drug problem, according to Bennett?
3. According to Bennett, how will increasing law enforcement affect drug-ridden, inner-city neighborhoods?

From William J. Bennett, "Responding to New Challenges in the War on Drugs," a speech delivered to the Heritage Foundation conference, "Winning the Drug War: New Challenges for the 1990s," March 20-21, 1990. Reprinted by permission.

In the summer of 1990, Health and Human Services Secretary Louis Sullivan and I released the findings of the 1988 National Household Survey on Drug Abuse. As I described the results then, we are fighting two wars. The first, more manageable front against casual drug use has turned in our favor. Overall, there are fewer Americans using drugs than in 1986. But we have a second front. It is against chronic, addictive drug use—cocaine use in particular—and we are not yet winning on that front. For every indication we have that overall drug use is declining, we have another reminder that chronic, addictive drug use remains a severe and stubborn problem. There is some evidence that things are not getting worse on the second front, but it will still be some time before things there will be better and seem better.

Habitual Cocaine Use

In a way, this stubborn front is the part of the problem we are most familiar with. The drug problem that we read about in our newspapers each day and see on TV at night is usually about habitual cocaine use and the crime that often accompanies it. On this front we see the hard-core addicts. We stare at and pity the cocaine babies. We are shocked by the crack houses. The drive-by shootings. The decaying neighborhoods. And although our data are not what they should be, it seems to most demographers that this part of the problem is concentrating increasingly in our poor, black, and Hispanic inner-city neighborhoods.

Having said that, let me hasten to add that this is by no means a problem of *every* inner-city neighborhood. Again, by a long shot, most black and Hispanic citizens are innocent of drugs, either as users or dealers. They are most often the victims, not the perpetrators, of drug crime. Most inner-city residents are people who, despite their poverty, despite their often run-down housing, and despite the dire predictions of the culture-of-poverty theorists, confront and resist drug use every day. They are America's new invisible men and women. We rarely hear about them. We rarely see them on TV. But they are there. They retain their dignity and pride by keeping their children away from drugs, obeying the law, and by opposing the drug dealers in their midst.

It is at the second front of the problem that many of these good citizens live, and life there can be very tough. The problem is tough not for any abstract, philosophical reason; not because we can't comprehend the culture of inner-city life; and not because we don't understand it. It is tough because of the facts on the ground, and the very tough nature of those facts. Life in some of these drug-torn neighborhoods is characterized chiefly by its murder and addiction rates. Here drug kingpins may be heroes to the young, and the meanest thugs can rule the streets. Open air drug markets are adjacent to elementary schools, crack vials are strewn across parking lots, and in some schools, students must walk through metal detectors to check for weapons.

Chuck Asay, by permission of the *Colorado Springs Gazette-Telegraph*.

I have been to 41 American cities where there are drug pronlems and it is no exaggeration to say that in some of these places, drugs have made life very much as [philosopher Thomas] Hobbes imagined it to be in the state of nature: solitary, poor, nasty, brutish, and short.

Fundamental Order

Now given these facts—facts not open to serious dispute—I confess that I still find it remarkable that there remains any debate over what our response should be to this specter. The position that I have taken all along is that the rehabilitation of a community cannot begin until some degree of fundamental order and basic civility has been established. Treatment and education stand little chance of succeeding if they must compete in a neighborhood where drugs and drug dealers flourish on every corner. Most people who use drugs cannot be made whole or made well in such an environment.

Yet some people think they know different. One critic insists that "until the root causes of drug abuse are addressed—the lack of education, housing, employment, health care, family, and above all poverty—the scourge of drugs will continue to expand." He and many others argue, essentially, that the real task of drug policy in these communities is not to create safety and order, but to rid society of poverty, unemployment, racism, illiteracy, disease. I say we need to get at these things too, but we must immediately, and directly, and with all deliberate speed, go after the drug problem. The larger conditions do exist, of course, and no one denies that they are important factors in *locating* chronic drug use. But I have grave doubts that we can *explain* the drug problem in our cities merely by pointing to surrounding social conditions.

Now let's agree on some things: unemployment makes people poor. Poverty deprives them of certain material goods. Prejudice keeps them excluded. Broken homes or non-existent families make children vulnerable. Bad schools do the same. All these things may indeed make people more likely to succumb to drugs; they sap the spirit and weaken the will. They are conditions that present us, all-together, with a kind of weakened immune system. But drugs are the invading virus. And you must attack the virus while you are pondering how to strengthen the immune system. Drugs are not merely a symptom, they are a cause, an efficacious and sometimes deadly one. They degrade human character. They sear the mind and they numb the soul. And that is why we oppose them.

Citizens into Victims

Drugs can make other serious problems seem modest. As John Jacob, president of the Urban League, has observed: "Drugs have destroyed more families than poverty ever did." I think he's right. Drugs can turn good citizens into victims. They can turn otherwise solid citizens into addicts, and even into criminals. That's why good citizens in bad neighborhoods need our help—active and aggressive help.

When drugs penetrate a neighborhood, all other efforts to improve the condition of the people who live there are weakened. Schools can't function when gang members roam or rule the halls. The local economy can't work when store owners, tired of risking their lives, move their businesses elsewhere. Young people don't bother looking for honest work when it seems as if only crime pays. Streets, parks, and recreational areas become places to purchase drugs, consume them, and wage gang war on a daily basis.

To save these communities, the legitimate forces for good—law enforcement officials, private citizens together, all the agents of the rule of law and civility—must assert themselves. Measures of enabling toughness are called for because, as Flannery O'Connor wrote: "You have to push as hard as the age that pushes against you." Only here, with drugs, you must push harder.

Suffering Consequences

Those who use, sell and traffic in drugs must be confronted, and they must suffer consequences.

By "consequences," I mean that those who transgress must make amends for their transgressions. This idea is central to any conception of just government. Consequences come in many forms. In terms of law enforcement, they include policies such as the seizure of assets, stiffer prison sentences, revocation of bail rights, and the death penalty for drug kingpins.

William J. Bennett, *New Perspectives Quarterly*, Summer 1989.

That means that in our inner-city quasi-states of nature the good guys must confront the bad guys, and they must win. They must do so responsibly, lawfully, and constitutionally. But they *must* also do so decisively. This is true and it is common sense. And I say it because the people who live in neighborhoods that most of us here would be too scared to walk through say it too. [In March 1990], a number of courageous local heroes—from Albuquerque, New York, Houston, Oakland, and other cities—came to Washington to have lunch at the White House and exchange stories about their experiences. Some of them organize neighborhood patrols; others bring anti-drug messages to schools or youth groups. But all of them know this to be true: where they live, as elsewhere, order must prevail over chaos. Similar men and women live in the towns and cities where your papers are published. Ask them.

Needing More Cops

When you meet people who have seen the drug epidemic up close, they'll tell you that there are two arguments they hate hearing. The first is that we should legalize drugs. The second is that their neighborhood doesn't need more cops. The fact is that they need more cops and they want them. If you disagree with me or with them, then let me suggest that you go see for yourself.

In the neighborhoods where they live, law enforcement is not a political option or a policy question; it's a moral imperative. The drug trade has succeeded in many places in eroding the basic sense of security that is a precondition of life, liberty, happiness, and so much else. So while others debate the fine points of root causes, and deride the role of basic law enforcement, the residents of poor neighborhoods are busy marching on crack houses, putting locks on their doors, and chasing dealers out of apartment courtyards. Sometimes, in the absence of enough police, they themselves help patrol the streets.

I think if we fail to see this part of the drug war, this second front, as *first* a question of restoring an essential level of security to citizens, then we risk ignoring the most pressing concern of the people who live there, the people who everyone involved in the debate say they want help. If we fail to act here, their lives will go on, but they will increasingly be lives shaped by drugs and the street culture drugs have produced. And on such streets, as we all know, drugs themselves will soon become a root cause of one more generation's misery.

Finally, let me point to the educational implications of what we do or fail to do. If we teach that crime is wrong and that, in the end, crime doesn't pay, we should be ready to back up those sentiments with action. Not for the sake of seeming tough, being tough, or acting tough, but for the sake of acting compassionately toward our children. What I mean is so obvious it seems to have been forgotten, but as [author George] Orwell said, sometimes our most important responsibility is a restatement of the obvious. Here's the obvious: there are two things children need more than anything else; they need love and they need order. And if you love children, the first thing you do for them is to secure their safety. I ask you: why might some people who work to provide these things for their own children deprecate the value of these things to the children of others?

Equal Right to Security

In my neighborhood, middle- to upper-class Chevy Chase, Maryland, if we see someone selling drugs on the street, there is no debate about what we do. We call 911. We do not convene a seminar on root causes. We expect action, and if we don't get it we raise hell. I think that is a natural, civilized, and appropriate reaction. And I don't believe for a moment that a single parent in Southeast Washington should behave any differently. Equality is the oldest promise of America. Parents—all law-abiding citizens—have an equal right to expect security regardless of where they live.

"It is not fair to ask law enforcement to take responsibility for solving society's drug problem. "

Increased Law Enforcement Efforts Cannot Solve the Drug Problem

Jerome H. Skolnick

Jerome H. Skolnick is a professor of law, jurisprudence, and social policy at the University of California at Berkeley. In the following viewpoint, Skolnick argues that as laws against drug possession, use, dealing, and trafficking become more stringent, they become less effective. He maintains that stricter enforcement of drug laws has failed to reduce chemical dependency.

As you read, consider the following questions:

1. What effect has interdiction had on substance abuse in the U.S., according to Skolnick?
2. According to the author, why have drug laws and law enforcement been so ineffective in solving the drug problem?
3. Why do some policymakers believe that stringent enforcement of drug laws will reduce chemical dependency, according to Skolnick?

Public anger about drug dealers, street crime, and violence is justifiable. However, the War on Drugs—which calls for an "unprecedented" expansion of police, prosecutors, courts, and prisons, in addition to military force and interdiction—seems more an expression of outrage than a sound appreciation of the limits of law enforcement. [Former] drug czar William Bennett and the President seem to believe that we have been losing that war because of a lack of resolve, but I believe the reasons are more fundamental.

It is not fair to ask law enforcement to take responsibility for solving society's drug problem. In thinking about what might work and what won't, we need to appreciate the conundrums they face in trying to combat crimes involving the sale of an illegal and highly addictive product. *The National Drug Control Strategy* (the red book the President held up in his address to the nation on drug policy, along with the now famous bag of crack) acknowledges that, "Despite interdiction's successful disruptions of trafficking patterns, the supply of illegal drugs entering the United States has, by all estimates, continued to grow." Why should that have happened? No matter how hard Federal, state and local police officers try, they encounter frustrating dilemmas and paradoxes.

The Demand-Supply Dilemma

For any product, demand generates supply. U.S. and European demand for drugs has contributed to a rise in the number of suppliers from a variety of producing countries. Some of these are political allies; others are not. The key fact is that demand has resulted in multiple drug producers, followed by a rise in output, with a subsequent drop in price. As Edmundo Morales has observed in *Cocaine: White Gold Rush in Peru*, "Unquestionably, drug production and traffic in Peru have addicted thousands of people to illegal sources of hard cash." Price reduction, in turn, further invigorates demand—once again stimulating the entire cycle.

Bennett and the President acknowledge that, "As we have expanded our interdiction efforts, we have seized increasing amounts of illegal drugs. Stepped up interdiction has also forced drug traffickers to make significant operational changes. . . . Every time we disrupt or close a particular trafficking route, we have found that traffickers resort to other smuggling tactics that are even more difficult to detect."

This is undoubtedly true, but it seems to argue against, rather than for, the stepped-up interdiction advocated by *The National Drug Control Strategy*. As we develop increasingly sophisticated tactics for reducing both narcotic production and smuggling, only the stronger and more efficient producers and smugglers

163

survive. This, in turn, heightens supply and lowers cost. As this occurs, suppliers seek wider markets, particularly in distressed populations, just as segments of the alcohol and tobacco industries do.

© 1990, Washington Post Writers Group. Reprinted with permission.

The borders can not be sealed, according to Rand Corporation economist Peter Reuter, who studied the question for the Department of Defense. The Mexican border is especially permeable. There are few barriers from the south to transporting drugs into that country, and they can be "brought across by small plane, private vehicle, or even by boat." A Mexican-American California narcotics agent made a similar observation to me in an interview in 1989: "Four hundred thousand of my people cross the border every year. How can you stop a much smaller number who are carrying a kilo or two of cocaine on their back?"

Interdiction is supposed to reduce street sales by increasing production and smuggling costs, thus raising the street price. This assumes that production and smuggling costs constitute a significant percentage of street price, but that is not true. It is relatively cheap to produce and refine a kilo of cocaine—about $1,000 for a kilo that eventually, when broken down into quarter- or even eighth-gram units, might retail for $250,000. Smuggling costs might amount to an additional few percent of the retail price. Most of that price is divided among those who distribute it on this side of the border. As Reuter explains, "Fully 99% of the price of the drug when sold on the streets in the United States is accounted for by payments to people who distribute it." Thus, a doubling or tripling of smuggling costs would have a negligible impact. Street prices of cocaine have dropped dramatically, by 60 to 75%, since the Reagan Administration introduced its War on Drugs in 1982, headed by then-Vice Pres. Bush. The evidence suggests that interdiction has had little, if any, positive effects, and that even these can be outweighed by unanticipated side effects.

The Drug Hardening Paradox

When the Nixon Administration succeeded in reducing the supply of low-potency Mexican marijuana to California in the early 1970's, agriculturally skilled drug entrepreneurs developed a high-potency marijuana (sinsimilla) industry in northern California, generating a market for a drug five or more times as potent. The paradox is this: the more successful law enforcement is at cutting off supply, the more incentive drug dealers have for hardening drugs, for developing varieties that are more potent, portable, and dangerous.

Contemporary interdiction policy—and its expansion, as advocated by the Bush/Bennett strategy—is grounded in an assumption concerning the stability of drug preference among those who enjoy faster living through chemistry. We know from history that demand for a specific drug is less related to its intrinsic properties than to the social definition of a particular substance as the drug of choice. Twenty years ago, heroin was the "problem" drug in American society. Today, it is crack cocaine.

Suppose we actually could destroy the Peruvian, Bolivian, and Colombian cocaine fields. Lurking in the background are a variety of manufactured drugs. It is likely that underground chemists could design and manufacture what addicts would consider the ideal drug—one with the kick of crack and the longevity of crank (methamphetamine). Indeed, a powerful new drug, a colorless and odorless form of crystal methamphetamine— street name "ice"—is said to be sweeping Hawaii and is threatening to invade the West Coast ports of San Francisco, Los Angeles, and Portland. Should that happen, it would be just a matter of time before ice found its way across the country to replace crack as the drug of choice during the 1990's. The only good news ice will bring is its economic challenge to the Medellin Cartel. Moreover, it is doubtful that the distributors of the new drug will prove more concerned for public health than the cocaine producers.

165

Whatever the latest fashion on drug use, manufacturers, smugglers, and distributors can operate more efficiently by corrupting public officials. As we attempt to put pressure on foreign producers, we will have to work with authorities in such countries as Colombia, Bolivia, Panama, and Peru. The bribe is a familiar part of law enforcement in these countries. Thus, the State Department's Bureau of International Narcotics Matters finds that Jorge Luis Ochoa, a major Colombian drug trafficker, "was able to buy his freedom through the intimidated and vulnerable Colombian judicial system."

The Fruits of Enforcement

During the years of the Reagan Administration's prosecution of the drug war, the US prison population rose by a stunning 90 percent—from 329,821 to 627,402. Already, Washington, DC has the highest per capita incarceration rate of black males outside of South Africa: of the nearly 200,000 black males that reside in the District of Columbia, 10,000 are in jail, the vast majority on drug-related charges. In New York City and Washington, DC, the most trenchant analysts argue, it is precisely law enforcement efforts to close down the drug trade that have sparked the sharp rise in violent turf wars over diminishing market share. And this is not to speak of the hundreds of deaths and casualties suffered by the Drug Enforcement Agency and local police in the doubtful cause of purging drugs from our society.

New Perspectives Quarterly, Summer 1989.

What of our urban police? We are all too familiar with the narcotics scandals that have bedeviled the police in various cities, especially New York. Such corruption is not confined to the East Coast. Deputies in the Los Angeles County Sheriff's Department were involved in what *The Los Angeles Times* called "one of the worst corruption cases" in the department's history. Although the possibilities of official misconduct exist in any form of vice investigation, only in drug enforcement do we encounter large sums of cash and drugs held by perpetrators who are in no position to complain about being ripped off by cops.

By no means am I suggesting that all narcotics police are corrupt. The Los Angeles deputies were caught in a sting operation conducted by Sheriff Sherman Block. I *am* suggesting that it is difficult to uncover narcotics corruption, particularly when a small number of individuals are involved; that whatever amount is discovered has to be the tip of the iceberg; and that such misconduct must be counted as one of the anticipated costs of an unprecedented expansion of drug law enforcement.

State and Federal prison populations virtually doubled in the 1980's and have tripled since the 1960's. Overcrowded jails and prisons are bulging with newly convicted criminals, as well as those whose probation and parole were revoked, largely because they failed their drug tests when released to the community. California, for example, had a 3,200% increase in parole violators returned to prison between 1978 and 1988. By the end of 1989, more than 1,000,000 Americans were behind bars.

Drugs and Jails

As our advanced drug-testing technology consigns more parolees and probationers to prison, however, we find we can not continue to convict them and impose longer sentences without building new penal institutions. Bennett and the President recognize the critical lack of prison space as we expand law enforcement. They acknowledge that "most state prisons are already operating far above their designed capacity." They also recognize that "many states have been forced under court order to release prisoners before their terms have been served whenever a court-established prison population limit has been exceeded." Their solution is for state governments to persuade their citizens to support new facilities. "The task of building [prisons]," they write, "remains with state governments, who poorly serve their constituents when prison construction is stalled or resisted."

Yet, there is not a word in *The National Drug Control Strategy* about how to finance, staff, and pay for the continuing and rising expense of maintaining prisons. Evidently, the slogan "No New Taxes" applies only to the Federal government. If the states are to serve their citizens as Bush and Bennett exhort, *they* will have to raise taxes.

Even those citizens who demand longer and more certain sentences are reluctant to pay for penal institutions and understandably even more reluctant to live next door to them. Highly publicized plans for a 700-bed facility to house convicted Washington, D.C., drug dealers at Fort Meade, Md., were withdrawn—with embarrassment—the day after they were announced, *The New York Times* reported, because "there was too much public resistance."

Even if we could build new facilities, imprisonment is not necessarily stigmatic or entirely foreboding for those who sell drugs. My students and I have been interviewing jailed California drug dealers. Imprisonment may offer a kind of "homeboy" status, specially for gang youth, for whom the institution can become an alternative neighborhood. Moreover, imprisonment often motivates prisoners in their illicit ways. Consigned to the margins of society anyhow, in jail they join gangs, use drugs, and make useful connections for buying and selling illegal substances. The penitentiary was perhaps once a place for experiencing penance. Today's correctional institutions, overcrowded as they are with short-term parole violators (many of whom have failed their court-mandated drug tests), often serve functions similar to those conventions perform for academics and business people—as an opportunity for networking. . . .

Time and Money

The major problems with traditional law enforcement procedures in combating drug abuse boil down to time and money. In 1988, police officers made almost 14,000,000 arrests, 8.3% of which were for drug violations. For all of their efforts, however, police "buy-and-bust" operations had little impact on the availability of drugs, and those street dealers arrested easily were replaced.

George J. Bryjak, *USA Today*, July 1990.

Is there *anything* law enforcement can do to impair the crack cocaine trade? There is little evidence to support the effectiveness of the law enforcement initiatives the Bush Administration proposes. Several colleagues at the Center for the Study of Law and Society and I recently evaluated such an initiative in Alameda County (Oakland), Calif. The sharp rise in drug selling and violence there persuaded the legislature and the Governor to provide $4,000,000 from 1985 to 1987 to bolster and expand prosecution, probation, and the courts—just the sort of expansion advocated by *The National Drug Control Strategy*. Following an ethnographic and statistical evaluation, we concluded that all of the law enforcement agencies carried out their mandate thoroughly and professionally, and that the intermediate goals of more prosecutions, convictions, and probation violations were met. That was the good news. The bad news was that it didn't seem to matter much. Crime—and narcotics felonies in particular—continued to increase. We concluded that, contrary to popular mythology, "The rise in narcotics crime in Alameda County can not be attributed to inefficient courts, prosecutors, probation officers, or police.". . .

Some law enforcement officials are skeptical about the positive effects of crackdowns. According to [former] Minneapolis Police Chief Anthony Bouza, "Focused, saturation street enforcement will clean up an area, but it is costly and inefficient. It robs other areas of their fair share of scarce resources and it does not eliminate the intractable problem of drug dealing, merely displaces it. It also focuses, inefficiently, on the lowest level of the criminal chain and is sure to lead to abuses and repression, with sweeps and round-ups."

So, it is not clear how to repair the damage drug dealing imposes on local communities or what the costs would be of an expanded police effort in this direction. Still, so long as demand remains, local law enforcement initiatives are at least responsive to the complaints of law-abiding residents whose neighborhoods are undercut by street dealers and crack houses. Since public safety and civility should be law enforcement's highest priority, that's where I would recommend allocating restricted law enforcement funds. At the same time, we need to understand that law enforcement is merely a holding operation. We must address the underlying causes of drug-selling and addiction in our society before we can hope for a solution.

Distinguishing Between Fact and Opinion

This activity is designed to help develop the basic reading and thinking skill of distinguishing between fact and opinion. Consider the following statement as an example: "Prohibition was repealed in 1933." This is a factual statement because it could be checked by looking up Prohibition in an encyclopedia. But the statement "Legalizing drugs will reduce crime" is an opinion. Many people may not think that drug legalization would reduce crime. Others might argue that even if legalizing illicit drugs did reduce crime it might still increase the number of drug addicts.

When investigating controversial issues it is important that one be able to distinguish between statements of fact and statements of opinion. It is also important to recognize that not all statements of fact are true. They may appear to be true, but some are based on inaccurate or false information. For this activity, however, we are concerned with understanding the difference between those statements which appear to be factual and those which appear to be based primarily on opinion.

Most of the following statements are taken from the viewpoints in this chapter. Consider each statement carefully. *Mark O for any statement you believe is an opinion or interpretation of facts. Mark F for any statement you believe is a fact. Mark I for any statement you believe is impossible to judge.*

If you are doing this activity as a member of a class or group, compare your answers with those of other class or group members. Be able to defend your answers. You may discover that others come to different conclusions than you do. Listening to the reasons others present for their answers may give you valuable insights into distinguishing between fact and opinion.

O = *opinion*
F = *fact*
I = *impossible to judge*

1. Using illegal drugs can cause physical problems.

2. People who use illegal drugs like heroin, marijuana, and crack can become addicted to them.

3. The drug problem is not a moral issue.

4. Legalizing drugs would shatter the Latin American drug cartels.

5. Alcohol and tobacco cause more deaths every year than all illegal drugs combined.

6. Drug laws never prevented anyone from using illegal drugs.

7. The U.S. government spends approximately $10 billion on enforcing drug laws.

8. Drug use in the United States is a symptom of recent cultural changes that led to an erosion of traditional family values.

9. A recent National Institute on Drug Abuse survey shows that between fifty million and sixty million Americans use illegal drugs.

10. U.S. prison populations rose 90.2 percent between 1980 and 1988.

11. It is possible for some people to use illegal drugs like crack without harm.

12. Enforcing drug prohibition adds to the violence associated with drugs.

13. In Holland, laws against using soft drugs are not enforced.

14. In Washington, D.C., 60 to 80 percent of all murders are connected to the drug trade.

15. Creating a drug-free society is both impossible and destructive.

16. In 1914, the U.S. government passed the Harrison Act outlawing drugs.

17. Legalization of drugs would increase levels of drug dependency in inner cities, resulting in more social control over these areas by the government.

18. The number of U.S. citizens using drugs has declined.

19. Increasing enforcement of drug laws is necessary to stop the spread of drugs.

20. Drug-law enforcement is responsible for the violence associated with the drug trade.

Periodical Bibliography

The following articles have been selected to supplement the diverse views presented in this chapter.

Mark Curriden — "No Mercy," *ABA Journal*, March 1991.

Jeffrey Eisenach and Andre Cowin — "Fighting Drugs in Four Countries: Lessons for America?" The Heritage Foundation *Backgrounder*, September 24, 1990. Available from 214 Massachusetts Ave. NE, Washington, DC 20002.

Eddy Engelsman — "The Dutch Model," *New Perspectives Quarterly*, Summer 1989.

Gerry Fitzgerald — "Dispatches from the Drug War," *Common Cause Magazine*, January/February 1990.

Anthony Lewis — "Insisting on Disaster," *The New York Times*, September 24, 1989.

Richard Mackenzie — "Borderline Victories on the Drug War's Front Line," *Insight*, January 14, 1991. Available from *The Washington Times*, 3600 New York Ave. NE, Washington, DC 20002.

D. Keith Mano — "Legalize Drugs," *National Review*, May 28, 1990.

John Clifton Marquis — "Drug Laws Are Immoral," *U.S. Catholic*, May 1990.

Michael Massing — "Crack," *Mademoiselle*, May 1990.

Brad Miner — "How Sweet Is Mary Jane?" *National Review*, June 25, 1990.

Charles Murray — "How to Win the War on Drugs," *The New Republic*, May 21, 1990.

James Ostrowski — "Has the Time Come to Legalize Drugs?" *USA Today*, July 1990.

Jeff A. Schnepper — "Drug Enforcement Economics," *USA Today*, March 1990.

Walter Wink — "Biting the Bullet: The Case for Legalizing Drugs," *The Christian Century*, August 8-15, 1990.

Charles P. Wohlforth — "Off the Pot," *The New Republic*, December 3, 1990.

Should Pregnant Women Be Prosecuted for Drug Abuse?

Chemical Dependency

Chapter Preface

In January 1989, Jennifer Johnson gave birth to a baby girl. In July 1989, a judge convicted Johnson of delivering a controlled substance to a minor. According to the judge, Johnson's newborn daughter and her two-year-old son were exposed to and damaged by cocaine while in utero. Johnson was found guilty and was sentenced to fifteen years of probation. She spent several weeks in jail and a year in a long-term drug treatment program with random monthly drug testing. Her sentence also includes educational and vocational training and intensive prenatal care should she become pregnant again. Johnson's case raises many questions about the best way to end the problems resulting from addiction in pregnancy.

Many experts are horrified by the number of children born addicted to cocaine and other illegal drugs. Most estimate that between 10 and 25 percent of all babies, or 375,000 children annually, are born addicted to drugs. Many of them are born with a variety of serious mental and physical problems. How these children can best be protected is a matter of debate.

Many judges and lawyers contend that prosecution is the most effective way to stop women from using drugs during pregnancy. For instance, Jeff Dean, the Florida prosecutor in Johnson's case, points out that Johnson "wasn't doing anything to help herself. The arrest is what motivated her to get help she wasn't getting on her own."

But other experts protest that prosecuting pregnant addicts exacerbates the tragedy. Prosecution, they maintain, may frighten addicts away from seeking the prenatal care their babies need and at the same time may reduce the opportunities for their own addiction to be detected and treated. As American Civil Liberties Union lawyer Lynn Paltrow states, "Pregnant women are terrified they will be punished or have their babies taken away if there's evidence they misbehaved during pregnancy."

Another objection to prosecution is that it unfairly punishes women who cannot get help even if they want to. Critics point out that only a small fraction of treatment programs accept pregnant addicts. Jennifer Johnson, in fact, sought treatment for her addiction to crack in 1988 and was refused entry into a program. Dorothy E. Roberts, a professor of criminal law and civil liberties, argues that more treatment programs, not more punishments, are needed to help pregnant drug addicts.

The authors in the following chapter debate ways of dealing with the problem of addiction in pregnancy.

"The state must take a strong interventionist stance by criminalizing prenatal substance abuse in order to contain its alarming practice."

Pregnant Addicts Should Be Prosecuted

Kathryn Schierl

Kathryn Schierl is a student at The John Marshall Law School in Chicago, Illinois. In the following viewpoint, Schierl argues in favor of new laws permitting the prosecution of women who take illegal drugs during pregnancy. She contends that the threat of prosecution will reduce drug use among pregnant addicts. In addition, she concludes, mandatory treatment and even imprisonment will get pregnant addicts off drugs before they harm their fetuses.

As you read, consider the following questions:

1. Why does the author advocate prosecuting pregnant drug addicts?
2. According to the author, how would laws prevent pregnant addicts from ingesting illegal drugs?
3. According to Schierl, how will thousands of drug-addicted babies affect society?

Excerpted and reprinted, with permission, from "A Proposal to Illinois Legislatures: Revise the Illinois Criminal Code to Include Criminal Sanctions Against Prenatal Substance Abusers," by Kathryn Schierl, *The John Marshall Law Review*, vol. 23, no. 393, 1990. Excerpts reprinted herein exclude the author's arguments regarding the constitutionality and practicality of her proposal.

Although prenatal substance abuse is an old phenomenon, the staggering rise in cocaine/crack-exposed newborns dramatically reveals that America must now confront this acute societal problem. Prenatal exposure to illicit drugs can cause lasting damage to the fetus which will impede the child's physical, emotional, and intellectual development. Maternal prenatal drug abuse also causes grave financial and intangible costs to society as a whole.

As this fetal abuse increases, America has found itself faced with a dilemma: how can we protect the fetus from this prenatal maternal substance abuse? To date, America is unable to cope with the growing problem. In an effort to confront this prenatal problem, recent legislation and case law have extended state child abuse statutes to include the unborn, labelling drug-exposed infants as neglected or abused children. In addition, a few prosecutors have brought criminal charges against the mother for the fetal damage that her conduct has caused. Like these cases, the pivotal question involved [here] . . . is whether the state can criminalize prenatal illegal substance abuse and force the mother to provide a drug-free environment for the fetus. . . .

Cocaine Use and Health Effects

Although drug users' abuse patterns for most illegal substances have remained constant or decreased since 1982, cocaine use has increased at an alarming rate. Significantly, the increase in cocaine use among expectant mothers has paralleled the dramatic rise in use among the general populace. In 1988, approximately 11 percent of all newborns were exposed to illegal drugs *in utero*. Cocaine was involved in 75 percent of these cases. At least one authority estimates that one out of every ten newborns have suffered from *in utero* drug exposure.

In addition to its alarming abuse pattern, cocaine has changed the traditional image of the drug abuser. Thousands of pregnant cocaine users are women from the middle and upper class. Although this increase in prenatal cocaine abuse is shocking, the effects of prenatal cocaine abuse on the child, mother, and the public health and welfare are even more frightening.

Results of medical research conclusively demonstrate that maternal conduct and emotional well-being directly affect the fetal environment and subsequent fetal development. The effects of *in utero* exposure to illegal drugs include fetal death, physical deformities, psychomotor abnormalities, and growth and mental retardation. Recent research results indicate that children exposed to drugs *in utero* are at risk for long-term developmental difficulties. Further, although drug-addicted infants are already [according to Cathy L. Trost] "[b]orn to [l]ose," their withdrawal behavior puts them at risk for physical abuse. Due to the alarming number of cocaine-exposed newborns, cocaine's effects on the fetus and neonate are now the perinatologist's and pediatrician's most serious concern.

Prenatal Child Abuse

Only a few prosecutions for prenatal child abuse have been reported and the applicability of current child abuse and neglect laws to prenatal conduct is uncertain. However, this avenue is constitutionally within state authority. It may turn out to be an effective tool for demonstrating society's intent to protect children and to deter egregiously harmful prenatal conduct in certain cases.

John Robertson, *ABA Journal*, August 1989.

Not only does the pregnant mother's illicit drug use seriously jeopardize the fetus, it also imperils the mother herself. Cocaine's effect on an individual's cardiovascular system is well-documented. Cocaine use can cause maternal hypertension and soaring blood pressure which may lead to a seizure or stroke. In addition, many women who have used cocaine in their third trimester report increased fetal activity and/or a sudden onslaught of uterine contractions within minutes of using the drug. Prenatal cocaine use also results in complicated premature deliveries and is associated with *abruptio placentae*, a serious complication in which the placenta is literally torn from the uterine wall. Maternal drug abuse also puts these women and the children they carry at high risk for infection by the AIDS virus.

Cocaine abuse has deleterious psychological effects on maternal health as well as physiological complications. Cocaine has a unique ability to undermine the maternal instinct, causing the mother to be completely oblivious to her fetus/newborn. Many of these women are so preoccupied with their drug habit that they abandon their newborns in hospitals (boarder babies), sometimes without even naming the baby. Many mothers also indicate that they feel tremendous guilt over the physiological and psychological effects that their drug use has had on their child. Currently, the ramifications of cocaine's psychological effects on maternal health are unknown. Certainly, the prognosis is quite negative.

The Impact on Society

Aside from the immense suffering involved, prenatal drug abuse has generated an enormous financial burden for society. Medical treatment costs for distressed, disabled, and/or withdrawing newborns are very high. In addition, hospital tabs for "boarder babies" are astronomical. Since Medicaid provides only

$6,100 maximum payment for these babies, the cost is passed on to private, insured patients and taxpayers.

Although these medical care costs are substantial, prenatal drug use has created even graver financial and social costs to the public health and welfare. One of these grave social costs is the impact of prenatal drug abuse in terms of stress on social institutions and existing structures. Throughout the nation, the dramatic rise in drug-exposed infants has overwhelmed America's medical community. A shortage of hospital staff, space, and equipment to care for these newborns already exists and the numbers are still rising. Soon, our current medical system will not be able to accommodate these babies.

The explosion of drug-affected infants has also overwhelmed America's child welfare system. Under child protection laws, some states have provided for postnatal state custody of infants born with illegal drugs or metabolites in their systems. Already facing a severe foster-care shortage, child welfare systems are unable to cope with the onslaught of drug-exposed babies. Caseworkers are already over-burdened with heavy caseloads. Nevertheless, doctors urge that these children will need extensive follow-up and their mothers will need extensive training in parenting and special handling of drug-affected offspring. This immense burden on states' child welfare systems has caused at least one state to reverse its policy of taking custody over drug-exposed infants.

The Drug Cycle

Of an equally grave nature, the financial and institutional stress that drug-affected children will place on America's educational system is unforeseeable. Doctors are already warning educators to begin to prepare for a new class of children who will require a specially structured educational environment.

Perhaps the singularly most devastating effect of maternal drug abuse, however, is the "drug cycle" and its intangible cost to the public welfare. Among many prenatal substance abusers, doctors note a cycle of parental drug abuse and violence that spans generations. Like their mothers before them, many of these infants will [according to Dr. Ira Chasnoff and colleagues] suffer through childhood in the "chaotic and transient nature of the drug environment."

Caught up in the drug environment, many of these children will not receive the special parental care that they need to avoid future developmental problems. These children are at high risk for neglect, physical abuse, and/or placement in foster care. The odds are that many of these children will become drug abusing parents, only to go through the same pattern with their future offspring, perpetuating the "drug cycle."

Without state intervention and treatment, the grip of the "drug cycle" on both the mother and infant is probable. This represents a loss to society of *two or more* productive citizens, depending on the number of children that the mother produces. When society's "double loss" is combined with the alarming incidence of drug-exposed neonates, the debilitating effect on the public health and welfare is incalculable.

Although the extent of the financial and social costs of prenatal cocaine abuse are unascertainable, one thing is very clear: prenatal drug abuse is a serious menace to the public health and welfare. If society does not deal with this menace in a swift and comprehensive manner, prenatal drug abuse will greatly undermine America's future well-being.

The Inadequacy of Available Remedies

To date, however, the remedies available to alleviate and/or cope with the prenatal drug abuse epidemic are inadequate. Noncoercive governmental programs such as public education, prevention campaigns, and voluntary treatment programs are vital elements in a comprehensive national attack on prenatal drug abuse. In light of the dramatic rise in drug-exposed births, however, a voluntary system of drug treatment alone appears to be largely ineffective in alleviating prenatal drug abuse.

With respect to available legal remedies, a few states have intervened in the prenatal drug abuse situation by way of civil child abuse and neglect statutes. Under these statutes, some legislatures have extended their legal definitions of neglect to include drug-exposed and/or addicted neonates. In addition, a few courts have held that neonatal drug withdrawal is probative of neglect under child abuse statutes.

By extending the definition of neglect to include drug-exposed neonates, the state is able to take custody over the infants. As custodian, the state can either remove the infant from the mother at birth, investigate the infant's home life, obtain court-ordered treatment and education for the mother, and/or initiate contempt or permanent custody proceedings against her if she fails to comply. Usually, the court makes mother/child reunification conditional on, *inter alia*, the mother's enrollment in a treatment program.

This policy of state custody over the drug-exposed child, however, is inadequate in several respects. First, as noted above, our child welfare system is too overburdened to handle the rising number of cases. Second, state intervention comes too late. The physiological damage done to the baby occurs *in utero* when the pregnant mother uses the cocaine. Third, custody is not a sufficiently coercive factor to compel many of these women to comply with court-ordered rehabilitation. As a result, the state simply has one more foster child, no rehabilitated mother, and, most likely, more drug-exposed offspring in the future.

179

Frustrated by this inadequacy, a few prosecutors have brought criminal charges against women for prenatal substance abuse. Although criminal legislation against the mother for prenatal drug abuse is currently non-existent, these prosecutors are basing charges on innovative interpretations of existing criminal statutes. The charges include criminal child abuse, delivery of a controlled substance to a minor, and involuntary manslaughter of an unborn child. However, these prosecutorial attempts are meeting with limited success.

Like the other remedies available to address prenatal substance abuse, ad hoc prosecutorial attempts are inadequate for several reasons. The underlying problem concerning prosecutorial attempts is the lack of a criminal statute directly addressing this prenatal misconduct. Because prosecutors are applying existing laws that were not meant to apply to prenatal conduct, there is an issue involving notice to the women that their conduct is subject to criminal sanctions. Further, if it is not clear that delivery of drug-affected newborn will subject the mother to criminal sanction, there can be no deterrence factor. Third, without clear legislative provision, a court or grand jury may find that the statute does not apply, and the mother will not receive compulsory drug treatment. Finally, and most importantly, ad hoc, innovative prosecutions will not aid in the establishment of a comprehensive, effective policy guided by the goals of deterrence and rehabilitation.

Legitimate Need for Police Power Action

While there is [according to the National Center for the Prosecution of Child Abuse] an "increasing willingness to use the legal system to force treatment" in the judicial and prosecutorial communities, only the legislature has the power to outline and establish a comprehensive, effective policy towards the menace of prenatal substance abuse. Under its police power, the state may *forbid* conduct that endangers the public health, welfare, and morals.

The purpose of criminal legislation is [according to H.L. Hart] "[t]o announce to society that these actions are not to be done and to secure that fewer of them are done." Criminal statutes [again, according to H.L. Hart] establish standards of conduct "to encourage certain types of behavior and discourage others. . . ." Criminalizing conduct serves the goals of deterrence and rehabilitation. Criminal sanctions have a particular deterrent effect on the offender in that she will "think twice" about her future conduct. In addition, penal sanctions have a general deterrent effect on the rest of society. Further, through penal threat, the state can coerce treatment and rehabilitation.

It is appropriate to use the criminal system to avert this threat to society, because prenatal drug use, as distinguished from drug use by non-pregnant individuals, causes harm to the actor, harm to society, and harm to a fetus. The advantage to explicitly criminalizing prenatal drug use over and above illegal drug use in general is that this type of drug use is detectable by urinalysis testing on the newborn. The state can test the newborn but not the mother nor any other non-pregnant individual.

MADONNA AND CHILD (CIRCA 1989)

Pat Crowley/Copley News Service. Reprinted with permission.

In this particular case, probable detection will be a good deterrence. Deterrence will be a weighty factor for pregnant women. They will know that they stand a greater chance of detection than the non-pregnant drug user. This risk alone will curb recreational users. In addition, ones who continue to use *will* be detected and *will be treated*. Most importantly, because of the pregnant woman's unique situation, *her* conduct causes suffering to all of us. Certainly, it is in the interest of society to criminalize this conduct, thereby discouraging prenatal drug abuse and encouraging maternal/fetal health and family order.

In light of the rapid increase in drug-exposed births, the existing non-coercive remedies appear to be woefully ineffective in attacking this societal problem. As a matter of policy, the state must take a strong interventionist stance by criminalizing prenatal substance abuse in order to contain its alarming practice. Incarceration alone, however, would be extremely unwise. By itself, incarceration will not alleviate any of the complex social problems associated with maternal prenatal substance abuse.

In order to eliminate the drug cycle and reduce drug-exposed births, the state must rehabilitate offenders. The legislature must establish a comprehensive system for drug treatment, parenting skills, medical services, and education in order for these women and their children to become productive citizens. Criminal sanctions are necessary to this overall system to coerce the mother's responsible participation in the treatment, parenting, and educational programs.

An Alternative to Prison

Under the criminal system, the state can offer the pregnant substance abuser in-patient treatment as an alternative to incarceration. The woman can be placed on probation with treatment as a condition of probation. In addition, upon successful treatment outcome, the woman's post-treatment conduct can be monitored by drug screening while on probation. Her post-treatment conduct will be influenced by the probation requirements, supervision, and the penal consequences of violating probation. Moreover, there is evidence that legal threat may be a positive factor in successful treatment outcome.

In the face of this epidemic, the legislature must do *something* to attack prenatal drug abuse. The threat of criminal prosecution when combined with the alternative of compulsory in-patient treatment and probation may well be the most effective policy towards *reducing* the rising incidence of drug-exposed births.

"Jailing women because of their conduct while pregnant infringes fundamental guarantees of reproductive choice and bodily autonomy."

Pregnant Addicts Should Not Be Prosecuted

Dorothy E. Roberts

Dorothy E. Roberts contends that criminal sanctions against pregnant drug addicts are wrong. She maintains that fear of prosecution and imprisonment would prevent pregnant addicts from seeking necessary prenatal care. Instead, Roberts argues that increasing the availability of drug-treatment programs will reduce maternal substance abuse and uphold the civil liberties of all women. She is associate professor of criminal law and civil liberties at Rutgers School of Law in Newark, New Jersey.

As you read, consider the following questions:

1. What sectors of society would sanctions against pregnant addicts affect most, according to Roberts?
2. Why does Roberts argue that women might not seek prenatal care if laws prosecuted pregnant addicts?
3. Why does the author believe prosecution will not reduce maternal substance abuse?

Dorothy E. Roberts, "Drug-addicted Women Who Have Babies." Reprinted with permission of *Trial* (April 1990), © 1990 the Association of Trial Lawyers of America.

When Judge O. H. Eaton, Jr., issued the verdict in a Florida courtroom in July 1989, it may have seemed like a run-of-the-mill drug-trafficking conviction. But it was a landmark decision. It was this country's first criminal conviction of a mother for exposing her baby to drugs while she was pregnant.

Jennifer Clarice Johnson, a 23-year-old crack addict, gave birth to her son, Carl, in 1987, and to her daughter, Jessica, in 1989. Both babies tested positive for cocaine. The Florida state attorney's office, which in December 1988 embarked on a policy of prosecuting pregnant drug addicts, decided to press for a conviction.

The state charged Johnson with two crimes: two counts of delivering a controlled substance to Carl and Jessica and one count of felonious child abuse against Jessica. Because neither Florida statute applied to fetuses, the prosecution came up with a novel theory. It based its case on the 60-second period that a cocaine metabolite may have passed through the infant's umbilical cords after they were delivered.

After a two-day bench trial, Eaton found insufficient evidence of child abuse. However, he declared Johnson guilty of delivering cocaine to her children. She was sentenced to 15 years probation under a number of conditions, including the requirement that she submit to random drug testing and complete a drug rehabilitation program. Johnson has appealed her conviction with the support of 14 public health and women's advocacy organizations, including the American Public Health Association, the National Association for Women, and the National Abortion Rights League.

The case illustrates a growing trend to prosecute women who give birth to drug-exposed babies. About 35 so-called "fetal abuse" cases have been brought nationwide. Criminal charges have been filed against women in California, Colorado, Connecticut, Florida, Illinois, Massachusetts, Michigan, South Carolina, and Wyoming, according to a February 5, 1990 New York Times article.

In addition, judges have sentenced pregnant drug addicts charged with unrelated crimes to prison sentences in order to protect their fetuses. For example, a 30-year-old woman who pleaded guilty to forging $700 worth of checks in Washington, D.C., had evidence of cocaine use in her court file. Judge Peter Wolf sentenced her to jail for the duration of her pregnancy.

Common Penalties

The most common penalty imposed on mothers who use drugs is the immediate removal of their newborns. Some child-protection agencies automatically institute neglect proceedings to obtain custody of babies with positive toxicologies. . . .

This unprecedented assault on the liberty of pregnant women

appears to be a response to two heated social issues.

• First, there is increasing public concern about the nation's drug problem, particularly the effect of drugs on babies born to addicts. In some inner-city areas, more women than men are now using crack, and many of them are pregnant. The statistics on the newborn drug victims are staggering. Some experts estimate that every year 375,000 babies are affected by drugs imparted to them in the womb. In many urban hospitals, the number of such newborns has nearly quadrupled [since 1985]. A 1988 study conducted by the National Association for Perinatal Addiction Research and Education (NAPARE) found that 10 percent of new mothers had used drugs, usually cocaine, during pregnancy. In some hospitals surveyed, the proportion was as high as 15 or 25 percent.

The Force of Law

If what we really want is to help women and children, the last thing we should do is use the force of law. Twenty-five percent of all American women have no financial coverage for prenatal care or delivery. Most drug treatment programs won't take women who seek help for drug addiction during pregnancy. The only constitutional and common-sense solution is to provide women with reproductive health services (including abortion), sex education, and a full range of health care services including prenatal care and drug-abuse treatment. Then we should leave the decision-making where it belongs—with the woman herself.

Lynn Paltrow, *ABA Journal*, August 1989.

These children may suffer a variety of medical, developmental, and behavioral problems, depending on the nature of their mother's substance abuse. Short-term effects include premature birth, low birth weight, stroke, and withdrawal symptoms. According to NAPARE, babies exposed to cocaine have a tenfold greater risk of suffering sudden infant death syndrome.

The harm may be long-term as well—mental retardation, congenital disorders and deformities, hyperactivity, and speech and language impairment. The problem is compounded by the fact that pregnant addicts often receive little or no prenatal care and may be malnourished.

• Second, the antiabortion movement has advocated expanded recognition of fetal rights. It may not have been mere coincidence that the Johnson conviction occurred just two weeks after the Supreme Court decision in *Webster v. Reproductive Health Services*. That decision upheld the state's authority to place certain restrictions on abortion in the name of fetal protection.

The legal standing of the unborn has changed radically during the last two decades. This evolution has included the right of a fetus to sue for prenatal injuries and to be protected by state criminal statutes. But until now, enforcement of these rights has never extended to the criminal conviction of the fetus's mother.

Rights at Issue

The tragedy of drug-exposed babies must be addressed. But is prosecuting their mothers the way to do it? Many women's rights advocates, legal scholars, and health-care professionals have said it is not.

Jailing women because of their conduct while pregnant infringes fundamental guarantees of reproductive choice and bodily autonomy. If criminal sanctions are used to enforce a duty of care on pregnant women, could they not be extended to less egregious behavior that also affects the fetus? Today drug and alcohol abuse are used as the basis for criminal charges; tomorrow it could be cigarette smoking, failure to follow a doctor's orders, inadequate prenatal care, or strenuous physical activity.

There are also equal protection concerns. Punishment on the basis of pregnancy affects only women. It imposes controls on women's lives that are not placed on men and thus limits women's ability to function equally in society. Legal scholars have argued that courts should carefully scrutinize laws that restrict pregnant women because reproductive capacity has historically served as the primary justification for denying women equal treatment under the law.

Women have been the only targets of prosecution for fetal abuse, even though certain conduct by men can harm the fetus. Conduct that causes genetic damage to sperm can result in miscarriage, birth defects, neonatal death, and early childhood illnesses. In 1987 a California woman named Pamela Rae Stewart whose son died shortly after birth was charged with criminal neglect in part because she failed to follow her doctor's orders to refrain from sexual intercourse while she was pregnant. Although her husband was aware of the doctor's instructions and initiated the sexual intercourse, he was not prosecuted.

Fetal abuse laws will have the greatest impact on poor and minority women. Drug use by low-income women is more likely to be detected and reported because these women are the most susceptible to government monitoring. They also receive the worst prenatal and health care. Jennifer Johnson is poor and black.

Prosecuting Pregnant Drug Addicts

Applying drug-trafficking and child-abuse laws to conduct during pregnancy also violates the defendants' due-process right to fair notice. Criminal penalties may not be imposed for conduct that is outside the plain contemplation of the penal code.

Prosecuting pregnant drug addicts is also unjust because many authorities regard addiction as an illness. The Supreme Court in *Robinson v. California* held that a statute that criminalized the status of being a drug addict violated the eighth amendment's prohibition against cruel and unusual punishment. The prosecution of addicted mothers punishes women for the combined status of being addicted and being pregnant. Defendants are not charged simply for using drugs, but for biological consequences from drug use that can occur only if they also happen to be pregnant. An addict who discovers that she is pregnant cannot definitely avoid this added punishment unless she aborts the fetus.

The unfairness of these prosecutions is increased by the scarcity of drug rehabilitation services for pregnant women. A survey of 78 drug-treatment programs in New York City, conducted by Dr. Wendy Chavkin, found that 87 percent excluded crack-addicted pregnant women on Medicaid. The handful of programs in this country for pregnant addicts have funds to treat only a tiny fraction of those women who seek help.

The most compelling reason for rejecting the proposed solution is that it will not work. Indeed, many experts agree that prosecuting pregnant addicts will ultimately cause even greater devastation. There are already signs that the threat of prosecution has scared pregnant drug users away from public hospitals and health-care programs. Many of these women may decide to get abortions or abandon their babies rather than risk going to jail. The recent prosecutions divert attention from the only real solution—freely available drug-treatment programs that meet the needs of pregnant women.

The trial of Jennifer Johnson highlights several of these legal and social policy issues. The prosecutor's legal theory shows the distortion that results from stretching a criminal statute usually applied to drug dealers to cover prenatal parental behavior. The testimony of the witnesses reveals how physicians and counselors are turned into informants against women who confide in them. The judge's opinion disregards Johnson's constitutional rights. The entire prosecution sends a dangerous message to pregnant women who use drugs: You may be convicted of a crime you never intended to commit, especially if you seek help for your addiction.

Clearing the Hurdle

The Johnson trial took place in the Seminole County Circuit Court on July 12 and 13, 1989. Assistant state attorney Jeffrey Deen was the prosecutor. James Sweeting, III, of Orlando, represented Johnson. The major evidentiary hurdle Deen faced was proving that Johnson had delivered cocaine to her children *after* they were born.

Johnson admitted in a sworn statement that she had smoked crack while pregnant. Counsel stipulated to the admissibility of toxicology reports on Carl and Jessica showing traces of cocaine. But Deen conceded that the Florida law did not apply to transferring drugs to a fetus. A Florida precedent, *Love v. State*, held that a fetus is not a person for purposes of the battery statute.

Deen got around this statutory roadblock through the testimony of the obstetricians who had delivered the babies, Drs. Randy Tompkins and Mitchell Perlstein. Tompkins, who delivered Jessica, testified that even after delivery "maternally altered" blood circulates between the placenta and the baby through the still-attached umbilical cord. He said that he believed Jessica's umbilical cord was functioning properly after he delivered her. He also testified that about 45 to 60 seconds elapsed from the time the baby had completely emerged to the clamping of the umbilical cord. Tompkins added that once Jessica was delivered from the birth canal she was a person and no longer a fetus, even though the umbilical cord was still attached. Perlstein, who delivered Carl, testified to similar facts with respect to Carl's birth.

Deen also put the county medical examiner on the stand. He testified that a cocaine derivative called benzoylecgonine remains in the bloodstream in decreasing amounts for 48 to 72 hours after cocaine is ingested.

Deen used this testimony, along with evidence that Johnson had smoked cocaine within hours of both deliveries, to establish an unprecedented application of the drug law. He asserted that Johnson had passed cocaine to her children after they were born via their umbilical cords in the 60 seconds before the cords were cut.

Serious Due Process Problems

This interpretation poses serious due process problems. True, Deen succeeded in presenting a theory that could be made to fit the words of the statute, but the plain reading of the drug delivery law did not give Johnson fair warning that it prohibited her conduct during pregnancy. The legislature enacted the statute with the intention of punishing drug pushers who give or sell drugs to minors. Sweeting argued that Deen's interpretation constituted an unforeseeable and improper judicial enlargement of the state's criminal code. Unfortunately, Eaton was undaunted. . . .

The testimony of Johnson's obstetricians shows another troubling aspect of the prosecution. Physicians and patients have historically cherished a confidential relationship. Yet Johnson's own obstetricians provided the most damaging evidence against her. Tompkins, for example, testified that Johnson told him that she had used cocaine the morning she went into labor. Dr. Riaz Arifuddin, the pediatrician who attended Carl after his birth, also disclosed that Johnson had told him about her cocaine use the night before the delivery. Indeed, Johnson and her children might not have been tested for cocaine had she not confided in her doctors that she had used the drug. The issue of doctor-patient privilege was not raised at trial. Under Florida law, doctors are required to report evidence of drug use.

Pregnancy and Addiction

It is the mother's status as an addict that creates the danger to the health of the fetus, and if maternal conduct or omissions are subject to criminal sanction, she will face the risk of punishment whether or not she continues to use the harmful substance. Thus, the criminal law would be used to punish a health status over which many women lack control. Just as attempts to use the criminal law to control public drunkenness were unsuccessful, so too are criminal prosecutions of women likely to be ineffective to eradicate substance abuse during pregnancy.

Molly McNulty, *Review of Law and Social Change*, Winter 1987-1988.

Other people in whom Johnson confided testified against her. Sandra Gomez, a child-protection investigator with the Department of Health and Rehabilitative Services, divulged what Johnson had said about her crack habit. Johnson's mother was declared a hostile witness in order to elicit testimony against her daughter.

One wonders whether Johnson would have answered her doctors' questions honestly if she knew then what she knows now. Would she have cooperated so freely in Gomez's investigation? Would she have discussed her problem with her mother? Clearly, the threat of prosecution will tend to make pregnant women who use drugs wary of providing health-care professionals with important information concerning their and their offsprings' health.

Constitutional and Social Issues

Johnson's attorney tried to raise constitutional and social policy issues that weighed against a conviction. But Eaton disallowed them at trial and ignored them in his opinion. For example, he refused to allow Montye Kelly, the director of a residential drug treatment center in Apopka, Florida, to testify about the availability of treatment to Johnson in 1988. In fact, Johnson had been turned away from a treatment program she had tried to enter during her pregnancy. The judge also excluded [expert witness for the defense, Dr. Stephen] Kandall's testimony about the nature of drug addiction and its effect on Johnson's volition.

189

At the end of trial, Sweeting asked for an opportunity to file a post-trial memorandum. Deen objected to "drag[ging] this out any longer so that social questions can be dragged in front of the Court that aren't relevant." Eaton issued the verdict after a three-hour recess.

The judge reasoned that Johnson had made three choices: she chose to use drugs, she chose to become pregnant, and she chose to allow her pregnancy to come to term. He concluded, "Upon making those choices the defendant assumed the responsibility to deliver children who were not being delivered cocaine or a derivative of it into their bodies."

Eaton's identification of Johnson's "choices" overlooks two important points. He failed to recognize the limitations on Johnson's exercise of true choice. It is doubtful whether, as a crack addict, Johnson freely decided to use drugs during her pregnancy. And the judge failed to respect her choice to bear children rather than to get an abortion or not to become pregnant at all. Instead, he punished her for making that decision and apparently did not even consider whether this impermissibly burdened her constitutional right to privacy. . . .

Eaton said, "This verdict gives further notice that pregnant addicts have a responsibility to seek treatment for their addiction prior to giving birth," despite having refused to hear testimony about the lack of available treatment programs. The true message of Johnson's trial was that addicts' very efforts to seek treatment could be used against them in a criminal prosecution.

Key Evidence

That is precisely what happened to Johnson. The state's entire proof of her criminal intent was based on her attempts to get help. Deen's theory was that her concern showed that she knew that her cocaine use harmed the fetus. The key evidence was that a month before Jessica's birth Johnson had summoned an ambulance after a crack binge because she was worried about its effect on her unborn child. Tompkins also testified that he believed Johnson told him about her cocaine use because she was concerned about its impact on Jessica's health.

Perhaps in Florida women will be prosecuted only if they remain addicted at the time of delivery. But how can a pregnant addict who wants a healthy baby be sure that she will be able to overcome her addiction in time? It is unlikely that she will be able to get treatment for it at all. Even if she does, it may be impossible for her to overcome her habit in a matter of months. In the end, she may decide not to risk being turned in by the people she would otherwise turn to for help.

"If state intervention is upheld in this context, a precedent will be created for state intrusion that will affect the right to bodily integrity of all women."

State Intervention to Stop Pregnant Addicts' Drug Abuse Violates Civil Rights

Kary Moss

Kary Moss is a staff attorney for the American Civil Liberties Union's Women's Rights Project in New York City. In the following viewpoint, Moss contends that the use of criminal and civil law to control and punish pregnant drug addicts will have potentially disastrous consequences for the health of the addicts, their babies, and the rights of all women.

As you read, consider the following questions:

1. How would mandatory reporting laws affect the health and welfare of pregnant addicts, according to Moss?
2. How does the author think the problem of pregnant addicts should be solved?
3. According to the author, what effect would laws criminalizing pregnant addicts have on women?

From "Substance Abuse During Pregnancy," by Kary Moss, *Harvard Women's Law Journal*, Spring 1990. Permission granted by *Harvard Women's Law Journal*. Copyright © 1990 by the president and fellows of Harvard College.

The incidence of fetuses exposed to drugs while in utero has generated nationwide attention from the media, social service agencies, state prosecutors, state legislatures, and Congress. A dominant theme that emerges from this attention is that women who use drugs during pregnancy are being singled out and punished for their behavior in ways that are unprecedented. The phenomenon of punishing pregnant women for being "bad mommies" because they did not behave "properly" while they were pregnant is not new. In the past, courts have authorized cesarean sections against the mother's wishes, or have taken guardianship over a fetus, but these cases were rare. Today's drug problem, however, has provided a new context in which state intervention into the lives of pregnant women becomes more acceptable because of the danger that drug use poses to the fetus. Some prosecutors, courts, and legislatures now believe that pregnant women may be punished and their rights curtailed in favor of "fetal rights." Yet, if state intervention is upheld in this context, a precedent will be created for state intrusion that will affect the right to bodily integrity of all women, even those not engaging in illegal behavior. . . .

Criminal Prosecution: The Johnson Case

On July 13, 1989, Jennifer Johnson became the first woman criminally convicted for giving birth to a drug-exposed infant after she had given birth to two such infants born fourteen months apart. Johnson, who had used cocaine during both pregnancies, was charged under section 893.13(1)(c) of the Florida Statutes, which makes delivery of drugs to a minor illegal. The prosecutor successfully argued to the court that Ms. Johnson had delivered a derivative of cocaine through the umbilical cord to her children during the sixty to ninety seconds after each child's birth and before the cord was clamped.

The court sentenced Ms. Johnson to fifteen years: one year to be served on "community control," followed by fourteen years of probation. As conditions of her sentence, Ms. Johnson must participate in a drug rehabilitation program and obtain a high school equivalency diploma. She cannot possess controlled substances, consume alcohol, associate with individuals who possess drugs, or enter a bar without the permission of her probation officer. Johnson must also perform 200 hours of community service and remain employed. If she becomes pregnant, she must enter a judicially approved prenatal care program. Ms. Johnson has appealed this verdict and the order denying her motion to dismiss. Appellate briefs were submitted in December 1989. . . .

The resolution of the Johnson case may have national impact, since the Florida District Court of Appeal's decision could significantly affect the willingness of other states to use their own criminal laws to prosecute pregnant women. Already, prosecutors in several states have used similarly novel interpretations of statutes to prosecute women who used drugs while pregnant. In Michigan, for example, K.H., a twenty-two-year-old single mother of three, is being prosecuted for giving birth to a baby born with traces of cocaine in his urine. The prosecutor alleged, as did the prosecutor in *Johnson*, that K.H. "delivered" drugs to her fetus in violation of Section 333.7401 of the Michigan Compiled Laws. The prosecutor has also alleged that K.H. committed second degree child abuse, which is punishable by up to four years in prison, by using cocaine prior to delivery of the child. The primary evidence relied upon by the prosecution was the positive toxicology of the newborn at birth. The defense filed a motion to quash which is still pending.

Human Freedom and Dignity

There will always be hard cases—times when a baby will die or suffer because a pregnant woman is negligent, unreasonable, or just plain wrong; when sensitive, dedicated doctors will wish they sold rugs for a living; when the most democratic-minded judge will have the impulse to sanction force. But even in those hard cases, the impulse must be resisted: the price in human freedom and dignity is simply too high. Not only do state controls over pregnancy violate particular women's right to self-determination, bodily integrity, and informed consent to medical treatment, in effect defining them not as people but as fetus-carriers; the degree of surveillance required to enforce such controls would violate the rights of all women of childbearing age.

Ellen Willis, *The Village Voice*, April 11, 1989.

In South Carolina, Candace Woolery was charged on August 11, 1989 with criminal neglect after giving birth to a baby found to have heroin in her blood. Ms. Woolery spent four days in jail and faces up to ten years in prison. Since that indictment, South Carolina prosecutors have similarly charged at least nine other women with criminal neglect. In Colorado, prosecutors have charged pregnant drug addicts with felony use of a controlled substance and misdemeanor child abuse. Women have also been arrested in Connecticut, Illinois, Indiana, Massachusetts, Michigan, and Ohio.

Legal Failings and Faulty Assumptions

In each of these cases, prosecutors have attempted to apply to fetuses state laws that were designed to protect children. If courts adopt these theories, they will be affording fetuses rights equal to or greater than those of women, despite a lack of legislative intent to create such a system. Additionally, the application of "delivery" and "drug pushing" statutes to pregnant drug users raises . . . due process concerns . . . since such statutory applications are novel and could not have given pregnant drug addicts requisite notice that their drug use would be in violation of those statutes.

It is also true that pregnant women are being singled out for criminal liability while similar behavior engaged in by men or nonpregnant women remains immune. For example, men and nonpregnant women who arrive at a hospital are not asked if they have children, they are not tested for drug use, and their medical records are not turned over to police or child welfare authorities. Men are not, and most likely will never be, arrested for child abuse after having used morphine or methadone, substances which animal studies have revealed will affect sperm.

Furthermore, each of these prosecutions is premised on erroneous assumptions that may have disastrous effects on these women's lives. One assumption of these prosecutorial theories is that pregnant addicts are indifferent to the health of their fetuses, or, alternatively, that they willfully seek to cause them harm. . . .

Understanding Addiction

However, it is not true that the majority of these women are insensitive to their children's needs and simply need reminders of the dangers of drug use. Real resource constraints often prevent these women from securing treatment or proper care during their pregnancies. Even when women can secure treatment, they still may be constrained by the nature of the addiction process itself. Addiction typically involves loss of control over use of the drug and continued involvement with the drug *even when* there are serious consequences. Thus, to treat pregnant addicts as indifferent and deliberate participants is to misunderstand the addiction process.

A second erroneous assumption is that drug treatment is available and pregnant women willfully seek to avoid it. For example, in *In re Troy D.*, the court reasoned in part: "To enable juvenile courts to protect drug-exposed infants and to compel parents to undergo drug rehabilitation therapy . . . courts must be able to assert jurisdiction over infants born at risk because of prenatal exposure to dangerous drugs." Yet the court did not examine the availability of drug or alcohol treatment programs open to the defendant. Had it done so, it would have found that many treatment programs will not admit pregnant women because they fear liability or lack obstetrical services. In New York, for example, 54% of the seventy-eight drug treatment programs surveyed by a New York physician refuse to treat pregnant women; 67% refuse to treat pregnant women on Medicaid; and 87% have no services available to pregnant women on Medicaid addicted to crack. Fewer than half of those programs that accept pregnant women provide or arrange for prenatal care. Lack of child care is also a major obstacle to participation in drug treatment for many women, yet only two programs make provisions available for clients' children. It is thus premature, at best, to talk about prosecuting a population for whom there are no treatment programs available.

A third assumption is that prosecution of pregnant drug users will deter such women from alcohol and drug use. Yet criminal prosecutions have shown so far that punitive measures will have the effect of deterring women from using the very health-related services that will most benefit themselves and their children. Punitive actions will drive these women away from the health care community as soon as they believe that their doctors also function as police. . . .

Implications for All Women

The problems posed by the cases discussed above have far-reaching implications for all women. First, when society chooses to punish pregnant women for their drug use, it opens the door to placement of additional restrictions on women's behavior during pregnancy. Preventing pregnant women from smoking or drinking alcohol is the most obvious such restriction, as the harmful effect of these actions on the fetus is well established. However, restrictions could go as far as to require a woman to obey all of her doctor's orders while pregnant, including instructions to quit her job or to stay in bed for a period of months. In addition, there would be rational arguments to extend such restrictions to all fertile women of childbearing age since it has been shown that alcohol consumption can harm a fetus even before a woman realizes she is pregnant. To criminalize lack of obedience to doctors' instructions merely to prevent possible harm to an unborn fetus would severely impinge on a woman's right of bodily integrity.

Second, the control over prenatal behavior will extend to other areas of women's lives. One dramatic example of such potential conflict is the Seventh Circuit case, *International Union, UAW v. Johnson Controls, Inc.*, which upheld an employer's policy that excluded all fertile women from jobs in which exposure to lead could *potentially* harm a fetus. While the majority went into great detail on the harm that might be done to a fetus exposed to lead on the job site, it did not discuss the effect that its decision would have on the lives of women excluded from these positions nor the effect it would have on their personal autonomy. The dissent estimated that the majority's rationale could possibly exclude fertile women from 15 to 20 million industrial jobs in the United States.

Social service agencies have recently begun to use child abuse laws that were never intended to apply to a mother's prenatal behavior to take custody of infants born with positive toxicologies. This focus on the prenatal activities of the pregnant women is misplaced since behavior during pregnancy is not predictive of "parental fitness," the prevailing legal standard which must be met before a court may find neglect. . . . Many hospitals report the results of positive toxicology tests to social service workers because they assume that the evidence of drug use indicates neglect. Yet, this assumption is problematic, because a positive toxicology test alone does not provide substantive information about the impairment of mother or child. Drug tests do not measure frequency of drug use. They indicate only that a person has used a drug in the twenty-four to seventy-two hours preceding the test. To presume parental unfitness given these facts is probably unconstitutional, since the Supreme Court has overturned laws that relied on a presumption of unfitness to deprive parents of custody without a substantive inquiry into the parents' actual fitness.

Moreover, drug tests are not always reliable. This means that some women will be erroneously identified while others will escape detection. Not all hospitals use the most reliable tests because they are the most costly. Even when a hospital uses a test with the greatest level of accuracy, false positives may still occur. Physiologic false positives can occur when an individual is exposed to passive marijuana smoke. There may be problems of "cross-reactions" in which a drug test returns a positive result due to the reaction of a non-"drug" substance in the body. Human error by lab technicians may also lead to false positives. . . .

State Legislative Acts

In a predictable move, state legislatures have begun to modify child abuse and neglect statutes to allow for the punishment of women who use drugs during pregnancy. For example, Illinois has amended the Juvenile Court Act definition of "neglected minor" to include infants born with controlled substances in their system, as have Indiana, Nevada, Florida, and Oklahoma. Although due process problems associated with novel application of existing laws are eliminated under these explicit statutes, the statutes are based on the same false assumptions and problems discussed above.

Other states are enacting laws which require health officials to report women who use drugs during pregnancy to child welfare authorities. For example, Minnesota amended its Reporting of Maltreatment of Minors Act to mandate the reporting of drug use by pregnant women. Minnesota requires, under certain circumstances, that doctors test pregnant women and newborns for the presence of drugs and report the results to the Department of Health. Oklahoma also requires mandatory reporting to social services. If social service agents find evidence of drug use, they are authorized to provide that information to district attorneys. Failure to report may be a misdemeanor. Utah now requires medical personnel to report a child's mother whenever they discover a child born with fetal alcohol syndrome or drug dependency.

Harmful Behavior

A physician should not be liable for honoring a pregnant woman's informed refusal of medical treatment designed to benefit the fetus.

Criminal sanctions or civil liability for harmful behavior by the pregnant woman toward her fetus are inappropriate.

Helene M. Cole, *Journal of the American Medical Association*, November 20, 1990.

One problem with this type of mandatory reporting is that it often affects poor women and women of color disproportionately. In some jurisdictions, women in government-subsidized health care facilities are labeled high-risk and are routinely tested for drug use, while women who can afford private health care remain untested. Additionally, hospital practices may vary from area to area, creating tremendous discretion as to who is reported to social services or county attorneys. . . .

The Patient's Privacy

Reporting requirements also violate a woman's right to confidential medical information. A patient's privacy interest, defined by the Supreme Court in *Robert Whalen v. Richard Roe* as "[the patient's] interest in the nondisclosure of private information and also [her or his] interest in making important decisions independently," encompasses a patient's right to non-disclosure of her or his medical history. Medical records are ordinarily entitled to a high degree of protection, and courts have upheld the sanctity of the doctor-patient relationship over threats posed by reporting requirements. The right to confidential medical information may be violated only upon the showing of a compelling state interest.

Thus, the privacy requirement should prevent hospitals from revealing patients' medical histories to county prosecutors or social service agencies. Yet, courts are violating this law. In *In re Troy D.*, the California Court of Appeals rejected plaintiff's argument that the hospital had violated the California Confidentiality of Medical Information Act by releasing her medical records. The court reasoned that the interests involved were not solely those of the plaintiff and that preventing disclosure of the newborn's records would not serve any important public policy.

A third problem with the requirement that health care professionals report test results is that it interferes with physicians' ethical and legal obligation to protect confidences told to them by a patient. Obviously, the pediatrician owes a duty of care to the child. However, requiring the doctor to report drug test results to social service agencies assumes that the woman will again engage in conduct that will harm the infant, a premise which is problematic for the reasons discussed above.

Mandatory reporting laws can also frighten pregnant mothers away from prenatal services as well as from drug treatment programs. In Minnesota the reporting statute imposes no criminal sanction and is designed only to get more women into drug treatment programs. Yet many doctors in Minnesota fear that the law is having an opposite effect, as pregnant drug users avoid treatment and withhold information from their doctors in order to avoid being reported.

Finally, reporting may not be in the best interests of the child given the current state of foster care in the United States. The acute shortage of foster care, particularly in major urban areas, must be considered when children are threatened with separation from parents, especially when the parents may be fit. . . .

Women's Rights

Actions taken by the state to "protect" the fetus from the woman carrying it conflict with a woman's rights to bodily integrity, liberty, and equality. Some addicted women who recognize that they will not be able to obtain adequate prenatal care or drug treatment will be forced to turn to abortion to avoid prosecution. Yet, these women may not even be able to obtain an abortion because of increasingly restrictive abortion laws. Legislative and prosecutorial actions that put alcohol and drug dependent women in this no-win situation necessarily jeopardize a woman's right to control her own body and must be challenged. Subjecting women to criminal sanctions or terminating their parental rights will not address the problems of children exposed to drugs in utero. Lawsuits against alcohol and drug treatment programs that discriminate against pregnant women and legislation that truly addresses the health care needs of pregnant women are two possible legal solutions to this problem. In an ideal world, this national health epidemic would not require the involvement of lawyers at all. Unfortunately, it does.

VIEWPOINT

"Civil commitment . . . offers a potentially effective and long-term solution to gestational substance abuse. "

State Intervention to Stop Pregnant Addicts' Drug Abuse Will Protect the Fetus

Kristen Rachelle Lichtenberg

In the following viewpoint, Kristen Rachelle Lichtenberg argues that states should intervene to stop pregnant women from using drugs. Lichtenberg believes that civil laws committing pregnant addicts to in-patient drug treatment programs are the most effective way of reducing the number of babies born addicted to drugs. Lichtenberg is a student at the University of Washington School of Law in Seattle.

As you read, consider the following questions:

1. How does the author justify committing pregnant substance abusers to treatment programs?
2. Why does Lichtenberg reject criminal prosecution of pregnant drug addicts?
3. According to Lichtenberg, how should the legal system solve the problem of too few treatment programs?

Kristen Rachelle Lichtenberg, "Gestational Substance Abuse: A Call for a Thoughtful Legislative Response," *Washington Law Review*, vol. 65, no. 377, April 1990. Excerpted and reprinted by permission.

Gestational substance abuse poses a significant risk to the physical and mental health of an emerging generation of Americans. Because abuse of cocaine and alcohol seriously threatens fetal health, the state has a strong interest in preventing pregnant women from abusing these substances. Recently, states have used manslaughter, child abuse, and drug delivery statutes to prosecute women who abused drugs while pregnant. Such prosecutions increasingly pressure state legislatures to find a solution directly addressing gestational substance abuse.

State intervention in pregnancies, however, poses several problems. First, states will face difficulty determining when intervention is permissible. States seeking to combat gestational substance abuse by intervention should abide by the abortion rights guidelines articulated in *Roe v. Wade*. Although *Roe* held that a right to privacy protects a woman's decision to abort during the first trimester [of pregnancy], *Roe* does not prohibit first-trimester intervention in cases of gestational substance abuse. Nonetheless, legislatures should treat gestational substance abuse consistently with abortion for reasons of public policy. Forbearance from early intervention is the only way to reconcile intervention with existing abortion law. Under this analysis, states can intervene only after the first trimester.

Second, states must decide what form intervention should take. Despite the recent increase in prosecution of pregnant substance abusers, criminalization is an inappropriate response to gestational substance abuse. Traditional justifications for punishment fail to support criminal liability. Criminalization also raises troublesome due process and mens rea [criminal intent] issues.

Civil commitment offers a better solution to the problem of substance abuse during pregnancy because it strikes at the heart of the matter. Civil commitment directly addresses the problem, lacks punitive aspects, and offers a potentially effective and long-term solution to gestational substance abuse. A state using civil commitment to intervene should adopt the Uniform Alcoholism and Intoxication Treatment Act (Uniform Act), amending it to include gestational substance abuse.

Gestational Substance Abuse

No physical contact is more intimate than that between a woman and her developing fetus. This close physical relationship creates special problems when the woman is a substance abuser. A pregnant woman abusing alcohol or cocaine harms not only herself, but also her fetus. Recently, states have attempted to address gestational substance abuse by criminally prosecuting women who abuse substances during pregnancy.

Use of alcohol during pregnancy poses severe risks to fetuses. Fetal Alcohol Syndrome (FAS) occurs in about one in a thousand live-born infants. Serious damage suffered by FAS infants includes heart defects, mental retardation, and neurologic abnormalities. Newborns with FAS are irritable, tremulous, and lack strong reflexes.

Court-ordered Treatment

Numerous courts have recognized a fetal right to safety that outweighs its mother's wishes, ordering caesarean sections or *in utero* medical treatment against the mother's will when the fetus's postnatal welfare was threatened. In limited situations, these cases might allow a court to order a woman into drug treatment.

Peggy Mainor, *Maryland Bar Journal*, May/June 1990.

The extent and severity of the fetal damage may vary according to which stage of pregnancy the woman abuses alcohol. Most alcohol-caused damage occurs during the first trimester, when the organs of the fetus begin to form. Continued alcohol abuse causes additional harm throughout gestation, however, because the brain develops during the entire pregnancy. If a woman stops drinking during the second trimester, the size and healthiness of the fetus will improve, but its intelligence may not.

Cocaine poses a unique risk to the physical and mental health of the youngest generation of Americans. The singular threat posed by cocaine stems from its relative popularity, particularly in the form of crack, among young women.

The most tragic aspect of gestational cocaine use is its potential to cause permanent physical and mental damage. By depriving the fetus of oxygen, cocaine use threatens fetal development. Malformations of the urogenital, cardiac, and central nervous systems can result from gestational cocaine abuse. Gestational cocaine use also places the fetus at a greater risk of suffering a stroke at birth, which leads to brain damage. Neurological problems caused by cocaine can permanently affect motor skills, reflexes, and coordination. Infants prenatally exposed to cocaine have lower birth weights and smaller head circumferences than do infants born drug-free. The majority of the fetal damage occurs during the first trimester, and it cannot be reversed by ceasing cocaine use. Halting cocaine use after the first trimester, however, improves fetal growth. Birth weights, lengths, and head circumferences of infants exposed to cocaine only in the first trimester do not differ significantly from nonexposed infants. . . .

The law does not specifically define the right of the state to intervene in the pregnancy of a woman whose substance abuse threatens her fetus. The state has three legal tools with which to address the problem: criminal liability, dependency proceedings, and civil commitment.

The state has the power to criminalize conduct, but no state has yet enacted laws specifically imposing criminal liability on a woman who harms her fetus through gestational substance abuse. States have, however, used existing criminal statutes to prosecute women who abuse substances during their pregnancies.

A state's *parens patriae* authority [to protect the health and welfare of the people] gives it the power to use dependency proceedings to transfer the custody of a child from a parent to the state. Prenatal substance abuse can be per se grounds for transfer of custody to the state after birth. The *parens patriae* power also gives the state authority to order treatment for a viable fetus in utero. The state can compel a woman to submit to a caesarean section or to a maternal blood transfusion for the benefit of the fetus.

The state's *parens patriae* power further permits the state to commit persons for treatment. Many states have adopted the Uniform Alcoholism and Intoxication Treatment Act (Uniform Act). The Uniform Act gives the state the power to commit alcoholics to an approved treatment facility. Under the Uniform Act, the state may commit a person who is either incapacitated by alcohol or an alcoholic who poses a danger to others and is likely to inflict harm on another unless committed.

The Uniform Act requires procedural safeguards. Before an alcoholic may be committed involuntarily, a physician must certify that he or she examined the alcoholic. The court promptly hears commitment proceedings. If the petitioner establishes a ground for involuntary commitment by clear and convincing proof, the court commits the alcoholic. At the end of the commitment term, the facility releases the alcoholic. However, when a person has been committed because he or she posed a danger to others, the facility applies for recommitment if the danger persists. If the likelihood of harm ends before the commitment term, the facility discharges a person committed because of dangerousness.

Legal and Illegal Drugs

Before the state can decide how to intervene in cases of gestational substance abuse, it must define the predicate behavior that will trigger state intervention. The state should consider both drug and alcohol abuse when deciding whether to intervene. Abuse of either alcohol or illegal drugs should establish predicate behavior for state intervention. However, the state must narrowly define actions that will spur state intervention,

202

because due process requires fair notice of what conduct constitutes a crime or predicate behavior for civil commitment.

State intervention predicated on drug versus alcohol abuse raises different legal questions. Abuse of illegal drugs creates the most convincing case for state intervention. Imposing sanctions on a pregnant woman for abuse of illegal drugs is not a significant infringement of her rights, because there is no fundamental right to use illegal drugs. Therefore, the state need not show a compelling interest to forbid their use by pregnant women. Alcohol, however, is legal. Prohibiting a pregnant woman from abusing alcohol thus represents a greater infringement on her rights. Yet, like use of illegal drugs, alcohol use is not a fundamental right, and the state can and does regulate its use.

The state should treat abuse of alcohol during pregnancy the same way it treats abuse of illegal drugs. Penalizing pregnant drug users while ignoring alcoholics is inconsistent and ignores the purpose of intervention, because the root of both problems is the same: both involve maternal addictions that endanger fetal health. If the state's goal is prevention of fetal harm, then gestational alcohol and illegal drug abuse must be treated similarly. To effectively prevent fetal damage, and to be consistent, the state must intervene in cases of alcoholism as well as drug addiction.

Harmonization with *Roe*

Gestational substance abuse requires thoughtful legislative consideration. State intervention in a pregnancy is an extremely intrusive action. Using a non-intrusive approach, the state could generously fund addiction prevention and voluntary treatment programs, with a special emphasis on averting gestational substance abuse. Before pursuing invasive solutions, the legislature should seriously consider making voluntary treatment more readily available. Unfortunately, however, prosecutors are calling for action and urging state legislatures to enact laws specifically allowing prosecution of pregnant substance abusers. The state undeniably has a tremendous interest in preventing fetal harm. Children physically and mentally damaged by gestational substance abuse will require many additional state services to meet their special medical, educational, and emotional needs. Yet prosecuting the mother fails to protect fetuses from harm.

The state should use the guidelines established in *Roe v. Wade* to determine when intervention is desirable. . . .

The right of privacy articulated in *Roe* should prohibit the state from intervening to prevent substance abuse in early pregnancy because the state's interest in protecting potential life is not compelling until [fetal] viability. If the state lacks a compelling interest in first-trimester fetal *life*, then it lacks a compelling interest in first-trimester fetal *health*. Without a compelling interest, the state cannot invade the cloak of privacy protecting a woman's first-trimester conduct. Although the Constitution does not mandate this conclusion, *Roe's* model of intervention harmonizes analysis of gestational substance abuse with abortion rights law.

Under *Roe*, the state has the right to intervene after fetal viability. Because the compelling state interest in post-viability potential life has justified invasive measures such as caesarean sections and maternal blood transfusions, similarly, this interest allows the state to intervene after viability.

It is futile, however, to allow state intervention only after viability, because most of the fetal damage happens during early pregnancy. Post-viability intervention may fail to prevent fetal harm. Nonetheless, departing from *Roe* is logically inconsistent with abortion rights law and creates undesirable maternal liability. The state should therefore apply *Roe* by analogy, and intervene only after the first trimester.

The Best Form of Intervention

A state electing to intervene must choose between criminalization and civil commitment. Criminalization is a poor choice because it lacks justification and raises *mens rea* and due process concerns. Moreover, criminalization misses the central problem—preventing fetal harm. . . .

Civil commitment is a better solution than criminalization because it focuses on the core of the problem, contains procedural safeguards, and protects both the woman and her fetus. A state choosing civil commitment should use the Uniform Act, and amend it to allow involuntary commitment of drug addicts as well as alcoholics. A state should also amend the Uniform Act specifically to include gestational substance abuse as part of the concept of posing danger to others.

The Uniform Act substantively and procedurally suits gestational substance abuse. Its substantive limits prevent arbitrary commitment and commitment of casual users. To trigger the civil commitment process, the pregnant substance abuser must first fit the definition of an alcoholic, or, under an amended Uniform Act, a drug addict. The Uniform Act's narrow definition of alcoholism and drug addiction thus decreases the risk of arbitrary or erroneous commitment. A threshold requirement of addiction makes civil commitment a solution carefully shaped to address gestational substance abuse, thus avoiding "slippery slope" problems. For example, under the Uniform Act a woman could not be committed for failing to eat properly, because the Uniform Act allows state intervention only in the case of substance addiction.

The Uniform Act's procedural safeguards and limits suit gestational substance abuse well by providing greater flexibility than criminal incarceration. Whereas criminal statutes fix the time of incarceration, the Uniform Act responds to the individual. An alcoholic or addict may be released when he or she is no longer a danger to others. If the danger persists, the substance abuser can be recommited. Like the substantive limits, the procedural safeguards also prevent erroneous or unjustified commitments. Because the Uniform Act requires a physician's certification, casual users would not be committed.

State Intervention

The state may legitimately intervene to control (the woman's) behavior during pregnancy by means narrowly designed to prevent or minimize harm to the child caused by prenatal conduct—just as it may legitimately intervene to prevent or minimize harm caused by postnatal conduct.

Nat Hentoff, *Liberal Opinion*, February 4, 1991.

Unlike penal incarceration, civil commitment recognizes and furthers the state's interest in protecting the lives and health of both the woman and the fetus. Civil commitment protects fetal health by treating the woman's addiction. Criminal incarceration may prevent further harmful substance abuse, but by ignoring the woman's health it fails to protect fetal health adequately. Nor does criminal incarceration guarantee treatment. Civil commitment protects fetal health, yet by making the woman's addiction the paramount concern, civil commitment treats her as a separate person and not as a mere vessel for the more-valued fetus.

Because civil commitment lacks a penal purpose, it does not involve complicated *mens rea* requirements. If the state amends the Uniform Act specifically to address gestational substance abuse, the state may commit once the predicate elements of alcoholism or drug addiction and threat of harm to a viable fetus are met. Thus, the issue of *mens rea* is avoided.

Civil commitment also has the advantage of speed. After the filing of a petition, a commitment hearing must be held promptly. The criminal process may take much longer. While it is true that much of the damage to the fetus occurs early in the pregnancy, before the state can intervene, civil commitment's speedy process prevents additional harm which might occur during a more lengthy criminal proceeding.

Civil commitment is not without difficulties. Even using civil commitment, the state should not intervene during the first trimester, despite the severity of the fetal damage during this period. Additionally, as with criminalization, civil commitment will not prevent damage that occurs before the woman suspects she is pregnant. Finally, civil commitment probably costs more than criminal punishment, because it involves treatment as well as incarceration. However, as the Supreme Court noted in *Roe*, pregnancy is temporary but capable of being repeated. Treatment, more than punishment, lessens the likelihood of abuse during future pregnancies. In the long run, treatment may be less expensive than prosecution or inaction, because it lessens the need for additional interventions, and because it decreases the number of children damaged by gestational substance abuse.

Conclusion

Gestational substance abuse presents troubling questions, and the law offers no ready answers. The best solution might not involve the law at all, but rather include increased state funding of drug abuse prevention and addiction treatment programs. Such programs are expensive, yet ultimately less costly than the effects of gestational substance abuse. Voluntary treatment programs avert the dilemma inherent in state intervention: although the United States Constitution probably does not prohibit early pregnancy intervention, policy and logic demand that the state not intervene before viability. Yet, tragically, most of the fetal damage occurs during early pregnancy.

If the state does intervene, it must speak to the real problem, and not attack its symptoms through highly publicized prosecutions. Prosecution has recently been the means for addressing gestational substance abuse, but this is a poor solution. Criminalization is unjustified by traditional rationales and offers no long-term solution to gestational substance abuse.

Civil commitment under the Uniform Act offers a better solution. It strikes to the heart of the issue, contains substantive and procedural safeguards, and protects the fetus by treating, not punishing, the woman. The only way the state can protect its future citizens is by treating its present citizens.

Distinguishing Bias from Reason

When dealing with controversial subjects, many people allow their emotions to dominate their powers of reason. Thus, one of the most important critical thinking skills is the ability to distinguish between statements based upon emotion or bias and those based upon a rational consideration of the facts. For example, consider the following statement: "White men want to punish all women who are poor, pregnant, and addicted to drugs by putting them in jail. They don't really care about the babies." This statement is biased. The author is basing her opinion on an emotional, unsubstantiated belief that all men want to punish women. In contrast, the statement, "Making treatment more available to pregnant addicts might reduce the number of babies born addicted" is a reasonable statement. Since many treatment programs are presently inaccessible to poor, pregnant addicts, these women are more likely to continue their addiction throughout their pregnancy. The author is using this fact to substantiate her opinion.

Another element the reader should take into account is whether an author has a personal or professional stake in advancing a particular opinion. For example, a pregnant addict who has been refused by a treatment program may write a scathing account of her experience. Note also that it is possible to have a strong interest in a subject and still present an objective case. This same woman is in a good position to discuss the lack of drug-treatment programs available for poor, pregnant women.

The following statements are adapted from opinions expressed in the viewpoints in this chapter. Consider each statement carefully. *Mark R for any statement you believe is based on reason or a rational consideration of the facts. Mark B for any statement you believe is based on bias, prejudice, or emotion. Mark I for any statement you think is impossible to judge.*

Compare your answers with those of other students. You may discover that others come to different conclusions than you do. Their answers may give you valuable insights into distinguishing between bias and reason.

> R = *a statement based upon reason*
> B = *a statement based upon bias*
> I = *a statement impossible to judge*

1. State attorneys have used laws designed to prosecute child abuse and drug dealing cases to prosecute pregnant drug addicts. It is unfair to punish women using laws they never knew applied to using illegal drugs during pregnancy.

2. Male attorneys have no right to prosecute women for what they put into their bodies during pregnancy.

3. Making treatment programs available and accessible to poor addicts who use drugs during pregnancy will help reduce the number of pregnant addicts.

4. Pregnant drug addicts should be thrown in jail as soon as possible to protect their babies and to teach them a lesson about harming children.

5. The prosecution of pregnant drug users is another example of wealthy, white men persecuting poorer Hispanic and African-American women.

6. If good prenatal care was universally available, there would be fewer pregnant addicts and fewer babies harmed by drugs.

7. Pregnant addicts hate their children and should never be allowed to reproduce. Any children they have should be permanently kept away from these women.

8. Minority women are indicted for drug abuse during pregnancy more often than nonminority women. Prosecutors should not discriminate against poorer women while letting wealthier women get away with their drug use.

9. Many people of different races and sexes are working together to prevent children from being addicted to illegal drugs their mother took during pregnancy.

10. Drug treatment programs and care for babies abandoned by drug-addicted mothers are a financial drain on state and federal government. Perhaps the threat of a jail term might frighten some pregnant addicts away from using drugs and contributing to the drain on government.

11. Only poor women are in danger of being jailed for using drugs during pregnancy. Wealthy women can enter expensive treatment and avoid prosecution.

12. The state has the right to intervene between a mother and a child to prevent the mother from doing harm to the child.

13. Hearing white males who make the laws advocating new laws that punish and harm women is deeply disturbing.

Periodical Bibliography

The following articles have been selected to supplement the diverse views presented in this chapter.

Douglas J. Besharov	"Crack Children in Foster Care," *The American Enterprise*, January/February 1990.
Wendy Chavkin	"Help, Don't Jail, Addicted Mothers," *The New York Times*, July 18, 1989.
Children Today	Entire issue on pregnancy and addiction, July/August 1990. Available from the Superintendent of Documents, U.S. Government Printing Office, Washington, DC 20402.
Mark Curriden	"Holding Mom Accountable," *ABA Journal*, March 1990.
Jane Doe	"Why Should I Give My Baby Back?" *The New York Times*, December 22, 1990.
Maggie Garb	"Must a Woman Battle Her Fetus and the Court for Autonomy and Civil Rights?" *In These Times*, February 7-13, 1990.
Jeffrey Hart	"Here Come the Crack Babies," *Conservative Chronicle*, October 3, 1990. Available from PO Box 11297, Des Moines, IA 50340-1297.
Jan Hoffman	"Pregnant, Addicted, and Guilty," *The New York Times Magazine*, August 19, 1990.
Barbara Kantrowitz et al.	"The Crack Children," *Newsweek*, February 12, 1990.
Kary Moss and Wendy Chavkin	"Pregnant, Addicted—and Excluded," *Christianity and Crisis*, May 28, 1990.
Katha Pollitt	"A New Assault on Feminism," *The Nation*, March 26, 1990.
The Progressive	"Pregnancy Police," special section, December 1990.
Anna Quindlen	"Hearing the Cries of Crack," *The New York Times*, October 7, 1990.
Abe M. Rosenthal	"How Much Is a Baby Worth?" *The New York Times*, December 15, 1989.
Andrea Sachs	"Here Come the Pregnancy Police," *Time*, May 22, 1989.

How Can Chemical Dependency Be Reduced?

Chemical Dependency

Chapter Preface

The federal government currently allocates less than a third of its budget for fighting the drug problem to treatment programs, choosing instead to focus on enforcing drug laws to reduce chemical dependency. Unfortunately the emphasis on law enforcement has failed to substantially reduce the problem. Although most public health experts agree that treatment is essential to reduce chemical dependency, it is not widely available.

The lack of publicly funded treatment programs and their effect on chemical dependency is dramatically illustrated in the story of Jeffrey Ellerbe. In September 1990, the *Wall Street Journal* documented Ellerbe's story. Ellerbe robbed a fast-food restaurant, taking about five hundred dollars. He then drove to a police station and attempted to turn himself in for the robbery. The police threw him out. A few hours later, after getting high, he robbed a McDonald's and then tried to turn himself in to a different police station, without success. Ellerbe, a crack addict, was stealing not to finance his drug habit, but to be sentenced to jail and placed in a drug-treatment program. Before the robberies, Ellerbe had contacted fifteen different treatment centers, all of which had refused to admit him. The police finally arrested Ellerbe after a third robbery. He pleaded guilty and, as part of his sentence, enrolled in a long-term treatment program called Rap, Inc.

Ellerbe's story is just one of many. Almost 6 million people in the United States are dependent on drugs and alcohol, according to a study published in September 1990 by a panel of experts convened by Congress. Nearly 2 million of these people are seeking treatment for their addiction, but according to William J. Bennett, the former director of the Office of Drug Control Policy, there are only enough publicly funded programs to treat 500,000 addicts. The congressional panel recommended that the government expand the availability of treatment programs dramatically, giving first priority to the 67,000 people on the waiting lists of treatment programs. The panel especially recommended increases in treatment for pregnant women, young mothers, and jailed criminals.

The viewpoints in the following chapter debate the value of treatment and other methods aimed at reducing chemical dependency.

"Participation in [Alcoholics Anonymous] helps many people stop drinking, stay sober and build a rewarding life."

Alcoholics Anonymous Can Help Alcoholics Recover

Stephen E. Schlesinger and Lawrence K. Horberg

Alcoholics Anonymous (AA) is a self-help group that uses peer support to end chemical addiction. In the following viewpoint, Stephen E. Schlesinger and Lawrence K. Horberg contend that AA's twelve-step program combined with strict abstention from all alcohol is the best way to end addiction. Schlesinger, a psychologist, teaches at Loyola University's Stritch School of Medicine in Chicago. Horberg, also a Chicago psychologist, teaches at Northwestern University Medical School in Chicago, Illinois.

As you read, consider the following questions:

1. According to Schlesinger and Horberg, what are the primary goals of AA members?
2. According to the authors, how does AA view moderate drinking during the program?
3. Why do the authors believe recovering alcoholics can never return to social drinking?

Excerpted, with permission, from *Taking Charge: How Families Can Climb Out of the Chaos of Addiction*, by Stephen E. Schlesinger and Lawrence K. Horberg. New York: Simon & Schuster, 1988. Copyright © 1988 by Stephen E. Schlesinger and Lawrence K. Horberg.

AA [Alcoholics Anonymous] has been in existence for more than fifty years. Its founders began their organizational efforts in the mid-1930's, and by 1938 AA was a functioning entity. AA groups exist all over the United States and in some 114 countries abroad. Estimated membership is 1 1/2 million; 800,000 members live in the U.S. and Canada.

For many years AA and alcoholism treatment were nearly synonymous in the U.S. AA remains a major form of treatment, and is the oldest and largest group of its kind. A great many people over the years have found AA to be extremely helpful. Some have found it to be the only effective form of treatment for them. Other AA members combine participation in AA with the other forms of treatment.

The AA Program

The AA program mirrors the population of problem drinkers in its diversity. Just as it is difficult to describe the typical problem drinker, it is also difficult to describe a typical self-help group meeting. Members gather in churches, synagogues, schools, hospitals, private homes, restaurants, corporate boardrooms and other meeting places. . . .

The traditions of AA explicitly discourage any form of activity that might distract members from their primary goals: to remain sober and to provide a supportive environment in which to achieve and maintain sobriety. An informal structure handles functions such as the maintenance of facilities and the distribution of publications. But, as a matter of principle, its organization is given little emphasis.

The general guidelines under which AA operates are known as the Twelve Steps and Twelve Traditions. The major components of the AA program remain the same around the world. Nevertheless, the AA program is adapted to meet the needs of each group. Each member contributes to the atmosphere, to the discussion and to the direction taken in the meeting.

Joining AA is very simple. In its official words, "The only requirement for membership is a desire to stop drinking." The way you join AA is to attend meetings. Period. There are no formal membership criteria, application procedures, referral forms or review boards, and there are no fees. Twelve-step programs are the only organized groups we know of that truly welcome strangers *unconditionally and at no cost.* A traveler can get off an airplane in most of the world's cities, call the central number of AA and quickly find people who will talk with him, take him to a meeting and share a common interest. AA views itself as a caring community; it lives up to its philosophy. . . .

The core of the AA program is the Twelve Steps, which were devised by the early members of AA. All meetings revolve around the Twelve Steps, and all writings are based on them.

1. We admitted we were powerless over alcohol—that our lives had become unmanageable.

2. Came to believe that a power greater than ourselves could restore us to sanity.

3. Made a decision to turn our will and our lives over to the care of God *as we understood Him.*

4. Made a searching and fearless moral inventory of ourselves.

5. Admitted to God, to ourselves, and to another human being the exact nature of our wrongs.

6. Were entirely ready to have God remove all these defects of character.

7. Humbly asked Him to remove our shortcomings.

8. Made a list of all persons we had harmed, and became willing to make amends to them all.

9. Made direct amends to such people wherever possible, except when to do so would injure them or others.

10. Continued to take personal inventory, and when we were wrong, promptly admitted it.

11. Sought through prayer and meditation to improve our conscious contact with God *as we understood Him,* praying only for knowledge of His will for us and the power to carry that out.

12. Having had a spiritual awakening as the result of these steps, we tried to carry this message to alcoholics, and to practice these principles in all our affairs.

The concept of the Twelve Steps is an important contribution made by recovering alcoholics to the culture as a whole. Applications can be found in everyday life, even for nonalcoholics. . . .

The first three Steps involve the surrender process. In this process, the drinker gives up his resistance to important facts about his life. He gives up the illusion that he can go on drinking without harm. He learns that many things in his life are not under his control but do follow some order and do have meaning. The religious AA member looks to God to understand that order and meaning. The atheist will look to nature and to other people as he tries to understand the sources of power and influence that shape his life. The drinker surrenders his lonely and desperate struggle to drink away the emotional consequences of problems in living. He learns that "there is no problem a good drink can't make worse.". . .

One Drink Is Too Many

During the process of surrender, many drinkers come to realize that they are not able to moderate their drinking. A popular AA slogan is, "One drink is too many, a thousand aren't enough." This process is not easy for most drinkers. Many relapses result when the drinker thinks, "I've been sober six months now. I can handle just one or two drinks." In the AA framework, this kind of thinking serves as evidence that this person has not yet "taken the first Step," that he does not yet see himself as truly power-less to control the effects of alcohol. . . .

The fourth through seventh Steps involve:

- Making an honest, fearless assessment of one's flaws
- Sharing the results of this assessment with another person
- Letting the higher power remove these character defects
- Asking the power to do so

Many people who relapse despite participation in AA have ig-nored one or more components of the assessment sequence.

Most of us are willing to admit to superficial flaws. However, the key word in the fourth Step is "fearless." In a fearless moral inventory we probe all those areas we do not usually let our-selves think about—for example, that we have failed our chil-dren, ruined our health or destroyed our marriage. . . .

The Strength of AA

AA . . . is the only institution in the United States that has any inkling whatsoever of the medical problems involved in alco-holism and the enormous human and economic costs of alco-holism in our society.

Only AA really understands that there are literally millions of un-declared alcoholics walking around, checking in and out of hospi-tals for masked disorders, killing themselves and others in a daily ritual of mayhem.

Joseph D. Beasley, *Wrong Diagnosis, Wrong Treatment*, 1987.

If the assessment is done well, it will undoubtedly bring a lot of painful memories to light. During the assessment, the mem-ber cannot help but become aware of certain weaknesses or flaws in himself. AA calls these flaws "character defects," and the process of exploring them is called "taking inventory." Some of these character defects may seem so shameful or embarrass-ing that the member cannot picture ever sharing that material with anyone. But through participation in AA, the material is of-ten gradually revealed. . . .

The sixth and seventh Steps are sometimes difficult for drinkers who do not have a sense of God. Once a drinker has honestly looked at his flaws and discussed them with someone else, he is usually ready—even eager—to change. And so he looks for the strength, understanding, courage and good judgment to alter his behavior. For the devout AA member, prayer is a natural way of focusing himself on the task of changing and asking for the strength to change. He asks God to remove his flaws. On the other hand, an atheist must create another focus in his yearning to change. He may focus on the group, humanism, health or self-actualization. He wishes for the strength and circumstances to allow him to grow. . . .

Understanding the Twelfth Step is central to correct stereotypes of AA. In the positive stereotype, selfless AA members will appear any time of the day or night to provide any form of help to a drunk. In the negative stereotype, AA fanatics go about preaching the AA gospel, badgering those with no significant drinking problems. As with all stereotypes, both are inaccurate.

Not a Religion

Spirituality is distinct from religion in AA. Members practice many different faiths, and some are atheists and agnostics. AA is not a religion. It does not promote beliefs about God and does not focus on the nature of the relationship between man and God. AA is a spiritual community whose members share some specific values and agree that certain types of behavior are admirable. For example, AA stresses the importance of caring, support and love. It emphasizes that it is important to structure your life to include giving and receiving support. Similarly there is value in taking good care of yourself. Getting worse through neglect is viewed as bad; doing what it takes to get healthy is good. It is good to find your place in the world, a base from which you can be involved assertively and comfortably with other people. Isolation is viewed as dangerous. Passively giving in to other people to seek their approval is termed "people pleasing" and is also viewed as dangerous. . . .

It is important to emphasize that the Twelve Steps constitute a circular, not a linear, process. In other words, the Twelve Steps are not a recipe for sobriety with which you start at Step one, go through to Step twelve and then expect sobriety to bloom. Instead, they are a process of continuing reappraisal and growth. For example, in doing Twelfth Step work, you can discover things about yourself that you did not know when you initially passed through the fourth Step. None of the Steps is ever irrevocably completed.

Also, not all AA members go through all the Steps, and many do not go through them in order. Some prefer to begin making amends before they have completed their assessment. The important thing is not to dismiss any of the Steps totally, while remembering that the program does not obligate anyone to do anything that appears foreign or senseless. . . .

As we said at the beginning, some people equate Alcoholics Anonymous with the treatment of alcoholism. There are, of course, many other forms of treatment.

There are some who say that no one can get sober without AA. Their response to someone who seems to get better without AA is that either he wasn't really addicted to alcohol in the first place, or he is not really sober but just on a "dry drunk."

Naturally, this whole line of reasoning is grandiose. It over-states the value of AA. Many people have stopped drinking and adopted a sober lifestyle without the use of AA or any other form of treatment. Some become sober through a religious experience, others for a variety of other reasons.

Nevertheless, participation in AA helps many people stop drinking, stay sober and build a rewarding life. Participation in AA makes a resumption of heavy drinking less likely.

"Programs designed explicitly to teach moderate drinking as a goal report success rates averaging 65 percent."

Controlled Drinking Can Help Alcoholics Recover

John S. Crandell

Recovering alcoholics can resume drinking in moderation, according to John S. Crandell, the author of the following viewpoint. Crandell maintains that while controlled drinking is unsuitable for some alcoholics, it can be an effective alternative to total abstention. Crandell argues that controlled drinking, while controversial in the United States, is a well-accepted treatment method in Europe and other parts of the world. The author is a clinical psychologist specializing in family therapy and substance abuse treatment in Winchester, Virginia.

As you read, consider the following questions:

1. According to Crandell, what form of treatment should problem drinkers participate in?
2. Why does the author believe that candidates for a moderate drinking program should first undergo two months of abstention?
3. Does Crandell consider a "slip" proof that a drinker cannot be treated in a moderate-drinking program? Why or why not?

Reprinted with permission of Lexington Books, an imprint of Macmillan, Inc., from *Effective Outpatient Treatment for Alcohol Abusers and Drinking Drivers* by John S. Crandell. Copyright © 1987 by the publisher.

There has been considerable controversy about whether alcoholics can resume asymptomatic drinking. Between 5 percent and 20 percent of patients treated in abstinence-oriented programs are found to be drinking without immediate problems at follow-up. Programs designed explicitly to teach moderate drinking as a goal report success rates averaging 65 percent. There is an important controversy about the quality of the controlled drinking. For example, Dr. George Vaillant [of the Harvard University Medical School] argues that the apparent success is not because of successful moderation of intake but is a result of more sustained abstinence. When they do drink, the controlled drinkers are likely to consume heavily or to have to employ stringent external restrictions that limit intake at the cost of removing most of the potential pleasure from drinking. Moreover, profiles of those who do return to asymptomatic drinking suggest that they do not accept the disease concept or see themselves as alcoholic, that they have few problems from drinking, that they have been using heavily for a short time, and that the increased intake is a transient response to a traumatic loss. In sum, many of those who return to asymptomatic drinking would be better classified as nonaddicted alcohol abusers, the heavy drinkers.

It is inappropriate to encourage abstinent alcoholics to resume drinking. Similarly, those who are clearly dependent on alcohol (those with middle- and late-stage symptoms) should set a goal of abstinence. But it would be naive and inappropriate to view abstinence as the only option for the less problematic drinkers who compose a significant proportion of the clients in an outpatient treatment program. To the extent that those who return to asymptomatic drinking can be identified, clients who resemble them and desire to learn to moderate their drinking should be given the opportunity to demonstrate that they can do so. [A controlled-drinking] exercise has those two objectives: to identify those who have a prospect of learning asymptomatic drinking, and to set a realistic test of their ability to do so.

Self-Diagnosis

[The] experiment allows clients to determine their self-diagnosis behaviorally. A sincere attempt to control that fails will be much more convincing evidence of alcoholism than a discussion of loss of control or the results of a paper-and-pencil test. Those who succeed in temporary control will have first-hand experience with the discipline needed to continue to drink while avoiding recurrence of destructive habits. There are secondary goals related to the fact that the "control test" begins with a requirement of two months of abstinence. Clients are less likely to distort their self-diagnosis simply to preserve their drinking if they know that nonalcoholics hoping to continue drinking will have to achieve temporary abstinence. This break from drinking, with its proof positive that it is possible to quit, often provides the opportunity for a client to reconsider whether abstinence might not be a desired objective. The dry period also forces the drinker to face withdrawal cravings or other evidence that controlled drinking is not an option. . . .

Controlled Drinking Works

According to Dr. William Miller, a leading alcoholism researcher [at the University of New Mexico at Albuquerque], there's increasing evidence that controlled drinking does work for some alcohol abusers.

Miller recently completed a long-term review of 140 problem drinkers who'd learned to imbibe in moderation after being taught self-control strategies. Eight years after treatment, 99 of those drinkers could be traced—and 14 were controlling their drinking. A surprising 23 were abstinent, often after a long period of tapering down. Another 22 had improved, but still had some problems with alcohol. Five were deceased; the remaining 35 were doing poorly. "Of some 28 studies of the controlled-drinking treatment of milder alcoholics, done by research teams in many countries, 23 show very similar favorable results—an average of 65%," says Miller.

Winifred Gallagher, *American Health*, June 1988.

Abstainers and those for whom control is not a realistic goal should not be deluded into believing controlled drinking is a option for everyone. The last thing they need is an additional rationalization ("I'm going to try to control it, like the doc told me to") to buttress their underlying desire to resume drinking. At times I have simply invited everyone who self-diagnoses as alcoholic to take a fifteen-minute break while controlled drinking is discussed with those who remain behind. More effectively, the discussion of control is preceded by a self-assessment step that indicates for whom it is *not* an option. Having been informed of the characteristics for whom controlled drinking is inappropriate, similar clients may be that much more aware of the need to aim for abstinence.

There is considerable agreement among researchers as to the characteristics of clients who may succeed in moderating their alcohol consumption. Clients can be asked to see if they meet the following eight criteria. If they fail more than three, they have poor prospects for changing their drinking and should seek to abstain. My experience indicates that only those who violate one or none have a good chance of succeeding, while those with two or three misses will have a continuing struggle to maintain asymptomatic drinking.

Criteria for Success

The criteria are:

1. The person should be under forty years of age. Older drinkers do better with an abstinence goal, while younger drinkers may have less relapse if they aim to moderate their drinking.

2. The person should have fewer than five years of heavy or problem drinking. Others have suggested that ten years of high-tolerance drinking is acceptable. But if problems have been recurring for that long, there is likely to be alcoholism or insufficient problem-solving energy.

3. Evidence of physical dependence should be absent. Even minor withdrawal would be evidence that this condition has been violated.

4. Few life problems because of drinking should exist. Vaillant found that most of those who achieved moderation on their own had two or fewer life problems because of drinking. Any more than four, including the DWI (driving while intoxicated), typifies those who need to abstain.

5. The person should have few alcoholic blood relatives. Although Vaillant found that this characteristic did not differentiate abstainers from controlled drinkers, the evidence for inherited vulnerability makes it unwise for alcoholism-prone individuals to continue drinking after developing premonitory symptoms such as the tolerance necessary for a drunk driving arrest.

6. The person should have made no prior attempts to moderate drinking. "The more the patient's history reveals past failures at controlled drinking, the more insistently clinicians should support a goal of abstinence rather than of reduced intake," says Vaillant.

7. The person should have incentive to change drinking. Vaillant found that many who changed without treatment did so because of concern about an alcohol-related health problem or because the beginning of a new love relationship changed the pattern of socializing so as to remove the temptation to drink. The educational and motivational components of the treatment program may supply additional incentive. But success requires a clear and sustained commitment on the part of the client.

8. The person should be strong-willed (hardheaded, field independent, and so forth). Some clients readily acknowledge that they are impulsive or easily influenced by peers. These clients are unlikely to maintain any changes. Conversely, willfulness and counter-dependence may now be assets for those intent on changing.

Once the criteria have been presented and discussed, most

clients can readily identify their score. More important, they can recognize the rationale for the course of action indicated by that score. It is, however, important to emphasize that it is appropriate to decide on abstinence even if the control questions suggest that moderated drinking might be possible.

The Control Test

There are risks in attempting controlled drinking. I have had clients rearrested during a slip sustained during the test. But the risk may be worthwhile for those who wish to demonstrate to themselves and to the counselor that they can drink in an asymptomatic fashion. They need to be reminded that the future drinking will differ from that of the past, in tone as well as in quantity. Because they will have to "keep their guard up," they can no longer engage in the carefree drinking of their favorite memories. They will need to make major changes in the circumstances and in the frequency of drinking. Bars and other "hot spots" will probably remain off limits. Consumption will have to be carefully observed and ritualized, as was the case with a woman who only drank three glasses of wine, once a week, with dinner, and when her boyfriend was present for support. If control fails, there must be a commitment to acknowledge the slip, openly and without rationalization, and to accept the need for abstinence as a goal.

Treatment Choices Are Needed

Fully 95% to 100% of those who enter treatment and/or self-help programs try at least once more to drink moderately, so it is unethical not to give them some behavioral tools, if for no other reason than to see which ones can learn to moderate successfully and move forward with normal, healthy lives—and which ones cannot.

Bill Talley, *Moderation as a Treatment Goal Choice*, 1990.

The control test is then outlined. It consists of two parts. First, there must be two months of abstinence from all alcohol. This is to break the old pattern, to get used to handling former drinking situations without imbibing, to develop confidence in the ability to change, and to allow the body time to recover from the effects of prior drinking. Controlled drinking proponents concur in the need for preliminary abstinence, although Roger Vogler and Wayne Bartz suggest only two weeks, and G. Alan Marlatt requires one month. The longer period suggested allows the client time to register protracted withdrawal, to begin to experience the benefits of being dry, and to develop enough of a pattern of abstinence so as to be able to think through the decision about whether resumed drinking is truly desired. Some clients choose to continue abstinence once they have achieved it.

The second part of the test is for the client to resume drinking in a controlled fashion for an additional eight weeks. I suggest a fixed limit of two standard drinks for women and small men, or three drinks for larger men on any day during which they imbibe. This limit is low enough so that adverse consequences are unlikely (for example, there is little risk of rearrest for driving under the influence). Yet the limit is high enough to "tease" their control. After a period of abstinence, the clients will likely feel some effects from this quantity of alcohol. Clients routinely report that it is more difficult to stop after three than after one or two drinks. This level provides a test. While there is no requirement that this amount be consumed on each occasion, and while it is strongly suggested that these clients not drink every day, consuming this amount regularly without continuing is evidence of control. Any excess, even if the fourth drink is put down before it is finished, should be regarded as a slip. This rigid limit prevents any uncertainty or excuses.

A Better Chance of Success

This test is more rigorous than the trials of other clinicians. Vogler and Bartz require that clients achieve control within the two-month period, believing that any learning takes time and that initial failure need not indicate ultimate lack of success. This may be true for clients who voluntarily seek treatment. For the clients with whom I work, who are court-ordered into treatment, clear-cut evidence of motivation to change is needed.

There are, however, two safety valves that give clients a better chance of success in this test. First, I inform them of the difficulty and urge a week or more of consideration before the challenge is accepted. Clients often use this period of preparation to inform friends, to seek support, and to consolidate determination—reducing the risk of early failures. Second, a single slip is permitted. The suggestion is made that it should be used as an opportunity to learn rather than as proof of alcoholism. A slip should be handled by returning to the beginning and repeating the current stage of the test. If the slip occurs in the second week of abstinence, then the entire test should begin again; but if the slip happens in the fourth week of control, then only the eight weeks of limited drinking need be repeated.

Clients who succeed in the test have demonstrated the ability to change and have laid the groundwork for a new and healthier pattern of drinking. Clients who fail have engaged themselves in a powerful process of self-confrontation that is likely to result in fuller acceptance of the self-diagnosis of alcoholism and of the need for abstinence as a goal. . . .

Some counselors reject the disease concept of alcoholism and try to make controlled drinkers out of all clients. This is clearly inappropriate. The criteria are evidence that even proponents of controlled drinking recognize as indicating that some clients must seek abstinence. There are other counselors, particularly if they are themselves recovering alcoholics, who reject even the prospect of resumed drinking by problem drinkers. This exercise will be seen as a challenge to their beliefs. It should be. . . . There is a need for different approaches, and alternative goals may be appropriate—including moderated drinking. . . . Some high-tolerance drinkers need not be addicted. The present exercise is intended to build on that understanding, by supporting selected clients in modified drinking. This goal is well accepted in Europe and in other parts of the world. It remains controversial in the United States.

"Drug rehabilitation, accessible for all who need it, is the best government can do."

The Government Should Fund Treatment Programs to Reduce Chemical Dependency

Los Angeles Times

In the following viewpoint, the *Los Angeles Times* argues that harsher penalties for drug use have been ineffective at reducing chemical dependency. The emphasis on imprisonment is expensive and has contributed to widespread prison overcrowding, according to the author. Rather than building more prisons to punish arrested drug users, the author advocates government-funded drug treatment programs as a less expensive and more efficient method of reducing chemical dependency. The *Los Angeles Times* is a daily newspaper in Los Angeles, California.

As you read, consider the following questions:

1. Why do law enforcement officers advocate treatment programs, according to the author?
2. Why does the author believe that tougher law enforcement and increased imprisonment have been unsuccessful in reducing the number of drug addicts?
3. Why, besides cost, does the author advocate increasing the number of treatment programs in the U.S.?

There is no magic pill to cure the wrenching addiction caused by crack cocaine. There is not even an equivalent to methadone, the narcotic palliative that suppresses the longing of heroin addicts for the drug that has them hooked. Rehabilitation offers the best hope as America looks for a way out of this social and human quagmire.

If drug treatment is the answer . . . what is the question? There are many. How many Americans need it? How much does it cost? Does it really work? And, perhaps, the question most on the minds of politicians: Does a buck spent on drug treatment pay off with a reduction in crime?

An estimated 860,000 Americans regularly use cocaine, according to a 1988 survey of households by the National Institute of Drug Abuse. That number excludes large groups of users—inmates, the homeless and people already in drug treatment programs. Other estimates put the figure as high as 2.2 million cocaine-addicted Americans.

Rehabilitation plus Law Enforcement

The budget debates on how to deal with such numbers boil down to prisons versus prevention and cops versus treatment. Beefed-up law enforcement is the historical response to higher rates of crime. But the numbers prove that more cops, courts and prisons can't provide the whole cure.

Even the nation's top cops—including Los Angeles Police Chief Daryl F. Gates—are beginning to call for additional rehabilitation. Out-manned and out-gunned on the streets, big-city cops are beginning to view the drug problem as more than a law enforcement nightmare. And they are right.

It costs about $71,600 in salary and benefits to put another cop on the streets of Los Angeles. Police can help stop drug abuse, but treatment costs less and does more good.

Getting people to admit they need help is often half the battle. When drug abusers want to go straight, are highly motivated and ready to change, they should get help quickly. But at the moment they get help only if they can pay.

Celebrities and other wealthy drug users can check into private, for-profit residential facilities that charge from $6,000 to $12,000 for 28 days of treatment, plus after-care. Research shows that residential facilities offer the greatest hope of success. But, at those prices, only the well-to-do or employees of companies with excellent health insurance plans can afford to stay 28 days and longer, or to go back again and again until they're able to control their craving.

No such help is available to the most vulnerable drug abusers: Poor city kids must be patient—very patient. The wait for an opening in some places can last longer than it takes a woman addict to deliver another crack baby.

Drug treatment on demand can save such babies, and their parents. It is costly, but not as costly as the millions of dollars involved in caring for drug-addicted babies from their tortured cradle through disabled adulthood to an early grave. Because of the cost in human terms, and to taxpayers, child-bearing women deserve first priority in government-supported programs. In those cases, drug treatment makes the most sense financially.

"You call this a drug treatment program?"

Paul Conrad, © 1989, *Los Angeles Times*. Reprinted with permission.

Residential treatment is a good investment because it removes users from an environment where cocaine is easy to come by and from friends who consider crack a seductive companion.

The optimal commitment is for at least 16 weeks, often followed by months of warding off relapses; the average addict suffers five relapses. Even when drug abusers learn to abstain, their cravings—triggered by a memory, a dream, a wad of money or a familiar face—may never go away. Through effective treatment, however, users can develop the will to resist drugs and master the secrets of staying clean. It may cost a lot—roughly $14,000 per year in public, nonprofit treatment centers—but it's more than worth it.

Drug rehabilitation is expensive, but not as expensive as building new prisons and running them at double the capacity. Tight government budgets and huge deficits demand spending priorities. But nearly 80% of the men arrested in large cities test positive for drug use, according to a study by the National Institute of Justice published in December 1989. Those numbers demand attention.

The Prison Climate

The prison climate—structured, highly disciplined and, in theory, largely free of drugs—could be conducive to successful rehabilitation. But few jails or prisons provide systematic drug treatment. That's a wasted opportunity.

Prison officials blame this failure on tight budgets that are being further squeezed by overcrowding, overtime wages and the cost of housing more dangerous criminals. Politicians blame voters who cast their ballots for more jail cells. But dollar-for-dollar, serious investment in drug treatment would do more to cut down recidivism and street crime.

Treatment—specifically residential programs—showed dramatic reductions in drug use and a significant decline in predatory crime, according to researchers who tracked more than 10,000 drug users in 41 residential and outpatient treatment programs nationwide for five years. The federally funded Treatment Outcome Prospective Study—the largest long-term study of treatment effectiveness—was done by the Research Triangle Institute in North Carolina.

An unusual and detailed cost-benefit analysis found that, in most cases, the benefits of providing treatment were substantially higher than the costs. According to "Drug Abuse Treatment: A National Study of Effectiveness," the published report of the TOPS findings: "Virtually all economic measures show that the burden of crime and other economic consequences of drug abuse are lower after treatment than before."

After drug treatment, crime-related costs declined significantly—for victims and the criminal justice system including cops, courts and prisons. Those encouraging findings—although based on drug use before crack put an intense and very addictive high within reach of anyone with as little as $5—are very

228

persuasive arguments that the best investment of scarce public dollars is drug treatment.

Drug abuse costs billions of dollars and drains productivity from every segment of society—from boardrooms and courtrooms as well as street corners. Drug rehabilitation, accessible for all who need it, is the best government can do to reduce the public and social costs—that is, unless this nation is willing to build a prison in virtually every neighborhood.

"Greed . . . must be fought and stopped before the chain can be broken and our country finally freed of its chemical, economic, and cultural addiction to illegal drugs."

Zero Tolerance for Drugs Can Reduce Chemical Dependency

Richard Nixon

Richard Nixon was president of the United States from 1969 to 1974. Since resigning as president, Nixon has written a number of books on U.S. domestic and foreign policy, including *No More Vietnams* and *1999: Victory Without War*. During his presidency, Nixon was an outspoken advocate of punishing drug users. Today, he continues to believe that a stringent crackdown on all aspects of the drug problem, from importation to recreational drug use, is necessary to reduce chemical dependency. In the following viewpoint, excerpted from his book *In the Arena: A Memoir of Victory, Defeat, and Renewal*, Nixon argues that all Americans must adopt a policy of zero tolerance for drugs.

As you read, consider the following questions:

1. According to the author, why has drug abuse continued to be such a widespread problem in the U.S.?
2. What specific measures does Nixon believe the government and society should take to end substance abuse?
3. Why does Nixon vehemently oppose legalizing drugs?

Despite the misery and death drugs have brought to our homes, neighborhoods, and schools, some still favor this permissive approach. They urge the government to go ahead and bomb the Colombian drug plantations and clean out the ghetto crackhouses, so long as the weekend cocaine and marijuana user is left in peace to unwind in whatever manner he pleases. This approach was proved wrong twenty years ago. It would compound the tragedy to let the elite, casual user off the hook again.

America's leadership class will be remembered for the role it played in helping lose two wars: the war in Vietnam and, at least so far, the war on drugs. The leadership class is made up of highly educated and influential people in the arts, the media, the academic community, the government bureaucracies, and even business. They are characterized by intellectual arrogance, an obsession with style, fashion, and class, and a permissive attitude on drugs. In Vietnam, they felt more comfortable criticizing the United States for trying to save South Vietnam than criticizing the Communists for trying to conquer it. In the drug war, they simply went over to the other side. For years, the enemy was them.

Past Leadership to Blame

Now that polls show a majority of the American people fear drugs more than war, poverty, crime, or the deteriorating environment, being against drugs is as fashionable as being on drugs was two decades ago. Every young politician who admits taking a puff of dope in the sixties is talking tough on dope in the eighties. But for years the elite class accepted and even celebrated "recreational" drug use. Some still say that the casual user is not the problem. But when the casual user is a powerful movie director, a millionaire rock star, or an influential columnist, he is more dangerous than a hundred Brooklyn drug pushers. Drug users in the leadership class helped create a climate of social, cultural, and political acceptance that permitted the drug plague to take root. As it began to spread through our colleges and schools, attempts to contain it were condemned in leadership circles as paternalistic efforts by the older generation to suppress the creative urges of its children. Those who did not openly condone drug use coyly looked the other way.

When I rejected the recommendation of a Presidential commission that called for the decriminalization of marijuana in 1972, one liberal columnist scoffed at our hard line. "There is no real cause for panic about drug abuse and its effect on crime," he wrote in *The New York Times*. "There is no evidence that a crackdown will be the answer: quite the opposite." Under the leadership of Dr. Jerome Jaffe, we did adopt a tough, coordinated policy, ranging from diplomatic pressure on Turkey to stop exporting heroin to the first treatment program for inner-city addicts.

But even more crackdown then and in the years that followed might well have meant less crack now.

Even today, when most of the prestige media have managed to crowd onto the anti-drug bandwagon, they could not help indulging in a revolting orgy of nostalgia during the twentieth anniversary of Woodstock in 1989. The smarmy retrospectives glossed over the fact that Woodstock's only significant legacy was the glorification of dangerous illegal drugs. At least the seven Woodstock performers who eventually died from drugs got obituaries in the newspapers. Thousands in the audience who also became victims of drug abuse weren't even that lucky.

Consequences of Drug Use

The necessary message for rich and poor, black and white, Hispanic and Indian is the same: Drug use is intolerable; use and the potential for use will be confronted on all fronts, and those who use and who sell will face certain consequences.

William J. Bennett, *Family Therapy Networker*, November/December 1990.

To erase the grim legacy of Woodstock, we need a total war against drugs. Total war means war on all fronts against an enemy with many faces. Some, such as the South American drug barons, are easy and even appropriate targets. But making the drug war largely a foreign-policy issue is a convenient way to blame others for our own domestic problems. Some people do not want to admit that the enemy is also as near as the face they see in the mirror—the inner-city or suburban father who walks out on young children who need his influence to avoid drugs, the Wall Street broker buying a couple of grams of cocaine in the subway station, the columnist smoking marijuana or snorting coke on Saturday night and then going to the office Monday and writing that drugs are really just a problem for poor blacks. All are links in a steel chain of greed, poverty, neglect, and self-indulgence that is being drawn tighter and tighter around our throats. All must be fought and stopped before the chain can be broken and our country finally freed of its chemical, economic, and cultural addiction to illegal drugs. But nothing can be accomplished, no anti-drug initiative will be successful, if our society does not face the hard fact that *any* tolerance of *any* use of *any* illegal drug is wrong.

For this reason, calls for legalization of drugs are totally misguided. Police, parents, and teachers in the inner cities, the soldiers on the front lines in the drug war, know that if drugs were legalized, they would be cheaper and easier to get. As a result, there would be far more people on drugs. The way to win a war is not to give all the ammunition to the other side.

The war also cannot be won on the cheap. If Abraham Lincoln had been worried about the budget in 1861, George Bush would need a passport to visit Atlanta. Instead, Lincoln spent what he needed to win the Civil War and ran up a $500 million deficit.

Provide Drug Treatment

The war on drugs is our second civil war. If winning it requires a tax increase, so be it. In that event the Bush administration should seriously consider proposing a new tax on cigarettes and alcohol, with the funds earmarked exclusively for drug interdiction, prosecution, treatment, and education. Timid advisers who warn the President that the political heat will be too great if he proposes such a tax are wrong. The American people expect him to do what is necessary to win the war no matter what the cost, so long as his measures are bold enough to have a chance to work. The war cannot be won without strong leadership from the top. Today, fifty-eight government agencies share responsibility for fighting drugs. Too often they end up spending more time fighting each other for turf than fighting the enemy. A drug czar who has little more than the symbolic power of a British king will not be able to knock heads together to end the civil war in the bureaucracy and make a victory possible in the civil war against drugs.

A tough policy can also be a compassionate one. When I visited the Daytop Village drug rehabilitation center in Swan Lake, New York, in 1988, I met scores of young people who had fallen into the drug trap. With guidance from [Daytop administrator] Monsignor O'Brien and his dedicated colleagues, they were now on the road to productive, drug-free lives. Daytop offers twenty-four-hour-a-day supervision, stiff punishments for patients who stray, and regular follow-up testing after they go home. Because many such programs rely solely on private donations, only a fraction of those who need them can get in. No matter what else President Bush does, he should make it a national goal to ensure that no one who really wants to beat drugs is ever excluded from treatment. Any American who saw the hopeful faces of the young people at Daytop Village would gladly open his heart and his checkbook if it meant saving even one more child from oblivion.

"In neglecting the task of transmitting our fundamental values, we lose everything for which this country and our Judeo-Christian religious tradition stand."

Teaching Moral Values Can Reduce Chemical Dependency

William J. Bennett

In the following viewpoint, William J. Bennett contends that schools should teach children the difference between right and wrong and other traditional moral values. These teachings, he argues, will help children learn that using illegal drugs is wrong. In this way, Bennett maintains, the demand for drugs will be reduced. Bennett is the former director of the Office of National Drug Control Policy and the former secretary of education. He is currently a senior editor at *National Review*, a weekly conservative newsmagazine.

As you read, consider the following questions:

1. Why does Bennett believe that the drug problem is a moral problem?
2. According to the author, why should schools be responsible for teaching moral values?

William J. Bennett, "Drugs and the Face of Evil," *First Things*, December 1990. Reprinted with permission.

One of the least understood aspects of the drug problem is the degree to which it is in the end a moral and spiritual problem. I continue to be amazed at how often people I speak to in treatment centers refer to drugs as the great lie, the great deception, indeed as a product of the Great Deceiver. An astonishing number of people in treatment have described crack cocaine to me simply as "the Devil." This has come up too often and too spontaneously in conversation to be ignored.

The Face of Evil

You will know what I mean, then, when I say that in visiting treatment centers, prisons, inner-city communities, and public housing projects across the country over the past twenty-one months I've seen what I can only describe as the face of evil. Those people who doubt that there is evil in the world need to travel a few weeks with me on the drug circuit.

Recently a police officer told me about going into an apartment after receiving a complaint and finding there a four-year-old child and a one-year-old child. They had been in there by themselves for three days. The four-year-old had been left by his mother to care for the one-year-old. Now my wife and I have a six-year-old and a one-year-old at home. I know something about four-year-olds and their capabilities. Babysitting is not one of them. I don't suppose that anyone would deny that for a four-year-old to be left in charge of a one-year-old for three days is not very wise child rearing. When the police entered and spoke to the children, the one-year-old was still holding on to the hand of her older brother. And the little boy said, "This is my sister and my mother told me to take care of her and I will." The little boy was manfully trying to do his best. While the police were there, the mother came in with a roll of money in her hand. She had been out walking the streets to get the money to support her crack habit.

That's not the kind of story that's going to make the headlines or the evening news. But that's the kind of story that is being told too often every day in communities all over America. Child-abuse experts tell me that they think that much of the dramatic increase in child abuse and neglect is due to drugs.

You may have heard the story from the West Coast of a six-month-old child who died of an overdose of crack. How does a six-month-old die of an overdose of crack? Because her mother or father, we're not sure which, inhaled crack and then, to quiet the baby, blew crack into the baby's mouth until the baby was destroyed.

Or you may have heard the story from Detroit of the woman who owed a debt to her drug dealer and handed over her thirteen-year-old daughter to the drug dealer in order to pay the debt.

If these kinds of incidents are not the face of evil in our time, I don't know what is. That is why a spiritual and a moral response is required. Those who believe that because of modernity the categories of right and wrong, of good and evil, no longer apply need to take a close, hard look at the drug problem. If one doesn't believe in the struggle of the *psychomachia*—what I was taught to recognize as the struggle between good and evil for possession of the human soul—then one might never get to the heart of this drug problem.

Moral Law

Public school students have been corrupted for years by the "nondirective," "nonjudgmental," "do your own thing," "situation ethics," "secular humanist" type of teaching. Under that type of teaching, children are *never* told that illegal drugs . . . or anything else is "wrong."

Instead, the schools for years have been aggressively teaching that students can "make their own decisions" by looking within themselves—without reference to their parents or moral law. This is why "drug ed" courses actually encourage children to experiment with illegal drugs. . . .

A new federal law requires public schools to teach students that illegal drugs are "wrong"—or else the school loses its federal funds!

This new law gives us *the tool* to bring about a change in the public schools. This new federal law gives us the opportunity to put a *stop* to the nondirective teaching which has had such a destructive effect on children by cutting them loose from respect for parents and moral law.

Phyllis Schlafly, *Eagle Forum*, November 1990.

I think that the drug question, although serious in itself, is really symptomatic of a much wider problem. And that has to do with the neglect of the most important things. The most important things have to do with the teaching and passing on of certain true and time-honored values to our children. When we neglect these things, it doesn't matter what wealth or knowledge we have. For in neglecting the task of transmitting our fundamental values, we lose everything for which this country and our Judeo-Christian religious tradition stand. A news report in the *New York Times* on teenage health problems makes the point inadvertently, but very well:

America's teenagers are plagued with an array of physical and emotional health problems that make them less healthy than their parents were at that age, the [National Association

236

of State Boards of Education and the American Medical Association] Commission said today. The panel, including medical, health, and business leaders, said hundreds of thousands of adolescents and teenagers suffered from excessive drug use, unplanned pregnancies, sexually transmitted diseases, social and emotional problems that can lead to academic failure or suicide. As a result, many teenagers are unprepared to achieve successful lives as adults, the panel says. Unlike the problems of earlier generations, the Commission said, those of today's teenagers are rooted in behavior rather than in physical illnesses like infections and diseases. Excessive drinking, drug use, sex, and violence are major threats to the current generation.

Note that one sentence: "Unlike the problems of earlier generations . . . those of today's teenagers are rooted in behavior rather than in physical illnesses . . .". So, having stated that teenagers' problems are rooted in behavior, what does the Commission recommend? It recommends that teenagers be guaranteed access to health services and that schools take on a larger role in improving their students' health. It says that schools should establish health centers as well as offer classes that go beyond customary hygiene lessons to include sex education. In other words, having pointed out that the problem is not, for the most part, a health problem, the Commission goes on basically to recommend better medical health as the solution.

Conventional Wisdom

Why is that? Because that's the only solution that the conventional wisdom—at least in some circles—understands. It understands physical health, but it does not understand spiritual health. The approach of the Commission indicates the intellectual poverty of modernity, with its reliance on technological, psychological, and governmental solutions for moral and spiritual problems. The evidence in this case is clear. Never has our scientific, technological, or governmental know-how been greater, and never has the condition of our young people been worse.

What's the answer? We need the decade of the nineties to be a time when once again we talk directly about right and wrong, about values and character, about education as the architecture of the soul. What our children need—and all one has to do is go to schools and talk to children to see it—is not for the most part medicine. Where medicine is needed, by all mean let it be provided. But what these children need most is guidance. They need an example. They need moral principles. They need to know what is worthy of being loved and what is worthy of being defended.

If we wish to help our children, we need the courage to say in classrooms in this country—including the classrooms in our public schools—that there is a difference between right and wrong.

"Acupuncture not only controls withdrawal symptoms and craving, but it also reduces fears and hostilities that usually disturb drug abuse treatment settings."

Acupuncture Can Reduce Chemical Dependency

Michael O. Smith

Acupuncture is an ancient Chinese method of healing that seeks to cure disease or relieve pain by using needles on certain parts of the body. More and more often, acupuncture is being used to reduce chemical dependency by alleviating a patient's symptoms of withdrawal. In the following viewpoint, Michael O. Smith maintains that acupuncture can treat crack and heroin addicts with greater success than any other treatment. He is the medical director of the substance abuse division of Lincoln Hospital's Department of Psychiatry in Bronx, New York.

As you read, consider the following questions:

1. According to the author, how can acupuncture be used to treat chemical dependency?
2. How is acupuncture different from traditional therapy, according to Smith?
3. What evidence does Smith give showing the effectiveness of acupuncture?

From Michael O. Smith, "The Lincoln Hospital Acupuncture Drug Abuse Program," testimony before the Select Committee on Narcotics of the U.S. House of Representatives, July 25, 1989.

Acupuncture is a foundation for psycho-social rehabilitation so that counseling, drug-free contracts, educational and employment referrals, and Narcotics Anonymous are essential parts of the program. Acupuncture not only controls withdrawal symptoms and craving, but it also reduces fears and hostilities that usually disturb drug abuse treatment settings. Acupuncture has a balancing effect on the autonomic and neurotransmitter systems as well as an apparently rejuvenating effect. Drug abuse treatment is accomplished by inserting three to five acupuncture needles just under the skin or surface of the external ear. Needles are sterilized by autoclave. The location of ear points and the technique of insertion can be taught easily so that most acupuncture components can be staffed by a wide range of substance abuse clinicians. . . .

In January, 1987, our [Lincoln Hospital substance abuse] clinic population was suddenly transformed by the avalanche of cocaine-based "crack" that continues to threaten our lives. We have all read about the bizarre, intractable nature of crack addiction. In professional meetings we have been told that there is no known treatment for the craving and fearful cycles of crack. From the beginning our experience at Lincoln has been strikingly different than these reports.

Eight thousand crack patients have been treated at Lincoln—many more patients than have been seen at any other program. Crack abusers seek treatment earlier in the course of their illness than other addicts. They often have a longer history of prior drug-free status than other abusers.

We have developed a protocol that is specifically intended to serve criminal justice clients rather than merely grafting probation and parole-referred clients onto a treatment structure designed for voluntary walk-in clients. I believe our program has had the highest success ever recorded in the treatment of an unscreened court mandated population seen on an outpatient drug-free basis. More than fifty percent of these clients have provided negative urine toxicologies for more than two months. We have received no adverse reports on these individuals. Certainly, the Lincoln Hospital Acupuncture Program has the best record in New York City [NYC] for the treatment of court referred crack abusers.

Clients on Probation

Fifty-five clients referred by the NYC Probation Department are listed in our 1987-88 records. Most of these clients have received probation with a requirement for drug abuse treatment. Some of our most successful clients have been referred to Lincoln during the pre-sentencing probation investigation. The statistical data can be summarized in the following manner: 11 of the 55 clients

(20%) attended Lincoln only once. Thirty (30) of the remaining 44 clients (68%) have responded quite well to treatment and have provided consistently negative urine toxicologies. This group of 30 successful clients has attended Lincoln for an average of 9 consecutive weeks over a total span of more than 4 months. The presentencing clients were assigned to probation instead of receiving prison time. One man who was facing 30 years of federal time for drug-related charges has been sentenced to probation because of his 6-month record of clean urines. This man still attends NA [Narcotics Anonymous] meetings here every Saturday with his 8-year-old son. The judges involved have been clearly impressed by our clients' long record of clean urines on an outpatient basis. The successful clients have been re-established. After completing the Lincoln Hospital program, clients often continue long-term drug-free recovery programs, including AA [Alcoholics Anonymous] and NA.

A joint project to provide long term evaluation of Lincoln clients is being conducted by the NYC Probation Department, the Police Foundation of Washington, D.C. and ourselves. Our plans include a properly matched controlled study with 2-year follow-up of a substantial number of clients.

In a preliminary study we have traced the outcomes of 34 clients referred to Lincoln by NYC Probation in 1978-88. Six (6) of the 34 clients (17%) attended Lincoln only once. Eighteen (18) of the remaining 28 clients (64%) have attended more than 10 visits over a range of 2-15 months. Only one of these 18 clients has had his probation revoked and has been sent to prison. Five (5) of the 18 clients have functioned so well on probation that they were given "early discharges" from the probation system. Five of the clients who attended less than ten visits were re-arrested and none were given early discharge. Hence frequent attendance at Lincoln correlates with a 5:1 improvement in outcome for this series of clients.

The possibility of diverting people from incarceration is a very high priority in our field because of overcrowding and the lack of revenue. The National Association of Criminal Justice Planners has placed a high priority on acupuncture detoxification in many jurisdictions where crack is rampant.

Nationwide Implementation

In April, 1987, I was invited to Portland, Oregon by Judge Nely Johnson and a criminal justice advisor to the mayor. A pilot program was established in the public detox unit. In June the county voted to allow $60,000 of their Federal Bureau of Justice Administration funds to create several acupuncture components. Presently 6 new programs have been established by David Eisen of the Hooper Foundation, the county's contract agency for drug and alcohol treatment. The detoxification program now reports that

85% of its patients complete their program. Before acupuncture was used, only 34% completed the program. The 6-month recidivism rate has dropped from 25% to 6%. The Oregon State Department of Correction has helped establish a Criminal Bed Reduction Program using acupuncture to treat men charged with drug and alcohol-related offenses up to the level of class C felony. A clinic for runaway youth and a community-based program have also been started. . . .

An Independent Report

Let me quote from an independent evaluation report prepared by Carolyn Lane for Multonomah County.

> The successful post-detox enrollment rate is somewhat higher for all acupuncture participants than for non-participants and much higher—nearly double, or 43% versus 25%—for participants who had 7 or more treatments. The size of the follow-up group, which is about one-third of all clients discharged from Hooper Center in a year, and the lengthy follow-up period of more than one-third of a year, make this finding very impressive.
>
> Out patients were asked, as part of their Acupuncture Progress Reports, to note their attendance at self-help recovery groups or their enrollment in other post-detox or recovery programs. Of those that did, about two-thirds attended Alcoholics Anonymous or Narcotics Anonymous meetings, most once or twice a week but some every day.
>
> Without exception, the clients interviewed were enthusiastic about acupuncture. One "needed less medicine to relax, to sleep", another felt the desire to use substances "just fade away", and several remarked they were less tense, less fearful, and "able to cope with things a lot better". Another commented that "with acupuncture, you're moving toward something".
>
> A major advantage of acupuncture is that treatment can begin immediately, while treatment programs require a client assessment, with its associated costs. The first of these is simply the fixed cost of performing a client evaluation. If the client drops out at this point, as frequently occurs with unstable individuals, the cost of evaluation plus any potential billing for treatment is lost. In addition, the loss is a source of endemic low morale among caseworkers and counselors. Acupuncture treatment does not require such an evaluation and can begin at first contact, in many cases thus retaining clients who would not return otherwise.
>
> In conclusion, acupuncture appears to be a very cost-effective modality in supplementing and supporting a comprehensive detoxification treatment program. Also, it provides an adjunct treatment that can be applied during the entire cycle of detoxification.

Judge Herbert Klein of Miami-Dade County has spearheaded the development of an acupuncture-based program in the prison stockade and an outpatient facility in Overton. The program, which focuses on criminal justice clients, began in May, 1989, and sees 100 people daily.

Reasons for Success

Acupuncture is a popular and effective treatment. Patients learn to have confidence in daily acupuncture visits and the relief that consistently occurs. Acupuncture is a treatment for craving and fear as well as withdrawal symptoms. This modality facilitates constructive, non-antagonistic counseling and breaks down the barriers that usually inhibit group process. The consistently calm atmosphere in the treatment area is a marked contrast to the tense mood of the streets and of even the best conventional drug program. Acupuncture acts physiologically by enhancing the patient's own balancing mechanisms. There is a renewed development of vitality and integrity from within *before* external challenges need to be taken up. In this clinical setting passive-aggressive dependency and adolescent acting-out are greatly reduced. Staff and patients alike can focus on stability and growth without the interpersonal static that usually limits communication.

We have applied many of the basic principles of chemical dependency which are often neglected in criminal justice related situations. The struggle for sobriety is "one day at a time". By testing urines on a daily basis, providing daily acupuncture, and encouraging brief daily counseling sessions—we are functioning in the same rhythm as the patient's struggle for recovery. Testing urines every two weeks, in contrast, functions as an external judgmental process that clashes with the potential rhythm of recovery. A common principle of AA is "keep it simple". . . .

The counseling process at Lincoln emphasizes a nonjudgmental, non-invasive, supportive approach. The firm challenge of sobriety is established, but the treatment relationship is quite flexible and open-ended. On some days patients may want to ventilate their feelings each day; at other times they may want to just say "hello" and take the acupuncture treatment. Patients often experience fear and resentment toward intrusive questions and advice. This phenomenon is particularly true with court-mandated clients. These fears often prevent frequent attendance at otherwise helpful programs. The therapy program cannot "hold a grudge" and put increasing pressure on the patient for previous failures to respond to treatment. Pressure and concern must be appropriate to the quality of today's struggle and not reflect the residue of the past. The use of acupuncture makes this non-judgmental process much easier.

Frequent urine testing provides an objective non-personalized measure of success that can be accepted equally by all parties. In this system, the counselor is the "good cop" and urine machine is the "bad cop". The counseling process can be totally separated from the process of judgment and evaluation. According to this approach, clients will not feel a need to be friendly to their counselor in order to gain a positive evaluation. The computer printout showing a series of drug-free urines is the only documentation they will need to gain a favorable report for the court.

Positive Results

Positive results have been obtained using acupuncture detoxification of patients dependent on cocaine, opiates, phencyclidine or alcohol.

Drug addicts are impressed by the fact that daily acupuncture can relieve withdrawal symptoms as reliably as the drugs they use. They also discover that acupuncture can prevent drug craving even if none of their personal problems are resolved. Nevertheless, it is very important to integrate the acupuncture treatment into counseling and other psycho-social services provided for drug-dependent persons.

Michael O. Smith and I. Khan, *Bulletin on Narcotics*, vol. XL, no. 1, 1988.

Clinical supervisors at Lincoln have developed an approach that encourages self-sufficiency in their colleagues. A counselor who perceives that his or her autonomy is respected will be much more able to develop autonomy in individual clients. The treatment field frequently neglects the principle that autonomy is a major component of health and sobriety. So much effort is focused on referrals to 24-hour facilities that this basic and practical reality often fades out of view. No matter how effective 24-hour rehabilitation is, the patient will spend 99% of the time is an independent state. The pressing reality of criminal justice is comparable. To help people, we need to help them function well independently of our agencies.

The fear and shame associated with impending incarceration or removal of a child is certainly an important factor in any success. In the chemical dependency field, it is considered beneficial for a prospective patient to face a fearful concrete reality. The myth of the well motivated walk-in patient is just that: a myth. Similarly, court-related referrals should always be made with definite requirements. Referrals of the type "why don't you see if this treatment can help you" lead to an unusually low rate of success. According to recent trends of budget deficit and court congestion, the threat of incarceration is often more symbolic than real. A temporary, more-or-less symbolic threat may often be quite effective in persuading a client to begin treatment and these clients continue in treatment long after the circumstances suggesting the threat of punishment have abated. This type of situation is actually quite typical of interventions and contracting in chemical dependency treatment.

"There is no such thing as a hopeless case" is another basic principle. The Lincoln program does not screen out prospective patients as "poorly motivated" or "unsuitable" as is frequently done in regard to criminal justice referrals. All referrals are accepted: a fact that makes these statistics all the more promising. . . .

Dr. Milton Bullock and acupuncturist Patricia Culliton of Hennepin County Medical Center in Minneapolis began to use a placebo protocol to evaluate our Lincoln Hospital acupuncture procedure in 1983. Their first article was published in the *Alcoholism* journal in June 1987. It showed that 37% of the treatment group responded well to acupuncture as compared to 7% of the placebo group which received non-specific acupuncture points.

The Hennepin group has just published a more advanced study in *Lancet*, June 24, 1989, the prestigious journal of the British Medical Association. Twenty-one of 40 treatment acupuncture patients completed the program compared to 1 of 40 controls. Significant treatment effects persisted at the end of a 6-month follow-up. These studies focus on severe recidivist alcoholics who are very rarely engaged in outpatient management.

Dr. Mindy Fullilove of the University of California at San Francisco is just completing a controlled placebo study using the Lincoln protocol with IV [intravenous] heroin abusers. Dr. Stephen Kendall and his staff at Beth Israel in New York have planned a controlled study using acupuncture in the treatment of addicted babies. Dr. Doug Lipton of the Narcotic Drug Research Institute (NDRI) is presently conducting a controlled placebo study using crack patients at Lincoln Hospital. In the recent submission of large scale AIDS prevention drug abuse treatment grants, acupuncture was the second most common procedure suggested for evaluation.

In a legislative meeting in Albany, New York, the chief representative of the Medical Society of New York stated that acupuncture was an important part of the health care field and that physicians were seeking more instructive and more active participation in the acupuncture field.

Relations with the Drug Abuse Treatment Field

I have always supported the position that acupuncture can only be a component part of the whole process of drug abuse treatment. Nearly all of the existing acupuncture drug abuse programs were developed within already existing licensed treatment programs. Our enabling legislation in New York State was written by Public Health Commissioner Deborah Prothrow Stith; the state drug abuse agency of Massachusetts funded four acupuncture-based programs during 1989. Numerous methadone programs have established acupuncture components in order to treat crack abuse and other secondary addictions. In a therapeutic community setting, such as the Phoenix House in London, staff members report that acupuncture helps reduce craving [and] tension among the clients and that most of the clients participate in the weekly acupuncture sessions.

The Lincoln Hospital acupuncture program has received a great deal of national and international attention. More than 60 clinics in the U.S. and another 25 in Europe, Latin America and Asia have been established explicitly on the model of our clinic in the South Bronx. Indeed Lincoln Hospital has become a "mecca" for visitors and journalists. Television networks from Spain, Italy, Brazil, Sweden, Britain, Latin America, Hungary and Japan have filmed our acupuncture drug abuse program.

The National Acupuncture Detoxification Association (NADA) was founded in 1985 by clinicians who wanted to extend the example of the Lincoln Hospital experience into other treatment settings. I am the chairperson of NADA. The organizational name also uses the Spanish connotation of "nada", suggesting a no-nonsense, drug-free approach. NADA has conducted many training programs for public institutions and communities in undeveloped areas. It has set standards of certification for acupuncture detoxification specialists that are widely accepted in the substance abuse field.

Empty Fire

I have just returned from a United Nations meeting in Spain scheduled to plan community-based treatment programs on a widely diversified basis. In the December 1988 issue of the Bulletin of Narcotics, we described NADA programs on the Pine Ridge Sioux reservation in South Dakota, in Kathmandu, Nepal, in La Perla in Puerto Rico, and Lincoln as an example of the effectiveness of this model in difficult socioeconomic settings.

It is easy to be confused by the aggressiveness that many addicts present and to conclude that the main goal should be symptom suppression. In fact, the addict himself takes this approach to the extreme by using sedative narcotics. In Chinese medicine the lack of calm inner strength is described as "empty fire" (xu huo), because the heat of aggressiveness burns out of control when the calm inner tone is lost. The hostile paranoid climate of communities vulnerable to drug abuse is a clear example of an energy-depleted condition with empty fire burning out of control.

Our patients seek greater power and control over their lives. Empty fire is the illusion of power—an illusion that leads to more desperate chemical abuse and senseless violence. Acupuncture is an effective treatment for empty fire. The patient is empowered, but in a soft, easy and long-lasting manner.

Recognizing Statements That Are Provable

We are constantly confronted with statements and generalizations about social and moral problems. In order to think clearly about these problems, it is useful if one can make a basic distinction between statements for which evidence can be found and other statements which cannot be verified or proved because evidence is not available, or the issue is so controversial that it cannot be definitely proved.

Readers should be aware that magazines, newspapers, and other sources often contain statements of a controversial nature. The following activity is designed to allow experimentation with statements that are provable and those that are not.

The following statements are taken from the viewpoints in this chapter. Consider each statement carefully. *Mark P for any statement you believe is provable. Mark U for any statement you feel is unprovable because of the lack of evidence. Mark C for any statement you think is too controversial to be proved to everyone's satisfaction.*

If you are doing this activity as a member of a class or group, compare your answers with those of other class or group members. Be able to defend your answers. You may discover that others will come to different conclusions than you do. Listening to the reasons others present for their answers may give you valuable insights into recognizing statements that are provable.

P = provable
U = unprovable
C = too controversial

1. Alcoholics Anonymous has no official procedure for becoming a member.
2. AA accepts members unconditionally.
3. The most difficult step for an alcoholic is admitting his or her powerlessness over alcohol.
4. A lack of willpower causes most AA members to relapse.
5. AA recommends a belief in God or a "higher power" in order to recover from alcoholism.
6. Controlled drinking is a more successful treatment method than abstinence.
7. Programs that allow problem drinkers to drink moderately report success rates averaging 65 percent.
8. Lincoln Hospital in New York City has the best record for treating court-referred crack abusers.
9. The waiting period to enter some drug treatment clinics is often more than a year.
10. The success of acupuncture as a treatment for chemical dependency is due to understanding and knowledgeable doctors.
11. The National Acupuncture Detoxification Association was founded in 1985.
12. Role models who abuse drugs help create a climate that permits the drug plague to continue.
13. The federal government cut funding for drug treatment by $200 million in 1990.
14. If drugs were legalized, there would be far more people addicted to drugs.
15. More than 800,000 Americans use cocaine regularly.
16. Drug addiction costs society almost $60 billion annually, according to the National Clearinghouse for Alcohol and Drug Information.
17. Rehabilitating drug users offers the best hope of solving the drug problem in the U.S.
18. The majority of males arrested in large cities test positive for illegal drug use.
19. Cocaine use in the U.S. is decreasing because people are returning to traditional American values.
20. A drug-free society is impossible because America is obsessed with taking drugs in order to feel good.

Periodical Bibliography

The following articles have been selected to supplement the diverse views presented in this chapter.

Celestine Bohlen	"Support Groups Are Offering Embrace to Cocaine's Victims," *The New York Times*, January 29, 1989.
Lily Collett	"Step by Step: A Skeptic's Encounter with the Twelve-Step Program," *Mother Jones*, July/August 1988.
Tim C. Criswell	"A Step in the Right Direction," *Corrections Today*, August 1989.
David Gelman, Anne Underwood, Patricia King, Mary Hagar, and Jeanne Gordon	"Some Things Work," *Newsweek*, September 24, 1990.
John J. Goldman	"Neglected Weapons in the Drug War," *Los Angeles Times*, April 6, 1990.
Howard Goodman	"When Herman Wrice Declared War," *Reader's Digest*, January 1991.
Kim A. Lawton	"Churches Enlist in the War on Drugs," *Christianity Today*, February 11, 1991.
Richard Leviton	"Staying Drugfree Naturally," *East West*, March 1988.
Mary Ellen Mark	"Turning Kids Off Drugs," *The New York Times Magazine*, May 24, 1987.
Michael Massing	"Desperate over Drugs," *The New York Review of Books*, March 30, 1989.
Peggy Mann	"Dogged Crusader Against Drugs," *Reader's Digest*, May 1989.
Pennell E. Paugh	"Drug-Abusing Juveniles: Conference Explores Alternatives to 'Just Say No,'" *Corrections Today*, June 1989.
Stanton Peele	"Cures Depend on Attitude, Not Programs," *Los Angeles Times*, March 14, 1990.
Joanne Scognamiglio	"How to Help Addicts Kick Their Habits," *USA Today*, July 1990.

Organizations to Contact

The editors have compiled the following list of organizations that are concerned with the issues debated in this book. All of them have publications or information available for interested readers. The descriptions are derived from materials provided by the organizations. This list was compiled upon the date of publication. Names and phone numbers of organizations are subject to change.

Action on Smoking and Health (ASH)
2013 H St. NW
Washington, DC 20006
(202) 659-4310

ASH is an anti-smoking organization that works to pass laws banning public smoking. Founded by John Banzhaf III, the lawyer who led the campaign to ban televised cigarette commercials, ASH has fought to obtain no-smoking sections on all major airlines and continues to support other rights for nonsmokers. It publishes the newsletter *ASH Smoking and Health Review* and provides information leaflets on smoking-related issues.

American Civil Liberties Union (ACLU)
132 W. 43rd St.
New York, NY 10036
(212) 944-9800

The ACLU, one of the oldest civil liberties organizations in the U.S., favors the decriminalization of drugs. It strongly opposes employers who terminate or refuse to hire people who smoke away from the workplace. The ACLU publishes information packets on drug legalization, decriminalization, and public smoking.

American Society of Addiction Medicine (ASAM)
5225 Wisconsin Ave. NW, Suite 409
Washington, DC 20015
(202) 244-8948

The society is a group of physicians with special interest and experience in the field of alcoholism and other drug dependencies. It believes all addicts should have access to government-funded drug and alcohol treatment. The society publishes the quarterly *Journal of Addictive Diseases*, the bimonthly *ASAM News* newsletter, and public policy statements on alcoholism and drug dependency.

Americans for Nonsmokers' Rights (ANR)
2530 San Pablo Ave., Suite J
Berkeley, CA 94702
(415) 841-3032

ANR is largely concerned with the danger of secondhand smoke to the nonsmoker. It supports legislation allowing communities to restrict public smoking. ANR publishes a newsletter, the *ANR Update*, as well as brochures such as *A Smokefree Workplace* and *Tobacco Smoke and the Nonsmoker*.

Cato Institute
224 Second St. SE
Washington, DC 20003
(202) 546-0200

The institute is a public policy research foundation dedicated to limiting the control of government and to protecting individual liberty. It studies the drug problem and strongly favors drug legalization. It publishes the *Cato Journal* three times a year, and the *Cato Policy Report* bimonthly.

Center for Alcohol Studies
Rutgers, The State University of New Jersey
Smithers Hall, Busch Campus
Piscataway, NJ 08854
(201) 932-2190

The center contains a large library on alcohol-related topics, and provides information on the use and abuse of alcohol. It publishes the quarterly *Journal of Studies on Alcohol* as well as bibliographies on the psychological, social, and physiological aspects of alcoholism.

Christic Institute
1324 N. Capitol St. NW
Washington, DC 20002
(202) 797-8106

The institute is an interfaith religious organization that works to expose wrongdoing by big business or government. It takes credit for exposing the Contragate scandal in which the federal government was accused of sanctioning drug trafficking in Central America. The institute asserts that the U.S. government passes stringent drug laws at home but uses drugs for political ends abroad. Publications include the bimonthly *Contragate Alert* and the quarterly *Convergence*.

Committees of Correspondence
57 Conant St., Rm. 113
Danvers, MA 01923
(508) 774-2641

The committees, a national coalition of community groups, fight drug abuse among youth by publishing data about drugs and drug abuse. The coalition opposes drug legalization and advocates treatment for drug abusers. Publications include the quarterly *Drug Abuse Newsletter*, the periodic *Drug Prevention Resource Manual*, and related pamphlets, brochures, and article reprints.

Do It Now Foundation
6423 S. Ash Ave.
Tempe, AZ 85283
(602) 257-0797

The foundation fights drug abuse by providing students and adults with facts on legal and illegal drugs and drug abuse. Founded in 1968, Do It Now offered one of the first drug-abuse hotline services in the country. The foundation publishes books, posters, and taped public-service announcements on drug abuse, as well as the pamphlets *Guide for Young People*, *Total Recovery*, and *Everyday Detox: A Guide to Living Without Chemicals*.

Drug Enforcement Administration (DEA)
1405 I St. NW
Washington, DC 20537
(202) 633-1000

The DEA is the federal agency charged with enforcing the nation's drug laws. The agency concentrates on stopping narcotics smuggling and distribution organizations in the United States and abroad. It publishes *Drug Enforcement Magazine* three times a year.

Drug Policy Foundation
4801 Massachusetts Ave. NW, #400
Washington, DC 20016-2087
(202) 895-1634

The foundation supports legalizing many drugs. It believes that increasing the number of treatment programs for addicts can reduce the demand for drugs. Its publications include the bimonthly *Drug Policy Letter* and the books *The Great Drug War* and *1989-1990, A Reformer's Catalogue*. It also distributes *Press Clips*, an annual compilation of newspaper articles on drug legalization issues.

Drugs and Crime Data Center and Clearinghouse
1600 Research Blvd.
Rockville, MD 20850
(800) 666-3332

The clearinghouse, an office of the U.S. Justice Department, compiles and distributes information on drug-related crime for use by policymakers and other researchers. Its publications include *Federal Drug Data for National Policy* and *State Drug Resources: A National Directory*.

The Heritage Foundation
214 Massachusetts Ave. NE
Washington, DC 20002
(202) 546-4400

The Heritage Foundation is a conservative public policy research institute that opposes the legalization of drugs and advocates strengthening law enforcement to stop drug abuse. It publishes position papers on a broad range of topics, including drug issues. Its regular publications include the monthly *Policy Review*, the *Backgrounder* series of occasional papers, and the *Heritage Lecture* series.

Libertarian Party
1528 Pennsylvania Ave. SE
Washington, DC 20003
(202) 543-1988

The Libertarian Party is a political party whose goal is to ensure respect for individual rights. It advocates the repeal of all laws prohibiting the production, sale, possession, or use of drugs. The party believes law enforcement should focus on preventing violent crime against persons and property rather than on prosecuting people who use drugs. It publishes the bimonthly *Libertarian Party News* and periodic *Issue Papers* and distributes a compilation of articles supporting drug legalization.

Methods of Moderation and Abstinence (MOMA)
1284 E. 130th Ave. #C
Thornton, CO 80241
(303) 457-4445

MOMA provides a network for nonreligious persons seeking self-help methods of treatment for alcohol and drug addiction as an alternative to programs that emphasize a reliance on God. The organization believes alcoholism should be treated as a disease and it strongly favors government funding for treatment. It publishes a newsletter at irregular intervals. A brochure and sample newsletter are available upon request.

Narcotics Anonymous (NA)
PO Box 9999
Van Nuys, CA 91409
(818) 780-3951

NA, comprised of more than eighteen thousand groups worldwide, is an organization of recovering drug addicts who meet regularly to help each other abstain from all drugs. It publishes *NA Way Magazine* and *Newsline* monthly.

National Acupuncture Detoxification Association (NADA)
3115 Broadway, #51
New York, NY 10027
(212) 993-3100

NADA promotes acupuncture as a treatment for chemical dependency. It favors government-funded drug treatment and opposes drug legalization. NADA publishes the *NADA Newsletter* annually.

National Association of Drug Abuse Problems (NADAP)
355 Lexington Ave.
New York, NY 10017
(212) 986-1170

NADAP attacks the drug problem through educating the public about drug abuse. It also focuses on rehabilitating drug users and helping them find job opportunities. NADAP publishes the monthly *Recent Development Memo* and the quarterly *Report*.

National Clearinghouse for Alcohol and Drug Information (NCADI)
PO Box 2345
Rockville, MD 20852
(800) 729-6686

NCADI is an information service of the Office for Substance Abuse Prevention of the U.S. Department of Health and Human Services. The clearinghouse provides alcohol and drug prevention and educational materials free, including technical reports, pamphlets, and posters. It publishes a bimonthly newsletter, *Prevention Pipeline: An Alcohol and Drug Awareness Service*, containing the latest available information on research, resources, and activities in the prevention field.

National Council on Alcoholism and Drug Dependence (NCADD)
12 West 21st St.
New York, NY 10010
(212) 645-1690

The council offers drug and alcohol prevention programs for schools, organizations, and communities. It considers alcoholism a treatable disease and advocates public funding of alcohol and drug treatment programs, especially those for women and their children. Its brochures include *Who Says Alcoholism Is a Disease?* and *What Are the Signs of Alcoholism?* It issues policy statements and fact sheets on alcoholism and drug-related birth defects.

National Federation of Parents for Drug-Free Youth
1423 N. Jefferson
Springfield, MO 65802-1988
(417) 836-3709

The federation is a national network of parent groups concerned about drug abuse in children. It created REACH, Responsible Educated Adolescents Can Help America Stop Drugs, to train high school students to educate younger children about the dangers of drugs. The federation also coordinates the Red Ribbon Campaign to increase public awareness of America's drug problem. Among the group's publications are a quarterly newsletter, the *Parent Group Starter Kit, Press/Media Guidelines,* and the *Anti-Paraphernalia Kit.*

National Organization for the Reform of Marijuana Laws (NORML)
2001 S St. NW, Suite 640
Washington, DC 20009
(202) 483-5500

NORML fights to legalize marijuana and to help those who have been convicted and sentenced for possessing or selling marijuana. It publishes a newsletter, *Marijuana Highpoints,* on the progress of all legislation concerning the legalization of marijuana throughout the country.

Smokers' Rights Alliance
20 E. Main St., Suite 710
Mesa, AZ 85201
(800) 562-7444

The alliance challenges antismoking legislation and discrimination against smokers. It believes that disputes about smoking should be settled by individuals, not by government regulations prohibiting smoking. The alliance publishes the quarterly *Smoke Signals.*

Smoking Policy Institute
PO Box 20271
Seattle, WA 98102
(206) 324-4444

The institute was the first organization in the U.S. to help companies establish smoke-free workplaces. It helps organizations develop and implement customized smoking control policies through information packages, products, and consulting services. The institute, in cooperation with the National Cancer Institute, publishes question-and-answer sheets on smoking.

The Tobacco Institute
1875 Eye St. NW
Washington, DC 20006
(202) 457-4800

The institute is the primary national lobbying organization for the tobacco industry. The institute argues that the dangers of smoking have not been proven and opposes smoking restrictions on airlines, in restaurants, and in public buildings. The institute also publishes many brochures and booklets such as *Environmental Tobacco Smoke and Health: The Consensus.*

Bibliography of Books

Howard Abadinsky	*Drug Abuse: An Introduction.* Chicago: Nelson-Hall, 1989.
Ernest L. Abel	*Fetal Alcohol Syndrome.* Oradell, NJ: Medical Economics Books, 1990.
Steve Allen	*The Passionate Nonsmokers' Bill of Rights.* New York: William Morrow & Co., 1989.
Ken Barun and Philip Bashe	*How to Keep the Children You Love Off Drugs.* New York: The Atlantic Monthly Press, 1988.
Joseph D. Beasley	*Wrong Diagnosis, Wrong Treatment: The Plight of the Alcoholic in America.* Durant, OK: Creative Infomatics, 1987.
Gilda Berger	*Smoking Not Allowed.* New York: Franklin Watts, 1987.
David Boaz, ed.	*The Crisis in Drug Prohibition.* Washington, DC: Cato Institute, 1990.
Dan Calahan	*Understanding America's Drinking Problem.* San Francisco: Jossey-Bass, 1987.
Frank Chaloupka	*Men, Women, and Addiction: The Case of Cigarette Smoking.* Cambridge, MA: National Bureau of Economic Research, 1990.
James Christopher	*How to Stay Sober: Recovery Without Religion.* Buffalo: Prometheus Books, 1988.
J. Christopher Clarke	*Alcoholism and Problem Drinking.* Elmsford, NY: Pergamon Press, 1988.
Michael A. Corey	*Kicking the Drug Habit.* Springfield, IL: Charles C. Thomas, 1989.
Norman K. Denzin	*The Recovering Alcoholic.* Newbury Park, CA: Sage Publications, 1987.
Michael Dorris	*The Broken Cord.* New York: Harper & Row, 1989.
Judith A. Douville	*Active and Passive Smoking Hazards in the Workplace.* New York: Van Nostrand Reinhold, 1990.
Ruth K. Engs	*Alcohol and Other Drugs: Self-Responsibility.* Bloomington, IN: Tichenor Publications, 1987.
John J. Fay	*The Alcohol/Drug Abuse Dictionary and Encyclopedia.* Springfield, IL: Charles C. Thomas, 1988.
Herbert Fingarette	*Heavy Drinking: The Myth of Alcoholism as a Disease.* Berkeley: University of California Press, 1988.
Kathleen Whalen FitzGerald	*Alcoholism: The Genetic Inheritance.* New York: Doubleday, 1988.
Richard J. Frances	*Concise Guide to Treatment of Alcoholism and Addictions.* Washington, DC: American Psychiatric Press, 1989.
Donald W. Goodwin	*Is Alcoholism Hereditary?* New York: Ballantine Books, 1988.
Ronald Hamowy, ed.	*Dealing with Drugs: Consequences of Government Control.* Lexington, MA: Lexington Books, 1987.

Robert L. Hubbard and Mary Ellen Marsden	*Drug Abuse Treatment: A National Study of Effectiveness.* Chapel Hill, NC: University of North Carolina Press, 1989.
James A. Inciardi, ed.	*The Drug Legalization Debate.* Newbury Park, CA: Sage Publications, 1991.
Stan J. Katz and Amy E. Liu	*Codependency Conspiracy: How to Break the Recovery Habit and Take Charge of Your Life.* New York: Warner Books, 1991.
Katherine Ketchman and Ginny Lyford Gustafson	*Living on the Edge: A Guide to Intervention for Families with Drug and Alcohol Problems.* New York: Bantam Books, 1989.
Edward Khantzian	*Addiction and the Vulnerable Self.* New York: Guilford Press, 1990.
Cheryl L. Lockett	*Smoking in the Workplace: A Review of Arbitrary Decisions.* Fort Washington, PA: LRP Publications, 1988.
Arnold Ludwig	*Understanding the Alcoholic's Mind: The Nature of Craving and How to Control It.* New York: Oxford University Press, 1988.
Gerald G. May	*Addiction and Grace.* New York: Harper & Row, 1989.
Richard Lawrence Miller	*The Case for Legalizing Drugs.* New York: Praeger, 1990.
David F. Musto	*The American Disease: Origins of Narcotic Control.* Oxford: Oxford University Press, 1988.
Craig Nakken	*The Addictive Personality.* Center City, MN: Hazelden Foundation, 1988.
Tara Ney and Anthony Gale, eds.	*Smoking and Human Behavior.* New York: Wiley and Sons, 1989.
Joseph Nowinski	*Substance Abuse in Adolescents and Young Adults.* New York: W.W. Norton, 1990.
Cardwell C. Nuckols	*Cocaine: From Dependency to Recovery.* 2d ed. Blue Ridge Summit, PA: Tab Books, 1989.
James Ostrowski	*Thinking About Drug Legalization.* Washington, DC: Cato Institute, 1989.
Stanton Peele	*The Diseasing of America: Addiction Treatment Out of Control.* Lexington, MA: Lexington Books, 1989.
Jean E. Rhodes and Leonard A. Jason	*Preventing Substance Abuse Among Children and Adolescents.* Elmsford, NY: Pergamon Press, 1988.
Jennifer Rice-Licare and Katharine Delaney-McLoughlin	*Cocaine Solutions: Help for Cocaine Abusers and Their Families.* New York: Haworth Press, 1990.
Diana Robertson and Robert M. Pinkerton	*Women, Drugs, and Babies: Guidelines for Medical and Protective Services' Response to Infants Endangered by Drug Abuse During Pregnancy.* Salem, OR: Oregon Department of Human Resources, Children's Services Division, 1989.
Nan Robertson	*Getting Better: Inside Alcoholics Anonymous.* New York: William Morrow & Co., 1988.
Ronald L. Rogers and Chandler Scott McMillin	*The Healing Bond: Treating Addictions in Groups.* New York: W.W. Norton, 1989.
Robert M. Rose and James E. Barrett	*Alcoholism: Origins and Outcome.* New York: Raven Press, 1988.

Stephen E. Schlesinger and Lawrence K. Horberg	*Taking Charge: How Families Can Climb Out of the Chaos of Addiction.* New York: Simon & Schuster, 1988.
Marc A. Schuckit	*Drug and Alcohol Abuse: A Clinical Guide to Diagnosis and Treatment.* 3d ed. New York: Plenum Medical, 1989.
Howard J. Shaffer and Stephanie B. Jones	*Quitting Cocaine.* Lexington, MA: Lexington Books, 1989.
Ronald K. Siegel	*Intoxication: Life In Pursuit of Artificial Paradise.* New York: E.P. Dutton, 1989.
Sherry Sonnett	*Smoking.* 2d ed. New York: Franklin Watts, 1988.
Peter Steinglass with Linda Bennett, Steven Wolin, and David Reiss	*The Alcoholic Family.* New York: Basic Books, 1989.
William M. Timmins	*Smoking and the Workplace.* New York: Quorum Books, 1989.
The Tobacco Institute	*An Assessment of the Current Legal Climate Concerning Smoking in the Workplace.* Washington, DC: The Tobacco Institute, 1988.
The Tobacco Institute	*Indoor Pollution: Is Your Workplace Making You Sick?* Washington, DC: The Tobacco Institute, 1988.
Robert D. Tollison	*Clearing the Air: Perspectives on Environmental Tobacco Smoke.* Lexington, MA: Lexington Books, 1988.
Michael Tonry and James Q. Wilson, eds.	*Drugs and Crime.* Chicago: University of Chicago Press, 1990.
U.S. Office on Smoking and Health	*Is Your Baby Smoking?* Rockville, MD: U.S. Office on Smoking and Health, 1988.
Joe Vaughn	*Family Intervention: Hope for Families Struggling with Alcohol and Drugs.* Louisville, KY: Westminster/John Knox Press, 1989.
Carol J. Verburg	*Substance Abuse in America.* Washington, DC: National Academy Press, 1989.
Arnold Washton	*Cocaine Addiction.* New York: W.W. Norton, 1989.
Larry C. White	*Merchants of Death: The American Tobacco Industry.* New York: William Morrow & Co., 1988.
Steven Wisotsky	*Beyond the War on Drugs.* Buffalo: Prometheus Books, 1990.
Barbara Yoder	*The Recovery Resource Book.* New York: Simon & Schuster, 1990.

Index

Moss, Kary, 191

Nadelmann, Ethan, 153
Nahas, Gabriel, 16
Nakken, Craig, 30, 36
Narcotics Anonymous, 239, 240
National Abortion Rights Action
  League, 184
National Academy of Sciences, 34
National Acupuncture Detoxification
  Association, 245
National Association for Perinatal
  Addiction Research and Education,
  185
National Association for Women, 184
National Association of Criminal
  Justice Planners, 240
National Center for the Prosecution
  of Child Abuse, 180
National Commission Against Drunk
  Driving, 122
National Drug Control Strategy, 163,
  167, 168
National Heart and Lung Institute,
  62
National Household Survey on Drug
  Abuse, 152, 157
National Institute of Justice, 228
National Institute on Alcohol Abuse
  and Alcoholism, 67
National Institute on Drug Abuse, 40,
  44, 139, 152, 226
National Research Council, 67
Native Americans, 110, 115, 116
New England Journal of Medicine, 74,
  109
New Perspectives Quarterly, 166
New York, 149, 166, 194-195
New York Times, 27, 116, 167, 184,
  231, 236
nicotine, 56, 58-59
Nixon, Richard, 165, 230
Nuckols, Cardwell C., 45

Ochoa, Jorge Luis, 166
Olinger, David, 118

Paltrow, Lynn, 185
Parker, J.A., 16
Parmley, William W., 70
Peele, Stanton, 38, 112
Perlstein, Mitchell, 188
physicians, 178
  and pregnant drug users, 188-189,
  196-197, 198, 202

poverty, 134, 148-149, 157, 159
pregnancy
  drinking during causes fetal alcohol
    syndrome, 105-111, 200-201
  con, 112-117
  drug use during, 27, 226-227
  prosecution for
    as necessary, 175-182
    con, 183-190
    violates civil rights, 191-198
    con, 199-206
  smoking during, 80, 186, 195
prenatal care, 117, 185, 195, 198
prisons, 152, 166, 167, 228
privacy rights, 197-198, 200, 203
Prohibition, 134, 137
Public Health Service, 76, 108,
public smoking
  should be restricted, 69, 79-85
  con, 75-78, 86-90
Puterman, Grace, 122
Puterman, Mark, 122

Ramirez, Mike, 143
Reagan, Ronald, 12, 152, 165, 166
Repace, James, 82
Reuter, Peter, 164, 165
Reynolds, R.J., Tobacco Company,
  56
Roberts, Dorothy E., 183
Robertson, John, 177
Robinson v. California (1962), 187
Roe v. Wade (1973), 200, 203-204, 206
Rosenthal, Elisabeth, 105, 114, 115,
  116
Rosett, Henry, 113, 115
Ryan, Elizabeth A., 47

San Diego Union, 120
Schierl, Kathryn, 175
Schlafly, Phyllis, 236
Schlesinger, Stephen E., 212
Schorr, Bill, 57
Schuster, Charles, 44
Seavey, David, 107
secondary smoke
  is harmful, 58, 63, 66-71, 80, 83, 85
  con, 65, 72-78
Shaffer, Howard J., 24
Shimp, Donna, 81
Shopland, Donald, 67-68
Siegel, Ronald K., 17
Skolnick, Jerome H., 162
Smith, Michael O., 238, 243
smoking, 20, 139, 186, 233

addiction to, 40, 41, 56
as harmful
to fetuses, 80, 117, 195
to nonsmokers, 58, 63, 66-71, 80,
83, 85
con, 65, 72-78
to smokers, 55-59, 67, 71, 74, 85, 144
con, 60-65, 89
to the public, 69, 79-85
con, 75-78, 86-90
chemicals in cigarettes, 56, 57-58
mortality rates from, 63-64, 67, 69,
71, 74, 134, 155
Snyder, Mitch, 75
Sokol, Robert J., 106-107, 110
Stamaty, Mark Alan, 164
Stellman, Jeanne Mager, 116
Stewart, Pamela Rae, 186
Stith, Deborah Prothrow, 244-245
Streissguth, Ann, 110, 111
Students Against Drunk Driving, 125
Sullivan, Louis W., 157
Sullum, Jacob, 72
Sununu, John H., 27
Sweeting, James, III, 187, 188, 190

Talbot, Doug, 47
Talley, Bill, 222
taxation, 139, 167, 233
terrorism, 134-135, 140
Tobacco Institute, 54, 62, 64
Tompkins, Randy, 188, 190
treatment programs
costs of, 43, 226, 228-229
for alcoholism
Alcoholics Anonymous, 212-217
are ineffective, 43, 102-103, 104
con, 32, 213, 216, 219, 220, 222
controlled drinking, 218-224
for drug addiction, 149-150, 154
acupuncture, 239-240
crack addiction, 194-195, 226, 228-
229, 239, 245
for pregnant women, 185, 187,
190, 194-195, 198, 206, 226-227
government should provide, 225-
229, 233
Trebach, Arnold, 151
Turner, Carlton, 12
Trost, Cathy L., 176

Uniform Alcoholism and
Intoxication Treatment Act, 200,
202, 204-205, 206

Vaillant, George, 43, 99, 219, 221
Vogler, Roger, 222, 223

Washington, D.C.
drug use in, 27, 161, 166, 167
murders in, 155
*Webster v. Reproductive Health
Services* (1989), 185
Weil, Andrew, 46
Weiner, Lyn, 113, 114-115
Willis, Ellen, 193
Witten, Mark L., 68
Wolf, Peter, 184
women
alcohol consumption, 108, 109
drug addiction, 149, 176, 185, 187,
194-195, 226-227
smoking mortality, 64
see also pregnancy
Woodstock, 232
Woolery, Candace, 193
World Conference on Tobacco and
Health, 74

zero tolerance, 230-233

262